ECCLESIASTES

William D. Barrick

ECCLESIASTES

The Philippians of the Old Testament

William D. Barrick

CHRISTIAN
FOCUS

William Barrick is Professor of Old Testament at Master's Seminary, Sun Valley, California. Dr. Barrick has been married to his wife Barbara for 45 years. They have four married children and fourteen grandchildren.

Unless otherwise indicated the English translation is that of *The Holy Bible: Updated New American Standard* (Anaheim, Calif.: Foundation Publications, Inc., 2003).

Scripture quotations marked "NASB" are taken from the *New American Standard Bible®*, Copyright © 1960, 1962, 1963, 1968, 1971, 1972, 1973, 1975, 1977, 1995 by The Lockman Foundation. Used by Permission. www.lockman.org

Scripture quotations marked "ESV" are taken from *The Holy Bible, English Standard Version*, copyright © 2001 by Crossway Bibles, a division of Good News Publishers. Used by permission. All rights reserved.

Scripture quotations marked "NIV" are taken from *The Holy Bible, New International Version®*. NIV®. Copyright © 1973, 1978, 1984 by International Bible Society. Used by permission of Zondervan. All rights reserved.

ISBN 978-1-84550-776-3

10 9 8 7 6 5 4 3 2 1

Published in 2011
in the
Focus on the Bible Commentary Series
by
Christian Focus Publications Ltd.,
Geanies House, Fearn, Ross-shire,
IV20 1TW, Scotland, UK.
www.christianfocus.com

Cover design by Alister MacInnes

Printed and bound by
Bell & Bain, Glasgow

MIX
Paper from
responsible sources
FSC® C007785

Contents

To my wonderful wife Barbara
with whom God has graciously allowed me to enjoy life
for most of the days which He has granted me 'under the sun.'

*Set your shoulder joyously to the world's wheel: you may
spare yourself some unhappiness if, beforehand, you slip the
Book of Ecclesiastes beneath your arm.*

– Havelock Ellis [1]

Introduction

The Jewish synagogue traditionally reads Ecclesiastes on
the third day of the Feast of Tabernacles (or, Booths) in late
September or early October (15-21 Tishri). This annual harvest
festival recalls Israel's wilderness experience (Lev. 23:33-43).
Reading the book during a festival of great joy (cf. Neh. 8:9)
provides a clue that at least Judaism does not consider the tone
of the book to be pessimistic. Ecclesiastes, as further study demonstrates, truly takes its place as the Philippians of the Old
Testament.

Derek Kidner compares the Old Testament's three major
wisdom books to houses:

> If one had to design a cover for each of the three canonical
> wisdom books, drawn from their own contents, one might
> represent them by the various houses they describe. For Proverbs
> it could appropriately be the seven-pillared house of Wisdom, or
> better still that gracious, well-stocked home of the accomplished
> wife, whose virtues bring the book to its serene close. For Job,
> a very different picture: perhaps the wreckage in which his
> family perished when 'a great wind came across the wilderness,
> and struck the four corners of the house;' or perhaps even the
> ash heap to which he banished himself. As for Ecclesiastes, its
> insistence on the transience of earthly glory could hardly find a
> better symbol than its own description of a great house (12:3-4)
> in the grip of slow, inexorable decay.[2]

Whereas many Bible teachers and expositors think that the Book
of Proverbs epitomizes *the practical path to wisdom*, the Book of
Ecclesiastes represents *the reflective path to wisdom* because of its

---

1. Havelock Ellis, *The New Spirit* (New York: Houghton and Mifflin, 1926), 33.
2. Derek Kidner, *The Wisdom of Proverbs, Job & Ecclesiastes*, 116.

deep philosophical and theological bent.[3] It is a book for thinkers – theological thinkers. It is not, however, a book of worldly philosophy. One of my early seminary professors claimed that Ecclesiastes contributed virtually nothing theologically. He believed that a carnal King Solomon produced the book while steeped in the pleasures and, in consequence, pains of life. Embittered and pessimistic, Solomon supposedly penned this book in order to share his dismal view of life with the people of Israel. Immediately upon hearing such a negative assessment of Ecclesiastes, I began a study of its theological content.

Ecclesiastes' Contribution to Theology
The contributions it makes to the doctrine of God offer sufficient reason alone to reconsider the so-called pessimistic and worldly view that many attribute to Ecclesiastes. Even a cursory study of the doctrine of God in Ecclesiastes results in a greater appreciation of the writer's eloquent examination of the character of man. Compared to the character of God, man clearly exists as an exceedingly sinful and thankless being. For this reason, the summarizing exhortation of Ecclesiastes commands the reader to 'fear God' (5:7; 12:13; cf. 7:18; 8:12-13). Confronted by an Almighty, Eternal, Holy, and Omniscient God, man ought to do nothing less.

'God,' as a title, occurs in Ecclesiastes forty times. Readers should confess Him to be 'the True God, the Exalted above the world, the Governor and the Ruler over all.'[4] God, and God alone, is the sole reason why life on planet Earth has any real significance. 'It is only God's work that endures, and only He can impart abiding value to the life and activity of man. "I know that, whatsoever God doeth, it shall be forever: nothing can be put to it, nor anything taken from it"

---

3. E.g., John Drane, *Introducing the Old Testament*, rev. ed. (Oxford, U.K.: Lion Publishing, 2000), 119, 280; William David Reyburn and Euan McG. Fry, *A Handbook on Proverbs*, UBS Handbook Series: Helps for Translators (New York: United Bible Societies, 2000), 15; Crawford H. Toy, *A Critical and Exegetical Commentary on the Book of Proverbs*, International Critical Commentary (New York: C. Scribner's Sons, 1899), xix; Michael V. Fox, *Proverbs 1–9: A New Translation with Introduction and Commentary*, Anchor Yale Bible 18A (New Haven, CT: Yale University Press, 2008), 17; Michael V. Fox, *Ecclesiastes*, JPS Bible Commentary (Philadelphia, Penn.: Jewish Publication Society, 2004), xi; C. L. Seow, *Ecclesiastes: A New Translation with Introduction and Commentary*, Anchor Yale Bible (New Haven, CT: Yale University Press, 2008), 68.

4. Delitzsch, *Song of Songs and Ecclesiastes*, 180.

(Eccles. 3:14).'[5] These represent but the first of the arguments that remove the idea that the ultimate theme of Ecclesiastes amounts to 'All is vanity' (cf. 1:2).

Here then, is a summary of the greater details concerning the doctrine of God in Ecclesiastes:

Theological Topic	References in Ecclesiastes [Key texts in bold]
God's Sovereign Control over Man	1:13 (cf. 3:10); 2:26; **3:1**, 11, 14, **18**; 5:18-20; 6:1-2; 7:14, 26; 8:15; 9:1, 7
God's Providential Grace	**2:24-26**; 3:13; 5:18-20; 8:15
God's Eternality	3:11, 14; 12:5, 7
God's Creatorship	3:11, 14; 7:29; 8:16-17; 11:5; **12:1**, 7
God's Perfection	**3:14**; 7:29; 8:16-17; 11:5
God's Justice and Holiness	2:24-26; **3:17**; 5:4, 6; 7:26, 29; 8:2, 12-13; 11:9; 12:14
God's Abode	**5:2**
God's Omnipresence and Omniscience	**5:2**, 6; 8:2, 16-17; **11:5**; 12:14
God's Omnipotence	**7:13**; 11:5
God's Preservation of His Saints	**7:26**; 8:12-13
God Requires Reverential Fear	3:14; **5:7**; 7:18; 8:12-13; 12:1, **13**
God Requires Obedience before Sacrifice	**5:1**, 4, 7; 8:2; 12:1, 13
God's Word	**12:13**

Bible expositors who think that Ecclesiastes is void of spiritual truth, doctrine, or theological content and value obviously engage in empty speculation. The evidence supports the theological nature of Ecclesiastes. The doctrine of God stands as but one aspect of the doctrinal teachings of this wisdom book. Within its verses a wealth of theological teaching contributes to the doctrines of man, salvation, and future judgment. Let the reader of Ecclesiastes draw near to listen to its wisdom rather than to offer the sacrifice of fools

5. Gleason L. Archer, Jr., *A Survey of Old Testament Introduction*, rev. ed., 475.

(cf. 5:1). As part of Scripture, Ecclesiastes bears the qualities of being God-breathed and profitable for doctrine and for guidance in daily living (2 Tim. 3:16-17).

'Vanity of Vanities'

For many people 'vanity' comes most readily to mind whenever someone mentions the Book of Ecclesiastes. One of my former teaching colleagues, Fred Brock, stated that soap bubbles came to his mind. He used to recite, 'Soap bubbles, soap bubbles, all is soap bubbles.' The bubbles are delightfully beautiful, multi-colored shimmering globes dancing in the air and gracefully changing their form until *poof!* they disappear in a brief shiny cascade of tiny droplets. Beautiful, but insubstantial; delightful, but ephemeral – just like life. The word 'vanity' (Hebrew, *hebel*; also translated 'futility,' 'futile,' 'emptiness,' and 'fleeting' in the NASU) appears thirty-eight times in Ecclesiastes. (See the commentary on 1:2 for a discussion about the meaning of 'vanity.')

The frequency of the occurrences of 'vanity' leads some commentators to identify the concept of vanity or uselessness as the overriding theme of the book – a skeptical and pessimistic theme. However, Ecclesiastes uses a number of words more frequently than 'vanity.' In view of the recurrence of such terms, a better choice for a theme consists of the good which God gives to mankind for enjoyment 'under the sun.' In his pursuit of wisdom, King Solomon discovers that wisdom is but one of the many gifts which God bestows upon His creatures. Repeated terms tend more toward the positive rather than the negative in determining the writer's intended tone. The repetitions and the overall teaching of the entire book lend little credence to the popular idea that Ecclesiastes is pessimistic in tone.

Occurrences	Word or Phrase
52	*good*
52	*wisdom/wise*
40	*God*
40	*heart*
38	*vanity/emptiness*
37	*time*

Occurrences	Word or Phrase
33	*trouble*
30	*evil*
29	*under the sun*
26	*live/life*
17	*rejoice/joy*
12	*give/gift*
6	*eat and drink*

The Purpose of Ecclesiastes

What is the purpose and meaning of Ecclesiastes? The book's epilogue (12:9-14) should be allowed to speak for itself:

9 In addition to being a wise man, the Preacher also taught the people knowledge; and he pondered, searched out and arranged many proverbs. **10** The Preacher sought to find delightful words and to write words of truth correctly. **11** The words of wise men are like goads, and masters of *these* collections are like well-driven nails; they are given by one Shepherd. **12** But beyond this, my son, be warned: the writing of many books is endless, and excessive devotion *to books* is wearying to the body.

13 The conclusion, when all has been heard, *is*: fear God and keep His commandments, because this *applies to* every person. **14** For God will bring every act to judgment, everything which is hidden, whether it is good or evil.

The primary purpose of Ecclesiastes appears to be didactic – the teaching of wisdom (cf. 2:24; 3:12, 22; 5:18-19; 8:1-9; 11:1-6). Its instructions emphasize obedience to God's commandments and the fear of God (3:17; 5:1-7; 8:12-13; 11:9; 12:7, 13-14). Such reverential fear of God resonates with the covenant teaching found in the books of Deuteronomy (4:10; 5:29; 6:2, 13, 24; 8:6; 10:12, 20; 13:4; 14:23; 17:19; 28:58; 31:12-13), Leviticus (19:14, 52; 25:17, 36, 43), and Proverbs (1:7; 10:27; 13:14; 14:27; 19:23; 22:4). Ecclesiastes stands rooted in the mainstream of Old Testament revelation.

Though many scholars tag Ecclesiastes with the label of skepticism, 'Qoheleth is no skeptic; he demolishes in order to build.'[6] As Gleason Archer put it, the author of the Book of Ecclesiastes writes 'to convince men of the uselessness of any world view which does not rise above the horizon of man himself.'[7] As a result of the biblical author's careful examination of man's environment, it 'leaves us hungry to know God.'[8] Christian Ginsburg, the eminent Hebrew scholar who produced one of the most detailed studies of Ecclesiastes, summarized the book in the following words:

> The design of this book ... is to gather together the desponding people of God from the various expediencies to which they have resorted, in consequence of the inexplicable difficulties and perplexities in the moral government of God, into the community of the Lord, by shewing them the utter insufficiency of all human efforts to obtain real happiness, which cannot be secured by wisdom, pleasure, industry, wealth, &c., but consists in the calm enjoyment of life, in the resignation to the dealings of Providence, in the service of God, and in the belief in a future state of retribution, when all the mysteries in the present course of the world shall be solved.[9]

Walter Kaiser suggests that Ecclesiastes should be viewed as a missionary outreach to Gentile peoples through the channel of wisdom.[10] Therefore, the book could be entitled *Euangelistes* (the Evangelist), a title especially suitable for the last half of the book (chapters 7–12).

The Title of Ecclesiastes
The English Bible adopts the title of *Ecclesiastes* from that employed by the ancient Greek translation of the Old Testament, the Septuagint. The Hebrew title is *Qoheleth*. The meaning attributed to either the Greek or the Hebrew title varies from commentator to commentator. The Jewish Midrash interprets *Qoheleth* as 'Preacher,' one who delivers discourses before a *qahal* ('congregation'). The great rabbi

---

6. Derek Kidner, 'Wisdom Literature of the Old Testament,' 126.
7. Archer, *Old Testament Introduction*, 475.
8. Stuart Olyott, *A Life Worth Living and A Lord Worth Loving*, 13-14.
9. Christian D. Ginsburg, *The Song of Songs and Coheleth*, 2:16-17. Ginsburg was a Polish-born (15 Dec. 1831) Jew who studied for the rabbinate, but converted to Christianity at the age of 15. He continued his studies in England and made Britain his home. He died at Palmers Green, Middlesex, on 7 March 1914.
10. Kaiser, *Ecclesiastes*, 32-33.

Rashi took *Qoheleth* to mean a 'Gatherer' of wisdom. Ginsburg follows the same line of thought, settling on the meaning 'Assembler' or 'Gatherer' of scattered people into the more immediate presence of God. Jerome, the translator of the Latin Vulgate,[11] took the meaning to be *Concionator*, 'one who gathers an assembly.'

Besides these major translations of the title *Qoheleth*, scholars have suggested a wide range of other possibilities throughout the history of the book's interpretation. They include Hugo Grotius' 'Collector' or 'Compiler,' Rosenthal's 'Eclectic,' Ibn Ezra's 'Accumulated Wisdom,' Coecejus' 'Penitent,' Simonis' 'Old Man,' Desvoeux's 'Sophist,' Spohn's 'Philosopher,' and Augusti's 'Departed Spirit (of Solomon).'

The English versions normally understand *Qoheleth* to mean 'Preacher,' but translate the same verb root in 1 Kings 8:1 with words like 'assemble,' 'convene,' and 'summon.' The record of Solomon's speech on that occasion comes in verses 55-61. Many have observed that the title in either Greek or Hebrew takes a feminine grammatical form. Why does Hebrew employ the feminine? Some answer by pointing out that it is a reference to Wisdom (a feminine noun in both Hebrew and Greek) and by concluding that Solomon is the exemplar of wisdom. References in Proverbs to Lady Wisdom (cf. Prov. 9:1-6) fill out that line of thinking. Both Greek and Hebrew utilize the feminine gender for many nouns referring to offices or vocations.[12] One example in Hebrew is 'scribe' (*sophereth*) and one example in Greek is 'prophet' (*prophētēs*).

The Canonicity of Ecclesiastes

As early as 190 B.C., Ben Sirach quoted from the Book of Ecclesiastes. Later, in the first century B.C. the apocryphal book 'The Wisdom of Solomon' took exception to the Book of Ecclesiastes.

---

11. Jerome (347–420) was the first to translate the Hebrew Bible into the Latin version known to this day as the Vulgate. The current edition of the Latin Vulgate represents the Roman Catholic counter-Reformation's revision of Jerome's edition under the supervision of Pope Sixtus V (1520–1590). Codex Amiatinus, produced in Northumbria, England, around the beginning of the eighth century, represents the earliest surviving copy of Jerome's Vulgate.

12. E. Kautzsch, ed., *Gesenius' Hebrew Grammar*, 2nd English ed., trans. and rev. by A. E. Cowley (Oxford, U.K.: Clarendon Press, 1910), 393 (§122.r); George A. Barton, *A Critical and Exegetical Commentary on the Book of Ecclesiastes*, International Critical Commentary (New York: Scribner, 1908), 66-67.

The New Testament writers do not quote Ecclesiastes direct, although there are possible allusions in Romans 3:10 and 8:20 and James 4:14. In the first century A.D. a controversy developed between the Jewish schools of Shammai and Hillel over the canonicity of Ecclesiastes. The former school rejected its canonicity, whereas the latter accepted it. Later Jewish literature accepts Ecclesiastes as part of the Hebrew Bible. The Midrash (*Shir Hashirim Rabba* 1:1, section 10) makes the claim that Solomon wrote the Song of Songs in his youth, Proverbs in his maturity, and Ecclesiastes in his old age.

The early church fathers accepted the canonicity of Ecclesiastes and cited some of its teachings. Hermas (died 150) was originally a slave. Church history remembers him best for having written 'The Shepherd,' in which he cites Ecclesiastes 12:13 at the start of his discussion of the fear of God as opposed to fearing the devil. Justin Martyr (ca. 100–165) was born in Palestine near Nablus in Samaria and studied at Ephesus. He was converted by a humble old Christian and taught in Rome until he suffered martyrdom under Marcus Aurelius. In his *Dialogue* with Trypho, Justin may refer to Ecclesiastes 12:7 as he speaks of the soul leaving the body and returning to the place from which it was taken. Clement of Alexandria (ca. 155–220) was born in Athens and was the teacher of Origen who himself refers to Ecclesiastes a number of times and includes it in his Hexapla. Clement cites Ecclesiastes 1:16-18 and 7:13. Tertullian's (160–225) fame arises from his declaration that 'The blood of the martyrs is the seed of the church' and being the first to use the term 'trinity' (*trinitas*) to refer to the persons of the Godhead. He cites Ecclesiastes 3:1 on three separate occasions. The canonical lists published by Melito, Origen, Epiphanius, and Jerome all include Ecclesiastes.

From the pre-Christian era, archaeologists have discovered four fragments of Ecclesiastes at Qumran's Cave 4. These fragments include 5:13-17; 6:3-8; 7:1-2, 7-9, and 19-20. It appears that the manuscript from which these fragments have come dates to the middle of the second century B.C.

Ultimately, however, the canonicity of Ecclesiastes is determined by its own apparent claim to divine inspiration in 12:11 – 'The words of wise men are like goads, and masters of *these* collections are like well-driven nails; *they are given by one Shepherd*' (emphasis added).

The Authorship and Date of Ecclesiastes

The words of the Preacher, the son of David, king in Jerusalem (Eccles. 1:1).

Views

In 1644 Hugo Grotius suggested that Solomon did not write Ecclesiastes. No one else in the Christian church had made such a suggestion prior to that time,[13] except for Martin Luther who identified the author as Jesus ben Sirach. Some evangelical scholars (e.g., Franz Delitzsch, Edward J. Young, J. Stafford Wright, and H. C. Leupold) have insisted that the author of Ecclesiastes is unknown. They argue that the Old Testament does not use 'king in Jerusalem' elsewhere. However, 1 Kings 11:42 comes very close to that statement: 'Thus the time that Solomon reigned in Jerusalem over all Israel was forty years.' 'Reigned' might also be translated 'was king' – it is the verb root (*malak*) for the Hebrew noun 'king' (*melek*).

Those who deny Solomonic authorship also point out that Ecclesiastes does not make specific reference to Solomon as the author even though both Proverbs 1:1 ('The proverbs of Solomon, king of Israel') and the Song of Songs 1:1 ('The Song of Songs, which is Solomon's') specify Solomon's authorship. However, readers must note that Ecclesiastes identifies the author as both 'the son of David' (1:1) and 'king over Israel in Jerusalem' (1:12) – exactly the same information Proverbs 1:1 provides about Solomon. The author might have considered that information sufficient for the readers of his day to know who composed the book.

A third argument offered by those rejecting Solomonic authorship involves what at first appears be a critical attitude toward kings: 'A poor yet wise lad is better than an old and foolish king who no longer knows *how* to receive instruction' (4:13); 'Blessed are you, O land, whose king is of nobility and whose princes eat at the appropriate time – for strength and not for drunkenness' (10:17); and, 'Furthermore, in your bedchamber do not curse a king, and in your sleeping rooms do not curse a rich man, for a bird of the heavens will carry the sound and the winged creature will make the matter known'

---

13. Leupold, *Ecclesiastes*, 16.

(10:20). However, the Book of Proverbs also makes declarations about kings that could be taken as equally critical: 'The fury of a king is *like* messengers of death, But a wise man will appease it' (16:14; cf. Eccles. 10:20); and, 'The king gives stability to the land by justice, But a man who takes bribes overthrows it' (29:4; cf. Eccles. 10:17). Should such proverbs be taken as evidence denying the involvement of kings (Solomon, Hezekiah, and Lemuel) in the writing and collecting of Proverbs?[14]

Linguistic Evidence

Franz Delitzsch argues that Solomon could not have written the Book of Ecclesiastes: 'If the Book of Koheleth were of old Solomonic origin, then there is no history of the Hebrew language.'[15] How tenable is Delitzsch's view? Scholars cite a number of Aramaisms (i.e., examples of Aramaic language influence on the Hebrew text) within Ecclesiastes.[16] In fact, some scholars claim that Ecclesiastes reveals substantial evidence of foreign influence, including Phoenician, Egyptian, Greek, Babylonian, and Persian.[17] The book's vocabulary includes seventy-seven words occurring five times or fewer in the Old Testament. Of those seventy-seven, a little over 57% are also employed in the Jewish Talmud.[18] Although some Old Testament scholars (like Delitzsch and Eissfeldt) believe that this kind of evidence favors a date for the writing of Ecclesiastes at least 500 years after the death of King Solomon, the vocabulary of the book is not a firm indication of date. The highly respected Old Testament scholar at Princeton Theological Seminary, Robert Dick Wilson (1856–1930), long ago pointed out that 'Solomon being the wisest man of his time and a poet, an observer of nature and of man, would, like

---

14. See the commentary on 8:1 for additional discussion demonstrating that the texts about kings actually argues favorably for Solomonic authorship.

15. Delitzsch, *Song of Songs and Ecclesiastes*, 190.

16. Barton, *Ecclesiastes*, 52; Delitzsch, *Song of Songs and Ecclesiastes*, 190-98. Whybray, *Ecclesiastes*, 15, writes, 'That Ecclesiastes contains a large number of Aramaic words – more, in fact, than any other Old Testament book except Esther – is an undoubted fact.'

17. Otto Eissfeldt, *The Old Testament: An Introduction*, trans. by Peter R. Ackroyd (New York: Harper & Row, Publishers, 1965), 491-500. Two Persian loanwords are also employed in Ecclesiastes: 'parks' in 2:5 and the one translated 'sentence' in 8:11. See, also, Bartholomew, *Ecclesiastes*, 48.

18. Robert Dick Wilson, *A Scientific Investigation of the Old Testament* (Chicago, Ill.: Moody Press, 1959), 109.

Shakespeare, Milton, and Carlyle, have a vocabulary much beyond the average.'[19] Indeed, the vocabulary is limited more by the subject matter than by the timeframe for the writing.

Aramaic influence need not indicate a date around the time of the Babylonian exile or following. It is true that Aramaic was the language of Babylon at the time of the exile and that the Hebrews returning from captivity brought the language back with them. However, from the time of the patriarchs Aramaic crops up in the history of the Hebrews and in their language.[20] Abraham probably spoke Aramaic in Haran. Genesis 31:47 provides evidence that Laban and his family conversed in Aramaic. During the united monarchy (the reigns of Saul, David, and Solomon), contacts with Aramaic-speaking peoples in the Syrian principalities of Hamath, Damascus, Hadrach, and Zobah increased. This contact would have broadened the vocabulary of Hebrew with terms borrowed from Israel's Aramaic-speaking neighbors. The events described in 2 Kings 18 indicate that King Hezekiah and his court officials understood Aramaic (v. 26). If Solomon, like Hezekiah, was conversant with Aramaic, there is no reason why we would not expect to find Aramaic influence in those biblical books penned by him.

Besides these very common-sense observations about Aramaic, the following points might also be made:[21] (1) Some so-called Aramaisms turn out to be Hebrew even though they might be more infrequent in a particular usage than in Aramaic. An example might be the word for 'grinding mill' in Ecclesiastes 12:4, which marks its only occurrence in the Hebrew Bible. However, another form of the same root takes the same meaning in Lamentations 5:13. (2) Some occurrences of so-called Aramaisms are merely vocabulary or grammatical forms well-known in Aramaic, but not previously recognized as existing in Hebrew. An example might be a Hebrew root used in a context in Ecclesiastes that does not occur in the rest of the Old Testament. In the Ecclesiastes context its meaning parallels one meaning of the same root word in Aramaic.

---

19. Ibid., 111.

20. For a full description of the relationship of Aramaic to the Old Testament, the reader is referred to Archer, *A Survey of Old Testament Introduction*, 137-41; and, Wilson, *Scientific Investigation*, 112-30.

21. Cf. James Barr, *Comparative Philology and the Text of the Old Testament, with Additions and Corrections* (Winona Lake, Ind.: Eisenbrauns, 1987), 121-24.

'Uproot' in Ecclesiastes 3:2 might qualify as this kind of usage. (3) The Aramaism might exist as a deliberate or non-deliberate effect of some Aramaic phenomenon on the author's choice of words or phraseology. Such an effect could be explained by the author's potential contacts with Aramaic speakers in northern Israel or with Ugaritic [22] speakers from north of Israel. The word for 'wealth' in Ecclesiastes 5:19 (Heb., 18) appears to have been borrowed from Aramaic as early as Joshua 22:8.[23]

Present-day commentators have come to the conclusion that the linguistic argument emphasized so strongly by scholars like Delitzsch does not hold up to careful scrutiny. Daniel Fredericks published a book in 1988 that acknowledges the diversity of the language of Ecclesiastes but attributes its dialectical uniqueness to the pre-exilic period of Israel's history.[24] Nearly a decade after Fredericks' detailed analysis, C. L. Seow observes that 'the presence of isolated Aramaisms in any book says nothing of its provenance; Aramaisms are attested sporadically in preexilic works, as well, particularly those texts from the north.'[25] Still, Seow concludes that the book originates in the post-exilic period.[26] Tremper Longman proposes that 'Fredericks's study should give rise to a healthy skepticism concerning the linguistic arguments used to date the book late.'[27] He concludes that 'the language of the book is not a certain barometer of date.'[28] Yet another decade passes and Craig Bartholomew, agreeing with Longman, declares that 'the arguments about language are not conclusive.'[29]

Internal and Contextual Evidence
Both internal and contextual evidence contribute support for Solomonic authorship of Ecclesiastes. At the very outset the

---

22. There is evidence of Aramaic intrusions in Ugaritic documents from Ras Shamra that date as early as the time of Moses (ca. 1500 B.C.). Cf. Archer, *Old Testament Introduction*, 144.

23. Seow, *Ecclesiastes*, 209.

24. Daniel C. Fredericks, *Qoheleth's Language: Re-evaluating Its Nature and Date* (Lewiston, Penn.: Edwin Mellen Press, 1988).

25. Seow, *Ecclesiastes*, 13.

26. Ibid., 15.

27. Longman, *Ecclesiastes*, 14.

28. Ibid., 15.

29. Bartholomew, *Ecclesiastes*, 52.

book identifies its contents as 'The words of the Preacher, the son of David, king in Jerusalem' (1:1). The writer labels the same king as 'king over Israel in Jerusalem' (1:12). Only four kings ruled over Israel (as opposed to Judah) in Jerusalem: Saul, David, Solomon, and Rehoboam. Another description compares the author to 'all who were over Jerusalem before me' (1:16; 2:7; cp. 1 Chron. 29:25). Three non-Israelite kings reigned in Jerusalem who might qualify for this description: Melchizedek (Gen. 14:18), Adonizedek (Josh. 10:1), and Araunah (2 Sam. 24:23).

Throughout Ecclesiastes the ties to Solomonic history and literature emerge again and again. The commentary will earmark these points of contact with Solomon in the course of interpreting the text. They include such associations as 'eating and drinking and rejoicing' in 1 Kings 4:20's description of life during the reign of Solomon. The same activities recur in Ecclesiastes with each refrain speaking of God's gifts (2:24-26; 3:12-13, 22; 5:18-20; 8:15; 9:7). Fredericks, in his own commentary, cites the nineteenth-century work of D. Johnston that provides an extensive list of parallels between Proverbs, the Song of Songs, Ecclesiastes, and the Solomonic histories.[30] The evidence presented in the following chart favors Solomonic authorship. No other king in all Israel fits the factors of wisdom, works, wealth, and words better than Solomon. These alone would seem to be adequate proof of Solomonic authorship of Ecclesiastes. Solomonic authorship would indicate a date for the book at approximately 940–932 B.C.

Factor	Ecclesiastes	1 Kings
W I S D O M	'I said to myself, "Behold, I have magnified and increased wisdom more than all who were over Jerusalem before me; and my mind has observed a wealth of wisdom and knowledge."' **(1:16)**	'behold, I have done according to your words. Behold, I have given you a wise and discerning heart, so that there has been no one like you before you, nor shall one like you arise after you.' **(3:12)**

---

30. Fredericks, 'Ecclesiastes,' 34-36. The Johnston manuscript is *A Treatise on the Authorship of Ecclesiastes*, available electronically on Google Books.

Factor	Ecclesiastes	1 Kings
W O R K S	'I enlarged my works: I built houses for myself, I planted vineyards for myself; I made gardens and parks for myself and I planted in them all kinds of fruit trees; I made ponds of water for myself from which to irrigate a forest of growing trees.' **(2:4-6)**	'Now King Solomon levied forced laborers from all Israel; and the forced laborers numbered 30,000 men.... Then the king commanded, and they quarried great stones, costly stones, to lay the foundation of the house ... and prepared the timbers and the stones to build the house.' **(5:13-18)** 'Now Solomon was building his own house thirteen years, and he finished all his house. He built the house of the forest of Lebanon;... He also made a house like this hall for Pharaoh's daughter, whom Solomon had married.' **(7:1-8)** 'So Solomon rebuilt Gezer and the lower Beth-horon and Baalath and Tamar in the wilderness, in the land *of Judah,* and all the storage cities which Solomon had, even the cities for his chariots and the cities for his horsemen, and all that it pleased Solomon to build in Jerusalem, in Lebanon, and in all the land under his rule.' **(9:17-19)**
W E A L T H	'I bought male and female slaves and I had homeborn slaves. Also I possessed flocks and herds larger than all who preceded me in Jerusalem. Also, I collected for myself silver and gold and the treasure of kings and provinces. I provided for myself male and female singers and the pleasures of men – many concubines. Then I became great and increased more than all who preceded me in Jerusalem. My wisdom also stood by me.' **(2:7-9)**	'Now the weight of gold which came in to Solomon in one year was 666 talents of gold, besides *that* from the traders and the wares of the merchants and all the kings of the Arabs and the governors of the country. King Solomon made 200 large shields of beaten gold, using 600 *shekels of* gold on each large shield. *He made* 300 shields of beaten gold, using three minas of gold on each shield,... Moreover, the king made a great throne of ivory and overlaid it with refined gold.... nothing like *it* was made for any other kingdom.' **(10:14-20)**

Factor	Ecclesiastes	1 Kings
W O R D S	'In addition to being a wise man, the Preacher also taught the people knowledge; and he pondered, searched out and arranged many proverbs. The Preacher sought to find delightful words and to write words of truth correctly.'(12:9-10)	'He also spoke 3,000 proverbs, and his songs were 1,005.' (4:32)

Literary Description

The Book of Ecclesiastes may be classified as wisdom literature. Extrabiblical examples of similar literature have surfaced in Egypt ('The Instruction of Amen-em-het,' 1995–1968 B.C.) and Babylonia ('A Pessimistic Dialogue between Master and Servant' and 'A Dialogue about Human Misery,' fifteenth or fourteenth century B.C.).

Scholars debate whether the book is prose (Delitzsch) or poetry (Hertzberg and Zoeckler), or prose narrative mixed with poetry (Eaton, Fox). Leupold's description of Ecclesiastes as poetic prose[31] might be considered the better part of wisdom and represents the view I have adopted in this commentary. Poetic portions include 1:2-8, 15, 18; 2:14a; 3:2-8; 4:5-6; 5:3 (Hebrew, 5:2); 6:7; 7:1-11; 8:1, 5; 9:7-8, 17-18; 10:1-3, 6-20; 11:1, 3a, 4, 6a, 7, 9-10; 12:1-8. Other classifications of the genre of Ecclesiastes include a royal testament (von Rad), a fictional royal autobiography (Longman), and diatribe (Bartholomew).

Each section of Ecclesiastes generally concludes with one of the following concepts:

- the weakness or transience of man's accomplishments

- the uncertainty of man's fate

- the impossibility of attaining true knowledge in this world

- the need to enjoy life

---

31. Leupold, *Ecclesiastes*, 22: 'a rhythmical prose which repeatedly soars to the level of poetic form with parallelism and like ornamentations.'

A refrain concludes three of the four major sections:

Section	Refrain
1:1–2:26	2:24 – 'There is nothing better for a man *than* to eat and drink and tell himself that his labor is good. This also I have seen that it is from the hand of God.'
3:1–5:20	5:18 – 'Here is what I have seen to be good and fitting: to eat, to drink and enjoy oneself in all one's labor in which he toils under the sun *during* the few years of his life which God has given him; for this is his reward.'
6:1–8:15	8:15 – 'So I commended pleasure, for there is nothing good for a man under the sun except to eat and to drink and to be merry, and this will stand by him in his toils *throughout* the days of his life which God has given him under the sun.'

Some commentators refer to these refrains as *carpe diem* ('Seize the day!') passages[32] or enjoyment passages. However, the final section (8:16–12:14) concludes the entire book with a different kind of statement: 'The conclusion, when all has been heard, *is*: fear God and keep His commandments, because this *applies to* every person. For God will bring every act to judgment, everything which is hidden, whether it is good or evil' (12:13-14). These verses provide the stimulus for considering the message of the book.

The Message of Ecclesiastes
Solomon develops three foundational spiritual truths in Ecclesiastes:[33]

(1) Mankind searches for happiness and enduring substance (2:24; 3:12, 22; 5:18; 8:15; 9:7-9; 11:7-10). Ecclesiastes presents mankind with an invitation to enjoy life.

- Unparalyzed by life's uncertainties, enjoy life as God's gift (11:1-6).

- Undepressed by life's shortness, enjoy life as God's gift (11:9-10).

---

32. Bartholomew, *Ecclesiastes*, 23; Longman, *Ecclesiastes*, 106.
33. Cf. Bullock, *Introduction to the Old Testament Poetic Books*, 193; and, Kidner, 'Wisdom Literature of the Old Testament,' 125-26.

- Showing reverence to and serving God in life, enjoy life as God's gift (12:1-14).

(2) Divine sovereignty and providence characterize human existence on planet Earth (2:26; 3:14; 7:13-14; 8:16–9:1; 11:5).

- We must believe that God is the Creator with whom we cannot trifle (5:2; 12:1).

- We must accept that God's world cannot be changed to our liking (3:1-8; 7:13).

- We cannot extrapolate the future on the basis of the present, because the pattern keeps changing in accord with God's plan (7:14; 8:17).

- We must believe that God is the Judge and will bring all wickedness into judgment (3:17; 5:6; 8:12-13; 11:9; 12:7, 14).

(3) The way of wisdom for human conduct requires the avoidance of excess.

- Be content with the present (7:10).

- Be conciliatory (10:12-14).

- Be cautious (8:1-9; 10:8-11; cf. 7:8-9).

One might encapsulate these three truths in the following exhortation: *Live without reserve; die without regret.* From a worldly, under-the-sun perspective void of biblical values, that sounds a lot like the philosophy of Aristotle (eudaemonism – happiness results from an active, rational life, and the morality of actions is determined by their capacity to produce happiness) or Epicurus (epicureanism – sensuous pleasure is the highest good since an afterlife and the influence of the divine upon this life are non-existent). From a biblical and heavenly perspective, however, the same exhortation applies, because the divine Creator gives life and He will judge any abuse of His gift. At the time of our death God will usher us into His presence as we transition from this life into the afterlife. Then we shall be held accountable for how we lived – how we invested the gift of life He gave us (cf. Heb. 9:27; Matt. 25:14-30). As we stand before Him, will we regret having squandered the opportunities of this life?

In addition to these three foundational truths, Ecclesiastes describes three problems faced by people in this life:

(1) *The uncertainty of time and chance* (9:11-12) demonstrates that man is not sovereign. It appears that individuals do not control their own destiny.

(2) *The endemic and incurable nature of wickedness* (3:16; 4:1; 5:8; 7:7, 20; 9:3) demonstrates that man is not inherently good.

(3) That *death has the final word in any human enterprise* (2:14-16; 3:18-22; 6:3-12; 8:8, 10; 12:1-7) is proof that mankind is not immortal.

The Book of Ecclesiastes does not proceed like a catechism with questions and very specific answers to those questions. Philip Ryken sums up its essence with the following words:

> It is not the kind of book that we keep reading until we reach the end and get the answer, like a mystery. Instead it is a book in which we keep struggling with the problems of life, and as we struggle, we learn to trust God with the questions even when we do *not* have all the answers.[34]

With these various themes and truths in mind, a basic outline of the contents of the Book of Ecclesiastes can be presented. This commentary will flesh out this basic outline with further detail as the study of Ecclesiastes progresses chapter by chapter and verse by verse.

Outline of Ecclesiastes [35]

I   From **experience**, the Preacher **learned that man is powerless** (1:1–2:26).

     • *Refrain:* 2:24-26   > There is no inherent good in man.
                                     > God alone is the Giver of good.
                                     > Enjoy God's gift of life.

---

34. Ryken, *Ecclesiastes*, 202.
35. Adapted from Kaiser, *Ecclesiastes*, *passim*.

II From **observation**, the Preacher **learned that God has a design for all things** (3:1-5:20).

- *Refrain:* 5:18-20   > Life is to be enjoyed.
  > Life is a gift from God to be lived
  – not to be analyzed endlessly.

III By **application**, the Preacher **found the explanation for apparent inequalities in divine providence** (6:1–8:15).

A. The evaluation of man's outward fortunes (6:1–7:15)
B. The evaluation of man's character (7:16-29)
C. The effect of righteous government (8:1-14)

- *Refrain:* 8:15   > Enjoy life.

IV In **conclusion**, the Preacher **determined to fear God, obey God, and enjoy life** (8:16–12:14)

A. What we cannot know (mystery) must not affect our enjoyment of life (8:16–9:9).
B. What we cannot know (mystery) must not affect our work (9:10–11:6).
C. The daily reminder of our short life and soon entrance into our Creator's presence should infect our God-given joy and work (11:7–12:8).

- *Epilogue:* 12:9-14   > Fear God with obedience.

STUDY QUESTIONS

1. What kinds of houses might depict the books of Job, Proverbs, and Ecclesiastes? Why?

2. What are some of the truths Ecclesiastes teaches about God?

3. How would you argue for Solomonic authorship of Ecclesiastes?

4. What are some arguments against Solomonic authorship of Ecclesiastes?

5. Where are the refrains in Ecclesiastes? Identify the general content of these refrains.

6. What are the three problems Ecclesiastes addresses that comprise the common experience of mankind?

7. Make a list of your personal experiences with these same three problems.

8. How do you cope with those kinds of experiences?

I

A Disappointing Discovery

From experience, *the Preacher* learned that
man is powerless *(1:1–2:26)*, Part 1

Discouragement, despair, and disappointment. It brings to mind the words of an American folk song:

> *Gloom, despair, and agony on me;*
> *Deep dark depression, excessive misery;*
> *If it weren't for bad luck, I'd have no luck at all …*

Discouragement, despair, and disappointment. 'When Solomon was old,… his wives turned his heart away after other gods' (1 Kings 11:4). Intriguingly, the Old Testament writers refer to idols ('other gods') as 'vanities' (or, 'empty things,' 'nothings;' Deut. 32:21; 1 Kings 16:13, 26). The Preacher employs the same Hebrew word for 'vanities' in the Book of Ecclesiastes. As an old man, the wisest, most accomplished and wealthy king of Israel discovers that life no longer possesses meaning. All satisfaction vanishes (Eccles. 1:8; 4:8; 5:10; 6:7; 12:1). Solomon, Israel's most powerful king, feels powerless – unable to control his life, unable to control what happens to his work and wealth after his death (2:18-19), and unable to prevent his death (9:12).

Surrounded by more success, opulence, and pleasure than any person could ever desire, Solomon hits rock bottom in his miserable existence. Then he begins a spiritual odyssey to return from the quagmire of nothingness in which he flounders

– a search for meaning in life. It begins with admitting his empty condition. Solomon concedes that his view of life is bleak and dismal.

Could it be that Solomon had never truly believed? Could it be that Ecclesiastes records his spiritual odyssey as a journey to faith in the Lord God of heaven and earth? Shortly after Solomon became king upon the death of his father David, the Scripture records that 'Solomon loved the LORD, walking in the statutes of his father David, except he sacrificed and burned incense on the high places' (1 Kings 3:3). That seems to indicate that Solomon had not yet placed his trust completely in God, or that he had but had not matured in his faith. When the Lord appears to Solomon for the first time in a dream (vv. 4-5), the young king confesses his immaturity ('I am but a little child; I do not know how to go out or come in,' v. 7). Responding to the Lord's invitation to ask for what he wants (v. 5), the king requests that he be given 'an understanding heart to judge Your people to discern between good and evil. For who is able to judge this great people of Yours?' (v. 9). Only after Solomon's reception of that discernment (equivalent to spiritual maturity) did he proceed with the building of the Temple.

At the dedication ceremony for the Temple, Solomon manifests his spiritual leadership and maturity repeatedly (1 Kings 8:1-66). Clearly, he understands fully the depraved nature of sin, the grace of God, and the importance of prayers of confession and praise. Solomon speaks of the Word of God as that which God will fulfill and by which His people must live (vv. 24-26, 56, 58, 61). Following the dedi-cation of the Temple, God appears to Solomon a second time (9:1-9), revealing that He hears the king's prayer and that He approves the completion of the Temple.

Would the Lord allow any book of Scripture to be written by an unbeliever? Solomon not only authored most of the Book of Proverbs, he also authored the Song of Solomon, Psalms 72 and 127, and, as argued in the 'Introduction' to this commentary, Ecclesiastes. If he were actually an unbeliever during his penning of these portions of Scripture, how could we believe that those writings were inspired (cf. 2 Tim. 3:16) and the writer of them borne along by the Holy Spirit (cf. 2 Pet. 1:20-21)?

If Solomon had not been a believer, how could the Scripture say that his wives were the cause of his turning his heart away from the Lord in his old age (1 Kings 11:1-6)? The very declaration of the king's departure from serving God advances proof that he had once rightly served God (cf. Neh. 13:26). He did not always indulge in idolatry. The sins of his youth raised their ugly head again in his old age. The spiritual journey that the Book of Ecclesiastes chronicles depicts the journey of a believer, not an unbeliever. A declaration in 2 Chronicles 11:16-17 seems to confirm the ultimate spiritual condition of Solomon when it speaks of those 'who set their hearts on seeking the LORD God of Israel' (v. 16) and then says, 'they walked in the way of David and Solomon' (v. 17).[1]

Vanishing Vapors (1:2)
Following the superscription of verse 1, this quote from the Preacher serves as an envelope for the entire book. It commences the book here in verse 2 and it concludes the book at 12:8 ahead of the closing postscript (12:9-14). In different contexts the Hebrew word translated 'vanity' in Ecclesiastes 1:2 has different meanings. The following chart reveals the variety of translations employed in the New American Standard Updated version:

Meaning	Reference (NASU)
vain	2 Kings 17:15
foolishly	Job 27:12
emptily	Job 35:16
nothing	Psalm 39:6
futility	Psalm 78:33
a mere breath	Psalm 94:11
vapor	Proverbs 21:6
fleeting	Ecclesiastes 9:9; 11:10
idols	Jeremiah 10:8
worthless	Jeremiah 10:15
useless	Lamentations 4:17

---

1. Cf. Benedikt Peters, *Das Buch Prediger; 'Sphinx' der hebräischen Literature* (Dillenburg, Germany: Christliche Verlagsgesellschaft, 2000), 25, to whom I owe this significant observation.

Other suggested meanings include the following:

Meaning	Reference and English Version
worthless idols	Deuteronomy 32:21 (NIV, REB)
worthless	Isaiah 30:7 (REB)
useless	Isaiah 30:7 (NIV)
no purpose	Isaiah 49:4 (REB)
nothing	Isaiah 49:4 (NIV)
a puff of air	Isaiah 57:13 (REB)
a mere breath	Isaiah 57:13 (NIV)
a sham	Jeremiah 10:3 (REB)
fleeting	Proverbs 31:30 (REB, NIV)
enigma	Ecclesiastes 8:10 (NET)

Several different contexts within Ecclesiastes present different potential meanings for this one Hebrew term. H. C. Leupold takes the position that 'vanity of vanities' means 'utterly transitory.'[2] In 3:16-19 it appears to focus on the painful condition that results from 'having to live with many questions unanswered.'[3] The text depicts a workaholic in 4:7-8. The success that he experiences lacks any understanding of the purpose of all his work. 'He never stops to ask the important question: "for what purpose am I doing all this?"'[4] In 6:1-2 Solomon deals with the matter of having material benefits but not being able to enjoy them. He talks, not about the meaninglessness of life, but about the frustration of not being able to enjoy the fruits of one's labor. A final example occurs in 8:14 where Solomon observes that good things happen to bad people while bad things happen to good people. It is one of life's great enigmas for which no one has the answer.

Thus, the word so often translated 'vanity' describes all of these situations. None of the texts proclaim that life is totally empty and meaningless. However, all of them do express the inability of mankind to fully understand these realities of life.

---

2. Leupold, *Ecclesiastes*, 41.
3. Ogden, 'The Meaning of the Term *Hebel*,' 229.
4. Ibid., 230.

Such realities produce frustration, puzzlement, and vexation, but they do not make life meaningless. In fact, the message of Ecclesiastes seems to be that the wise individual will learn how to accept such realities and live happily in the knowledge that there is Someone who really does comprehend the reasons for apparent inequities and who sovereignly controls life's enigmatic twists and turns.

One more observation concerning the phrase 'All is vanity' requires attention. In the Hebrew language a mere two words make up the phrase. At the time Solomon penned the Book of Ecclesiastes, Hebrew did not include written vowels. Consonants alone constituted the written text. This phrase not only exhibits assonance, its visual representation displays a repetition: הכל הבל (*hakkol hebel*). Look at it this way:

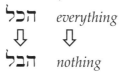

הכל   *everything*

⇩   ⇩

הבל   *nothing*

Jarick presents the following description of this intricate interplay between the words:

> Like the proverbial butterfly flapping its wings in the Brazilian rainforest and setting in train the tornado that sweeps across the Florida coastline, so too the merest stroke of a pen can change everything. In Hebrew, 'everything' is הכל, made up of the letters he, kaph and lamedh. But if the poetic imagination takes a pen and adds the smallest of marks at the heart of this word – that is to say, an extra stroke is added on to the bottom right corner of the letter kaph, transforming that letter into a beth – an entirely different word appears: the word הבל, 'a breath, transience, futility, nothingness.'[5]

Life is just that way. The tiniest of deeds can cause one's entire existence to collapse like a house of cards. We cannot, at any time, make the mistake of thinking, 'This decision or choice is insignificant – it's not going to affect anything.' In one moment of selfishness or recklessness, or just plain inadvertence, our *everything* becomes *nothing*.

---

5. Jarick, 'The Hebrew Book of Changes,' 79.

Round and Round, and Round and Round ... (1:3-8)

Sometimes readers interpret this passage as descriptive of the utter futility of life due to its endless succession of empty repetitions. On the other hand, we can understand as speaking about 'the *limits* within which nature – including human nature – must run its course.'[6] In His omniscience the Creator established the earth's cycles at creation (Gen. 1:14-18) and reiterated the natural ordinances after the Noachic flood (8:22). Thus, the 'past repeats itself ad infinitum, so there is nothing new under the sun. Things only seem new because of a human tendency to forget the past.'[7]

Divinely-ordained cycles in creation elicit awe and admiration as well as providing an individual with an accurate assessment of his or her insignificance. It is no wonder that the psalmist exclaimed, 'What is man that You take thought of him, And the son of man that You care for him?' (Ps. 8:4). The humbling reality of our insignificance also elevates the majesty and authority of the Creator. The contrast between our lowly estate and the majesty of the Creator produces a deep reverential awe, the fear of God (Eccles. 3:14).

Mankind's existence is ephemeral against the backdrop of the permanence of the world in which we live. Kaiser describes the situation in the following words: 'The transitory state of man is strikingly contrasted with the permanently abiding condition of the earth. Now why should this be? Wasn't man made a little lower than the angels? Yet he, not the earth, appears to be in a state of passing away.'[8] References to man's labor bracket descriptions of the never-ending cycles of the created order (1:3, 8). Solomon focuses on the frustration of having too short a time on earth to enjoy the fruit of one's labors, to taste all the potential gusto that life on earth has to offer. It is obvious that Solomon longs for the good life – a life that satisfies spiritually and emotionally. Nowhere does he indicate that such satisfaction remains inaccessible in this life. Indeed, his remarks implicitly state that satisfaction is accessible. However, the brevity of life leaves little time to

6. Whybray, 'Ecclesiastes 1:5-7 and the Wonders of Nature,' 239.
7. Crenshaw, 'Nothing New Under the Sun: Ecclesiastes 1:4-11,' 241.
8. Kaiser, *Ecclesiastes*, 49-50.

enjoy life to its full. King Death comes too soon for old King Solomon.

Mere existence requires exertion and Solomon is often exhausted by it. That situation has existed since the Fall of Adam. Man spends his days in labor in order to be able to eat. In the end, however, his body returns to the dust from whence it was originally taken (Gen. 3:19; cf. Eccles. 12:7). Exhaustion goes with the territory.

Paul Henri Spaak, the first president of the United Nations General Assembly in 1946, closed the session with the words: 'Our agenda is now exhausted. The secretary general is exhausted. All of you are exhausted. I find it comforting that, beginning with our very first day, we find ourselves in such complete unanimity.'[9] All who are reading these pages probably reach the same opinion repeatedly – we are exhausted just with the daily pressures and stresses of life.

In the final fleeting days of his life Solomon longs for the knowledge that all his accomplishments have been worthwhile (v. 3). He searches for a sense of satisfaction that is deeper and more lasting than just what his senses are capable of perceiving. Eyes and ears in this passage (v. 8) fittingly represent the entirety of physical perception.

Only Ecclesiastes employs the phrase 'under the sun' (v. 3) in the entire Old Testament.[10] However Phoenician, Akkadian, Elamite, and Greek writers also used the same phrase.[11] The phrase refers to existence on planet Earth where the sun dominates the daytime sky providing light, warmth, and energy for the sustenance of life. 'In this life' or 'on earth' provide two less colorful and more prosaic ways to make the same statement.

Poetic prose dominates the Book of Ecclesiastes. Poetry in ancient Israel (as also in all lands, languages, and times) helped the audience (readers or hearers) to sustain their interest in the subject matter. The recipient must 'be charmed by

---

9. Clifton Fadiman, ed., *The Little, Brown Book of Anecdotes* (Boston, Mass.: Little, Brown and Company, 1985), 517.

10. Eccles. 1:3, 9, 14; 2:11, 17, 18, 19, 20, 22; 3:16; 4:1, 3, 7, 15; 5:13, 18; 6:1, 5, 12; 8:9, 15 (2×), 17; 9:3, 6, 9 (2×), 11, 13; 10:5.

11. Eaton, *Ecclesiastes*, 58; Longman, *Ecclesiastes*, 66.

the familiar, yet aroused and captivated by the unexpected.'[12] Not only does poetry sustain the immediate interest, it preserves the memory of its contents. Who has not been unwittingly captivated by a clever jingle, a jaunty tune, or an unforgettable phrase? Words can be powerful – especially when served up in an attractive form and flow. Wise King Solomon uses poetry to convey his thoughts about life because he intends his words to goad the recipient into action (12:11). If he aims to convince the reader of the utter hopelessness and meaninglessness of life, he leaves them in the stagnating quagmire of futility. Dull prose would have sufficed; poetry would not have been necessary.

The Spirit of God superintended the writing of Ecclesiastes (cf. 2 Pet. 1:21). The divine Shepherd Himself guided Solomon's words and, through him, presents His Word to Israel and the world (Eccles. 12:11). The poetry of Ecclesiastes does not consist of lament, but of thoughtful contemplation leading to a more satisfying and happy existence 'under the sun.' As Eaton explains, the message of Ecclesiastes comes from God rather than from mere human endeavor.

> But, says the Preacher, take away its God, and creation no longer reflects his glory; it illustrates the weariness of mankind. When Adam fell, creation fell (Gen. 3:17-19). If man is weary, creation is weary with him. If our outlook is merely 'under the sun,' no doxology can arise to one who is 'in heaven' (Eccles. 5:2). The prophet's hope of mankind redeemed and an earthly paradise regained (Isa. 11:6-9; 65:17-25) cannot stand on secular premises.[13]

The poetry of divinely-revealed wisdom lifts the hearer above and beyond this earthly realm – beyond the sun itself – into the heavenly presence of the Creator. An invitation to enter the throne room of the sovereign Lord of the universe demands elevated language.

Some commentators read these verses and come away with a much different picture. Consider, as an example, the following observations by William Brown:

---

12. Watson, *Classical Hebrew Poetry*, 33.
13. Eaton, *Ecclesiastes*, 58.

This is a cosmos devoid of *telos* and full of toil, a world without direction and seemingly deprived of its own genesis. Creation elsewhere in the Bible consistently weds genesis and purpose, ontology and teleology, as determined by the divine will. But there is nothing, properly speaking, *creative* about Qoheleth's cosmos; indeed, God does not even appear to be involved.[14]

This commentator is not yet finished, however. He pushes forward in his own discourse which, 'like the wearisome cosmic courses, is afflicted with incessant monotony,'[15] and reaches a conclusion summarized by a very familiar metaphor of futility:

For Qoheleth, the cosmos seems to move on its own frenetic inertia, ever repetitive and wearisome, with human history mirroring its lifeless movements.... Like a hamster in a wheel, everything is feverishly running in place but to no avail.[16]

Does this accurately represent the intent of Solomon's discourse? Absolutely not. The Preacher does not exclude God from his picture of the cosmos. God is involved in the lives of human beings in this life (1:13; 2:24-26; 3:10-13). God is continuously at work in His creation (3:11, 14). Why is there no mention of the Creator in 1:4-7? Poetry may be the reason. An Israelite audience might expect reference to the Creator, in the same way Brown seems to expect it. 'Defeated expectancy,' however, is a poetic device 'intended to jar interest.'[17] God's noticeable absence in this section also helps to create increasing dramatic tension, making the audience think, stimulating their internal response, rather than allowing them to behave as a mere recording device for Solomon's words.

The rest of the book makes it clear that Solomon does not exclude God from his picture of the cosmos. Indeed, the farther one reads in Ecclesiastes, the more he or she becomes aware of God's intimate relationship with mankind 'under the sun.' People are not caged hamsters mindlessly running in place. Solomon's Spirit-superintended goal purposes to

---

14. Brown, *Ecclesiastes*, 24.

15. Ibid., 26. Brown himself applies this statement to his own commentary on Ecclesiastes: '"of making many books there is no end," notes the book's epilogist (12:12), a conclusion that is all the more true today (and applies even to Bible commentaries!).'

16. Ibid., 27.

17. Watson, *Classical Hebrew Poetry*, 34.

help readers obtain true spiritual satisfaction that will allow them to enjoy the life God has given to them – even if it is ephemeral.

One of Christ's parables speaks of a rich man whose fields produced an abundant harvest for which he had insufficient storage (Luke 12:16-21). Planning to build bigger and better silos for his grain, the rich man thought that he would then cease his labors and enjoy his riches. However, God had other plans. God said, 'You fool! This *very* night your soul is required of you; and *now* who will own what you have prepared?' (v. 20). Christ's summary and application was, 'So is the man who stores up treasure for himself, and is not rich toward God' (v. 21). Note that Jesus condemns the selfishness of the man and his exclusion of God from his worldview, not the enjoyment of the fruit of his labors. For that reason, the passage is not the equivalent of the enjoyment of the fruit of one's labor about which Ecclesiastes 2:24 speaks (also, 5:18; 8:15).

Similarity does not equate with identity. Christ precedes His parable of the greedy rich man with the declaration that 'not *even* when one has an abundance does his life consist of his possessions' (Luke 12:15). The same message comes through loud and clear in Ecclesiastes.

- No real profit ensues from material wealth (1:3; 2:10-11).

- Abundance does not satisfy (1:8; 5:10).

- Just as God denied the rich man his anticipated enjoyment of his wealth in the parable, so also the Preacher says that God does not empower the rich person to eat of his abundance (6:2).

Note that key differences exist between the parable and Ecclesiastes:

- Selfishly, the foolish rich man focused on what he considered '*my* crops ... *my* barns ... *my* goods' (Luke 12:17-18). Ecclesiastes, however, views the fruits of one's labor as gifts from God (5:19).

- Ecclesiastes teaches people to keep busy with God-given joy (5:20), rather than taking their ease and doing nothing (like the fool Jesus describes).

Solomon exhorts people to pour themselves into whatever their 'hand finds to do' (9:10).

- In the parable, the foolish rich man is condemned for leaving God out of his life, condemned for maintaining what Solomon describes as a life limited to 'under the sun.'

'All things are wearisome' (Eccles. 1:8) most likely refers to the ceaseless activity of the natural phenomena described in verses 5-7.[18] Job uses a related verb form to ask 'Why then should I toil in vain?' (Job 9:29). Fascinatingly, he uses the same word for 'vain' (*hebel*) as Solomon in Ecclesiastes. 'Man is not able to tell *it*' indicates that mankind falls silent before the repetitive wonders of creation. Instead of 'joy inexpressible and full of glory' (1 Pet. 1:8), human beings experience an inexpressible frustration. That which mankind sees in creation cannot bring the satisfaction and joy that the unseen Son of God can bestow. Unregenerate men see clearly the evidence of creation (Rom. 1:20), but become 'futile in their speculations' (v. 21). 'Professing to be wise, they became fools' (v. 22) because they 'exchanged the truth of God for a lie, and worshiped and served the creature rather than the Creator' (v. 25). That is why they experience difficulty in finding words to express the meaning of the sun, the wind, and the rivers.

Nothing New (1:9-11)

The past is the future; the future is the past (v. 9). Earthly existence does not consist of an unending series of discoveries – going where no man has ever gone before. Yes, there are things such as nuclear power and manned landings on the moon that never happened in prior history, but the vast majority of events are merely repetitions in a slightly different costume. There is a constant yearning for new things and new experiences, and yet, what is new for one person is old hat to someone else. Try as we might, we cannot change history. God alone has the power to 'make all things new' (2 Cor. 5:17; cf.

---

18. Whybray, *Ecclesiastes*, 39; and Whybray, 'Ecclesiastes 1:5-7 and the Wonders of Nature,' 236.

Num. 16:30[19]). Michael Eaton observes that that which is truly new must come from the realm above the sun, heaven itself:

> The Preacher's point is that this cannot be viewed secularly. Consider life 'under the sun' and the concept of God's ruling from heaven no longer holds good. No-one can appeal to God to 'look down' and intervene (Isa. 63:15). There can be no redemption, for no new factor can be introduced. The heavenly realm is the source of what is really new, the psalmist's 'new song' (Ps. 96:1) and the prophet's 'new thing' (Isa. 43:19).[20]

By means of a rhetorical question, Solomon confronts his audience: 'Is there anything of which one might say, "See this, it is new"?' (Eccles. 1:10). Before they can try to weasel out of the dilemma, he blurts out the truth: 'Already it has existed for ages which were before us.' Men and women take pride in their discoveries, advancements, and increasingly superior intellects. A new method for determining whether a woman is pregnant was 'discovered' in 1926. It involved the testing of the pregnant woman's urine. However, the ancient Egyptians were already employing a urine test over 3,000 years prior. They soaked small bags of wheat and barley with the urine. 'If the subject was pregnant, the urine would accelerate the growth of the wheat if the child was to be a boy, or the barley if it was to be a girl.'[21] Not until 1933 would modern laboratory tests rediscover and confirm the acceleration of wheat and barley by the pregnant woman's urine. In a related matter, a Chalcedonian who had taken up residence in Alexandria, Egypt described the ovaries and the thin tubes that run from them to the womb. His name was Herophilos and he is known as the Father of Anatomy. Nearly 2,000 years later, in 1561, Gabrielle Fallopio rediscovered the tubes running from a woman's ovaries to the womb. In recognition of his discovery, we call them fallopian tubes.[22]

---

19. Although English translations of Num. 16:30 employ the word 'new,' the Hebrew has 'create a created thing' (b^{e}ri'a yibra'), in other words, something that only God can do.

20. Eaton, *Ecclesiastes*, 60.

21. Colin Roman, *Lost Discoveries: The Forgotten Science of the Ancient World* (New York: Weathervane Books, 1976), 84.

22. Ibid., 86.

It seems that mankind labors under a continual case of cultural and historical amnesia (v. 11). Each generation automatically assumes that their parents and grandparents and great-grandparents lived in a backward age without the benefit of the advances of the most recent times. But, there is something more here than just being oblivious to the past. As Brown makes explicit, Solomon 'is undercutting [human beings'] deepest and vainglorious aspirations to secure some permanent place or "remembrance" in history. A life oriented toward ensuring its legacy for posterity only pursues the wind.'[23]

Solomon's reign had begun with such promise, but near the end of his forty years on the throne of David, his legacy fails to impress. His spiritual life declines and the nation of Israel declines. Very shortly after his death civil war ensues and the kingdom divides with ten of the twelve tribes seceding from the union. Solomon pursues the wind of *nothings* (idols) and the nation reaps the whirlwind. King Solomon sees it coming, but it is too late to alter the course. His only hope is to at least salvage his own spiritual life before death steals away his opportunity.

Advancement in the future builds on recovering the past. This remains especially true in the spiritual realm. God enjoins Israel to preserve their memory of His actions: 'remember that you were a slave in the land of Egypt, and the Lord your God brought you out of there by a mighty hand and by an outstretched arm' (Deut. 5:15). In the Song of Moses, the nation was exhorted to

> *Remember the days of old,*
> *Consider the years of all generations.*
> *Ask your father, and he will inform you,*
> *Your elders, and they will tell you.*
> *When the Most High gave the nations their inheritance,*
> *When He separated the sons of man,*
> *He set the boundaries of the peoples*
> *According to the number of the sons of Israel.*
> *For the Lord's portion is His people;*
> *Jacob is the allotment of His inheritance.* (Deut. 32:7-9)

---

23. Brown, *Ecclesiastes*, 28.

Solomon needs to remember what God has accomplished for him. He can no longer ask his father David. Solomon himself now stands among the elders – he should have known better than to get involved with idolatry. The time has come for him to apply his past wisdom, that is, his God-given wisdom. With the Lord's help and guidance, the king can be restored to spiritual vitality. Along the way, he will record his spiritual journal for others to read so that they might avoid the traps that have ensnared him.

In Pursuit of Wisdom (1:12-18)

Ecclesiastes 1:12–2:23 documents Solomon's personal testimony, his confession to his inability to resolve life's most important issues without God. He determines to examine a great range of human activities in search for anything of lasting value. In case his readers should purpose to take up the same search, 'he warns us of the outcome (1:13b-15) before he takes us through his journey (1:16–2:11); finally he will share with us the conclusions he has reached (2:12-26).'[24] Such royal autobiographical texts are well-known in the ancient Near East outside the Bible. Kings produced such material in abundance. A king's autobiographical account possessed propaganda value. Political opinion assumed that a king must toot his own horn if he desires to keep his enemies at bay, his people in subjection, and his place in history secure. Ancient Near Eastern royal autobiographical texts like the following display hyperbole (exaggeration) and a patent rewriting of history:

> Amen-hotep-the-God-Ruler-of-Heliopolis…. He is a king very weighty of arm: there is none who can draw his bow in his army, among the rulers of foreign countries, or the princes of Retenu, because his strength is so much greater than (that of) any (other) king who has existed. Raging like a panther when he treads the field of battle; there is none who can fight in his vicinity…. Prevailing instantly over every foreign country, whether people or horses, (though) they have come in millions of men,…[25]

---

24. Kidner, 'The Search for Satisfaction: Ecclesiastes 1:12–2:26,' 250.
25. John A. Wilson, translator, 'The Asiatic Campaigning of Amen-hotep II,' in *Ancient Near Eastern Texts Relating to the Old Testament*, 2nd ed., ed. by James B. Pritchard (Princeton, N.J.: Princeton University Press, 1955), 247. Amen-hotep II reigned in Egypt 1447–1421 B.C.

Tiglath-pileser, the legitimate king, king of the world, king of Assyria, king of (all) the four rims (of the earth), the courageous hero who lives (guided) by the trust-inspiring oracles given (to him) by Ashur and Ninurta, the great gods and his lords, (and who thus) overthrew (all) his enemies; son of Ashurreshishi, king of the world, king of Assyria, (grand)son of Mutakkil-Nusku, also king of the world, king of Assyria.[26]

In contrast to these royal pronouncements, Solomon's journal avoids hyperbole. Other biblical texts adequately document his accomplishments. Unlike his royal peers, Solomon admits to failure, frustration, and folly. The detailed listing of the king's accomplishments plays an important role in Ecclesiastes. Without this background, the reader might wonder if Solomon's credentials are valid – or, at least, appropriate to the huge task of research being conducted. After all, Solomon claimed to 'seek and explore by wisdom … all that has been done under heaven' (v. 13). Did he control the resources required to conduct such investigations? 'The world is the king's classroom, his laboratory.'[27] At his command emissaries travel to India, to Egypt, to Ethiopia, to Babylon, to Greece, and to the uttermost parts of the world in search of answers to life's most perplexing questions. How did other wise men and women deal with the brevity of life and the certainty of death? Had anyone succeeded elsewhere in ensuring what would happen to his hard-earned gains after his death? Solomon has ships and men to command. His wealth funds wide-ranging expeditions in search of answers to these questions. Even the realm of nature yields to his quest for potential clues – his knowledge of the fauna and flora excels that of any other living person (1 Kings 4:33). His wisdom, though tainted by his disobedience, is still vast and capable of collating the results and reaching a conclusion.

As his search for answers continues, Solomon begins to see that the only One who can answer life's questions is the Creator Himself. Absence of viable human solutions drives the king inexorably back to God. Daily his awareness of his God grows

---

26. A. Leo Oppenheim, translator, 'Texts from Hammurabi to the Downfall of the Assyrian Empire,' in *Ancient Near Eastern Texts*, 274-75. Tiglath-pileser I was king of Assyria 1114–1076 B.C.

27. Brown, *Ecclesiastes*, 29.

and, with it, God renews his wisdom. The first mention of God in Ecclesiastes comes in 1:13. Solomon depicts God as supreme in His authority over mankind. The Lord appoints man to his task in life on earth – a task divinely reserved for mankind. Animals are moved by instinct, not by a search for meaning. 'Someone has said that it is better to be Socrates discontented (because he cannot solve his problems) than a contented pig.'[28]

However, the task proves 'grievous' (v. 13). Some go so far as to translate the word as 'evil ... because no solution is found after much hard work.'[29] The word for 'task' occurs only in the Book of Ecclesiastes (1:13; 2:23, 26; 3:10; 4:8; 5:3 [Heb., 2], 14 [Heb., 13]; 8:16). The term basically means busy-ness that is humbling. God Himself appoints humans to this task. From the perspective of one 'under the sun,' such a task is difficult and, seemingly, unrewarding. However, 3:10-11 ('a kind of commentary on this verse'[30]) sets the task in its proper perspective: the perspective of eternity. Deep within each human being God implants the urge to seek truth. As sinful human beings, however, the desired result is fraught with frustration and failure. Without God the quest for truth and for eternity is fruitless.[31]

'I have seen all the works which have been done under the sun' (v. 14). Solomon's exhaustive search for answers meets with failure. All his wisdom and resources cannot turn up the answer to his most basic question: What is the purpose of life on this planet? He attempts to make order of chaos. Brown explains the difficulty of this task: 'The universe, in effect, is hopelessly stubborn; it cannot be molded to correspond to any human models of moral sense and order.'[32] In our own times another very knowledgeable man has undertaken a similar task with a strange twist to it. World-renowned physicist, Stephen Hawking, investigates the origin of the universe while seeking to disprove the existence of God.[33] So far, like Solomon of old, he has failed. Could it be that people like

---

28. Wright, 'Ecclesiastes,' 5:1154.

29. Longman, *Ecclesiastes*, 78. Longman's understanding of the situation is flawed by the assumption that the Preacher is subtly criticizing God throughout the book (80).

30. Whybray, *Ecclesiastes*, 49.

31. Cf. Leupold, *Ecclesiastes*, 53.

32. Brown, *Ecclesiastes*, 30.

33. Stephen W. Hawking, *A Brief History of Time: From the Big Bang to Black Holes* (New York: Bantam Books, 1988), x, 140-41, 174.

Solomon and Hawking are looking but not seeing? They take into account the visible, but what about the invisible?

With this question in mind, Charles Swindoll tells about a native American who was visiting New York City. Walking with a friend near the center of Manhattan, the Indian suddenly stopped his companion and whispered, 'Wait, I hear a cricket.' His friend was disbelieving. A cricket? In downtown New York? Impossible. The cacophony of sounds from passing taxis, impatient honking, people shouting, brakes screeching, and subways roaring would make it virtually impossible to hear a cricket, even if one were present. But, the Indian was insistent. He stopped his friend and began to crisscross the street and sidewalks with his head cocked to one side, intently listening. Then, in a large cement planter where a tree was growing, he finally found the cricket and held it up for his friend's benefit. Amazed, his friend asked how he could have possibly heard that cricket. Reaching into his pocket, the Indian grasped some coins, held them waist high, then dropped them on the sidewalk. Everyone within a block turned to look in their direction. As Swindoll says, 'It all depends on what you're listening for. We don't have enough crickets in our heads. We don't listen for them. Perhaps you have spent all your life searching for a handful of change and you've missed the real sound of life.'[34] In our own pursuit of truth in this world, we must train our hearts and minds for observing the evidences of God's presence and work.

'Shepherding the wind' is another way to translate 'striving after wind' (v. 14).[35] Chasing after life's unanswerable questions certainly plays into Satan's hands. Sometimes men and women can be so busy endlessly analyzing life that they fail to live it for God one day at a time. Ecclesiastes reveals that the search to answer all of life's conundrums is like trying to shepherd the wind – to attempt to push the wind into a pen of one's own making. Anyone trying to control the weather knows how impossible that task is.

Verse 15 concludes this section (vv. 13-15) with a proverb. Solomon is renowned for his proverbs – he had spoken at least 3,000 (1 Kings 4:32). What he did not compose, he

34. Swindoll, *Living on the Ragged Edge*, 26-27.
35. Bartholomew, *Ecclesiastes*, 124.

had collected and collated into an incomparable collection of wisdom (Eccles. 12:9). The Hebrew word for 'proverb' (*mashal*) means 'be like,' 'resemble,' or 'represent.' That is why many proverbs employ 'the characteristic words *like* and *as* with *so*.'[36] According to this proverb, 'What is crooked cannot be straightened and what is lacking cannot be counted.' In other words, '*Just as* what is crooked cannot be made straight and what is not there cannot be counted, *so mankind cannot change all that is done under heaven.*' No one but God can alter the realities of mankind's existence.

Solomon returns to this observation later in the book: 'Consider the work of God, For who is able to straighten what He has bent?' (7:13). This proverb falls into the same category as Jeremiah 13:23, 'Can the Ethiopian change his skin or the leopard his spots? *Then* you also can do good who are accustomed to doing evil.' In Ecclesiastes the context favors an application to the immediately preceding verse (v. 14). The proverb drives home the conclusion that the labors of mankind living under the sun ultimately prove unprofitable (v. 3), unsatisfying (v. 8), unremarkable (vv. 9-10), and unremembered (v. 11). That's life. That's the way it is – we cannot alter it.

If the task of investigation through wisdom (Eccles. 1:13) could not bring about the change, could wisdom itself (v. 16) be profitable, satisfying, remarkable, and memorable? Solomon considers himself to be the wisest and most knowledgeable man alive in his day. Obviously, his wisdom had not prevented his demise and dissatisfaction. Obtaining additional wisdom and knowledge likewise proves to be nothing more than 'striving after wind' (v. 17).

Ever ready with a proverb, Solomon recites another: 'With much wisdom comes much grief; the greater one's knowledge, the greater the sorrow' (v. 18, paraphrased). The more knowledge the old king obtains, the deeper his grief becomes – everything he learns keeps bringing him to the same conclusion. Humanly speaking, there is no way out of the quagmire into which he has fallen. Each new titbit of information only plunges him deeper into his hopelessness. As Jesus declares, 'the one who did not know *it*, and committed deeds worthy of

---

36. Louis Goldberg, *The Practical Wisdom of Proverbs* (Grand Rapids, Mich.: Kregel Publications, 1990), 17.

a flogging, will receive but few. From everyone who has been given much, much will be required; and to whom they entrusted much, of him they will ask all the more' (Luke 12:48). Solomon knows better than to worship idols. Given fantastic wisdom from God, the king has squandered it. A brilliant beginning moves inexorably to a sordid ending. Everything confirms his humanity, his sinfulness, his accountability, and his inevitable death. With an increasingly heavy heart, Solomon's research is driving him to a heart-wrenching conclusion: he cannot save himself. No person can.

What more can he do? Is it time to give up? With time so very short, what might possibly provide the greatest benefit? Like many an individual before or since, King Solomon turns from serious pursuits to the pursuit of pleasure (2:1-11).

STUDY QUESTIONS

1. What evidences can you present that would argue for Solomon being a true believer?

2. How many different translations exist for the Hebrew word *hebel*? Which ones does Ecclesiastes use most frequently?

3. How does Solomon depict the transitory nature of man's existence on earth?

4. What is the meaning of 'under the sun'?

5. Compare the parable in Luke 12:16-21 with what Solomon speaks about in Ecclesiastes. How does that comparison impact how you yourself live today?

6. Why did Solomon list his various accomplishments in Ecclesiastes 1?

7. What are the benefits and the disadvantages of wisdom?

2

A Disappointing Discovery (continued)

From experience, *the Preacher* learned that
man is powerless *(1:1–2:26)*, Part 2

People often claim that education resolves almost every conceivable problem that individuals and communities face. If only everyone had a better and higher education, so the argument goes, there would be no political instability, international tension, teen pregnancies, and hospital wards filled with patients suffering from stress and chronic depression. A college or university degree in hand, graduates are supposedly prepared to storm the heights of mankind's loftiest advancements to solve the worst of mankind's problems. Solomon certainly did not find that human wisdom could supply the solution to his personal depression. Human knowledge holds no answer for the seeming futility of life and inevitability of death. Life's most profound and psyche-wracking problems remain unresolved after the best of man's wisdom tackles them. Thus, Solomon turns to another potential means for defeating depression and death: unfettered pleasure.

In Pursuit of Pleasure (2:1-9)

Pleasure for Solomon involves play (vv. 1-3), property and parks (vv. 4-6), and possessions (vv. 7-8) – or, put another way, *entertainment, edifices,* and *earnings.* He has already tried *erudition.*

Ancient Near Eastern peoples expected their kings to accomplish much during their reigns. Their own inscriptions tend to list their accomplishments as evidence that they had ruled well and had provided the benefits their subjects required for a healthy and happy existence. Much of it sounds a lot like politics in our own day. Consider the inscription on the Moabite Stone by King Mesha of Moab (ca. 830 B.C.), who is mentioned in 2 Kings 3:

> I (am) Mesha, song of Chemosh-[...], king of Moab,...
>
> And I built Baal-meon, making a reservoir in it, and I built Qaryaten....
>
> It was I (who) built Qarhoh, the wall of *the forests* and the wall of the citadel; I also built its gates and I built its towers and I built the king's house, and I made both of its reservoirs for water inside the town.... And I cut *beams* for Qarhoh with Israelite captives. I built Aroer, and I made the highway in the Arnon (valley); I built Beth-bamoth, for it had been destroyed; I built Bezer – for it lay in ruins ...[1]

Hammurabi, king of Babylon (ca. 1728–1686 B.C.), commemorates his accomplishments by means of various dating formulas employed to refer to each year of his reign. He identifies each of his forty-three years as king by what he established, constructed, or restored, or whom he defeated. The following provides a partial listing:

1. Hammurabi (became) king.
   ....
3. He constructed a throne ...
4. The wall of (the sacred precinct) Gagia was built.
5. He constructed ...
6. He constructed ...
   ....
9. The canal (called) Hammurabi-hegal (was dug).
   ....
12. He constructed a throne ...
    ....
14. He constructed a throne ...
    ....

---

1. W. F. Albright, translator, 'The Moabite Stone,' in *Ancient Near Eastern Texts Relating to the Old Testament*, 2nd ed., ed. by James B. Pritchard (Princeton, N.J.: Princeton University Press, 1955), 320-21. (cf. 2 Kings 3:4 and its mention of Mesha.)

25. The great wall of Sippar was built …
    ....

33. He redug the canal (called) 'Hammurabi-(spells)-abundance-for-the-people, the Beloved-of-Anu-and-Enlil,' (thus) he provided Nippur, Eridu, Ur, Larsa, Uruk (and) Isin with a permanent and plentiful water supply …

34. He built the temple … for Anu, Inanna and Nana.[2]

In light of Mesha's and Hammurabi's claims, Solomon's list of accomplishments (Eccles. 2:4-9) run according to expectations. The difference, however, consists of the fact that Mesha and Hammurabi speak as though they are fully satisfied with their lives, but *Solomon confesses that all such accomplishments bring him no lasting satisfaction.* Why the difference? Solomon worships the true God while Mesha and Hammurabi worship idols. Their idolatry causes them no loss of sleep, but Solomon's does. *One who knows the true and living God can never be satisfied merely with what this world offers.* Solomon knows better than to pin his hope on things under the sun. He retains a true perspective of the value of earthly achievements and success.

An interpretive problem. Ancient versions and modern translations alike exhibit uncertainty in the translation of verse 8. The New King James Version's (NKJV) translation – 'musical instruments of all kinds,' also KJV – contrasts with that of the New American Standard Updated (NASU) and New Revised Standard Version (NRSV) which read 'many concubines.' The Hebrew word is somewhat obscure, but some scholars relate it to the word meaning 'breast' (*shad*), indicating a colloquialism for women who provide pleasure.[3] The Hebrew could be related to the Akkadian term meaning 'mistress' or 'lady' (*shaditum*).[4] A letter from Pharaoh Amen-

---

2. A. Leo Oppenheim, translator, 'Texts from Hammurabi to the Downfall of the Assyrian Empire,' in *Ancient Near Eastern Texts Relating to the Old Testament*, 269-70. Date of inscription: approximately 1750 B.C.

3. Garrett, *Proverbs, Ecclesiastes, Song of Songs*, 292. The English Revised Version (ERV), Revised Standard Version (RSV), and Today's English Version (TEV) offer this interpretation.

4. Murphy, *Ecclesiastes*, 17. See, also, Kidner, 'The Search for Satisfaction, Ecclesiastes 1:12–2:26,' 252 footnote 5.

hotep III (ca. 1417–1353 B.C.) to Milkilu prince of Gezer demanding forty concubines employs a very similar term in a Canaanite explanatory note. In order to make certain that the prince and his court understood the Egyptian term for concubine, the scribe inserted the Canaanite word.[5] Some Jewish versions prefer to follow the Mishnah's rendering of the term as a 'chest' or 'treasure chest.'[6]

Judges 5:30 employs a very similar phraseology (*racham rah^amatayim*) that the NASU translates 'A maiden, two maidens' (NKJV: 'a girl *or* two').[7] The phrase involves a singular and a dual form of the noun that could also be translated 'womb' – 'a womb, two wombs.' If the same grammatical treatment were applied to Ecclesiastes 2:8, the meaning of *shiddah w^eshiddot* could be something like 'a breast, even [two] breasts.' Finally, the Masoretic accentuation indicates that 'the pleasures of men' relates to what follows that phrase. It is but one more piece of evidence tipping the scales in favor of a translation like 'many concubines' (NASU, NRSV).

Still Pursuing the Wind (2:10-11)

In his pursuit of pleasure Solomon denies himself nothing. He thoroughly enjoys his task. Indeed, he even considers it his reward – he has earned it (v. 10). What better excuse can a man offer for indulging in worldly pleasures? 'I earned it. I deserve it because of all I have done. I worked hard to be able to enjoy myself for a season.' Pride in his toil drives Solomon to pursue pleasure with gusto.

However, such pleasure is short lived. Why? Is the pleasure flawed in and of itself? Yes, but that is not the reason for its failure to last. Solomon examines his 'activities' and finds them

---

5. W. F. Albright and George E. Mendenhall, translators, 'The Amarna Letters: RA, xxxi' in *Ancient Near Eastern Texts Relating to the Old Testament*, 487: 'To Milkilu, prince of Gezer. Thus the king. Now I have sent thee this tablet to say to thee: Behold, I am sending to thee Hanya, the commissioner of the archers, together with goods, in order to procure fine concubines (i.e.) *weaving women.*' The italicized translation represents the Canaanite gloss explaining 'concubines.'

6. Thus, the New Jewish Publication Society's (NJPS) translation, 'as well as the luxuries of commoners – coffers and coffers of them.'

7. Judges 5 is a very ancient Hebrew poem. The fact that Eccles. 2:8 employs a similar construction provides evidence antagonistic to the view that Ecclesiastes was written very late in Hebrew history. Cf. Garrett, *Proverbs, Ecclesiastes, Song of Songs*, 259 footnote 32.

unprofitable (v. 11). How can pleasure be the reward for works when works themselves do not endure? Products of man's labor are ephemeral and useless in light of eternity. In every way they are inferior to that which God has created. Wind, flood, fire, and earthquake make a heap of rubble out of man's accomplishments. Time itself takes its toll with its insidious ravages.

True joy cannot originate within man himself. That is the bottom line after all Solomon's searching, testing, and consideration. 'Under the sun' there exists no lasting happiness or pure pleasure.

Solomon's Assessment of Life under the Sun (2:12-17)

Solomon now says, 'So I turned to consider' (2:12). The same verb begins verse 11 ('Thus I considered'). Its sense is something like 'I faced the facts' or 'turned my full attention to.'[8] Note that consecutive verses commence with the same word (a literary device known as anaphora).[9] With these back-to-back phrases Solomon changes the subject. Solomon has completed his pursuit of both pleasure and wisdom and takes stock of the results one after the other.[10]

Although the second half of verse 12 might be somewhat enigmatic, there is no reason to emend the Hebrew text to try to make sense of it. One suggestion translates this portion as follows: 'for what kind of person is it who will come after the king, in the matter of what has already been done?'[11] Eaton suggests translating this portion as follows: 'for what kind of person is it who will come after the king, in the matter of what has already been done?'[12] In other words, how would Solomon's successors handle the same kind of investigation? Could they do any better than he? Finding this rendering without adequate sense, Garrett suggests that the reference is to Adam as the king of humanity and offers the paraphrase, 'Is a human likely to come along who will be better than the king – Adam – whom God made long ago?'[13] Though a clever suggestion, it does not present a material change in

8. Eaton, *Ecclesiastes*, 68.
9. Murphy, *Ecclesiastes*, 17, 20.
10. Reichart and Cohen, 'Ecclesiastes,' 2:37.
11. Ibid.
12. Eaton, *Ecclesiastes*, 68.
13. Garrett, *Proverbs, Ecclesiastes, Song of Songs*, 293.

the ultimate meaning. As Brown points out, the statement 'is more a lament than a boast.'[14] In spite of his exhaustive and detailed investigation, Solomon obtains no answers to his questions – even after pursuing wisdom and its opposites, 'madness and folly.'

Due to the extent of his observations, Solomon has no doubts about the relative value of wisdom over folly (v. 13). He *himself* (the Hebrew employs an emphatic personal pronoun to stress this point) has observed it sufficiently to reach that conclusion. The two are as different as night is from day, darkness from light. 'Excels' means 'there is more profit,' the same word the writer uses in 1:3 ('What advantage does man have…?') and 2:11 ('there was no profit under the sun'). In all his searching Solomon finds something relatively profitable: wisdom. How is wisdom profitable? Just as a torch makes walking in darkness much easier and safer, wisdom proves to be a benefit to a person (cf. v. 14). Hengstenberg concludes that 'The wise man is like one who sees, and who can therefore avail himself of many advantages and avoid many inconveniences.'[15]

With all of its advantages, however, wisdom cannot overcome the ultimate equalizer of sage and fool alike: death (vv. 14-16). Pursuing wisdom and education has limited advantages – advantages limited to this life. Wisdom cannot prevent death and does not supercede death. Therefore, an individual is unwise who occupies himself or herself too deeply with it. How could Solomon reach such a conclusion? After all, if nothing exists after death and the totality of a person's existence consists of his or her presence here on earth, then would it not be the better part of wisdom to acquire every advantage for this life? What could be so bad about dedicating oneself to the acquisition of knowledge and wisdom? 'Why then have I been extremely wise?' (v. 15) implies more than just futility; the question implies that there is something better with which Solomon might occupy himself in this life. It is better for a person to prepare for eternity than to immerse oneself in preparing for this life alone.

---

14. Brown, *Ecclesiastes*, 34.
15. Hengstenberg, *Ecclesiastes*, 82.

The seeming equality at death of both the fool and the wise (v. 16) does not negate the superiority of wisdom over folly. Solomon does not denigrate wisdom, he merely points the reader to the ultimate reality of death. True wisdom involves the fear of the LORD (Ps. 111:10; Prov. 1:7) and those who possess such wisdom will experience everlasting life (Dan. 12:1-3).

'So I hated life' (v. 17) concludes this section.[16] As Hengstenberg wisely observes, hating life 'is by no means in itself true repentance,' but such feelings are 'for the well disposed a powerful motive to return to God.'[17] Perhaps Solomon's feelings were much deeper than those normally experienced by others. We should not expect that someone imitating Solomon's investigations would come to the same dramatic conclusion. After all, Solomon is a believer, not an unbeliever. The unbeliever holds no means of evaluating the difference between their lost condition and the experience of one who possesses eternal life and divine forgiveness. Solomon has tasted the glorious wonders of divine grace. God granted him the best of divine wisdom. Previously he had basked in the warmth of the divine presence while he prayed. Solomon knows that there is something more than this life and he is fully aware of how he has lost its joy.

Solomon can identify with Adam's feelings in his fall from divine favor and expulsion from Eden. Outside the garden of Eden, Adam must have felt overwhelmed by the stark reality of his loss. What a contrast between God's blessing and God's judgment. For the believer fellowship with God involves a fullness of joy, peace, and love (cf. Ps. 16:11; Eph. 2:4; 3:19; Phil. 4:7; 1 Pet. 1:8) that is absent when sin breaks fellowship with God. The difference is as stark as that between darkness and light. Such a difference drives John to speak of fellowship with God in such terms:

> … what we have seen and heard we proclaim to you also, so that you too may have fellowship with us; and indeed our fellowship is with the Father, and with His Son Jesus Christ. These things we write, so that our joy may be made complete. This is the message we have heard from Him and announce to you, that God is Light,

---

16. Note that anaphora ('I hated' begins both v. 17 and v. 18; cf. vv. 11 and 12) demonstrates the conclusion of one section (vv. 12-17) and the commencement of another (vv. 18-23).

17. Hengstenberg, *Ecclesiastes*, 84.

and in Him there is no darkness at all. If we say that we have fellowship with Him and *yet* walk in the darkness, we lie and do not practice the truth; but if we walk in the Light as He Himself is in the Light, we have fellowship with one another, and the blood of Jesus His Son cleanses us from all sin. If we say that we have no sin, we are deceiving ourselves and the truth is not in us. (1 John 1:3-8)

Like his father David, Solomon learns that the joy of the Lord's salvation needs restoring (Ps. 51:12). Solomon does not commence the writing of Ecclesiastes until that restoration has been completed. His ability to reflect upon his folly and to compare it with true wisdom provides evidence of his prior restoration. The first two chapters of the book consist of a confession of what Solomon's unrestored condition had been. More than that, however, it is his way to fulfill what his own father had declared would be the result of restoration: '*Then* I will teach transgressors Your ways, and sinners shall be converted to You' (Ps. 51:13).

By explaining his intense disgust with life as he has been living it, Solomon invites his readers to consider his reasons for feeling so strongly. After all, many of them (especially those who are unbelievers with their hands on the reins of power within their own political realms) experience the best that this world has to offer. Privileged people in high positions occasionally contact people living in poverty and ill health, but cannot relate to their lowly condition. Solomon did not rise from the dung heap to sit on the throne of David. He never experienced life in the gutter, the leper colony, or the beggar's shanty. Since Solomon was raised in the palace, how can he properly understand the contrast? Some of his peers might think that he has discovered another kingdom where life is even better than what he is experiencing. Such is not the case, however. To put it simply, Solomon stoops to be a king and the heir of an earthly domain when, in truth, he is a child of the King of kings and an heir of a heavenly domain. His backslidden condition helps highlight the distinction (cp. Luke 15:11-32).

Solomon's Assessment of Labor under the Sun (2:18-23)

Two observations highlight this section: (1) 'under the sun' occurs repeatedly in a crescendo and (2) 'this also *is* vanity' closes each sub-section. 'Under the sun' occurs four times in the first twenty-nine verses of the book (1:3, 9, 14; 2:11), but five times in these six verses (2:17, 18, 19, 20, 22). 'This too is vanity' concludes verses 18-19, 20-21, 22-23, and 24-26.

Verses 12-17 contrast wisdom and folly, light and darkness, and life and death. An additional contrast between rest and labor arises in verses 18-23. 'I hated all the fruit of my labor' in verse 18 is the second half of the anaphora that starts with 'I hated life' in verse 17.[18] Irony exists in this declaration since Solomon has already said, 'my heart was pleased because of all my labor' (v. 10).

'I completely despaired' (v. 20) reads literally, 'I turned my heart to despair.' Solomon admits to bringing his own heart into a condition of despair. His disillusionment with life is his own creation. He is his happiness's worst enemy! Why does he plunge himself into such despair? For him the future of his kingdom is paramount. Ultimately, he obsesses over his life's work. As far as he can tell, that kingdom will pass into the hands of someone inept (v. 21) – his own son, Rehoboam, who will not appreciate what he receives because he has expended no labor for it. In fact, God has already revealed to Solomon that his kingdom will be divided and his son will keep only a small fraction of it after Solomon's death (1 Kings 11:9-13).

Selfishness produces Solomon's complaint: 'For what does a man get in all his labor and in his striving with which he labors under the sun?' (v. 22). In the end, Solomon does not fret over the kingdom or its wealth or power – he stresses over his own reputation and self-image. It even leaves him sleepless at night when his weary and exhausted body and mind desires rest (v. 23). Ecclesiastes records the spiritual journey that took Solomon from sleepless nights to the restful slumber of the righteous. Psalm 127:1-2 explains this matter more fully in Solomon's own words:

> Unless the LORD builds the house,
> They labor in vain who build it;
> Unless the LORD guards the city,
> The watchman keeps awake in vain.

---

18. See the discussion of 2:11, 12 above.

> It is vain for you to rise up early,
> To retire late,
> To eat the bread of painful labors;
> For He gives to His beloved *even in his* sleep.

In our own day workaholism drives men and women so that they do not get the proper amount of sleep to maintain good health. Does the job make us workaholics? Is it the rapid pace of modern technology? No. It is our own self-centeredness. Like Solomon we rob ourselves of joy and rest. We obtain true joy and rest only when we cast all our cares upon the Lord (1 Pet. 5:7) and allow Him to work within us that with which He is pleased (Phil. 2:13).

The Search's Conclusion (2:24-26)

Solomon's conclusion may be summarized simply as three basic principles:

> Man is not good.
> God is the Giver.
> There is no enjoyment in life apart from God.

Commentators dispute the first of these principles. The variety of English versions contributes to the controversy. In order to properly interpret and translate the first sentence in verse 24, one must compare it with what appears to be the identical sentence in 8:15. In 2:24 the sentence reads literally, 'There is no good in man that he eat and drink and see his soul good [an idiom = *get satisfaction*] in its labor,' while 8:15 reads literally, 'There is no good for man beneath the sun except to eat and to drink and to be happy.'

Context confirms 'There is no good in man' (v. 24) as the correct translation. Verse 26 reiterates the concept of sinful man when Solomon contrasts the gifts God gives to good men and sinners. However, we are still left with the problem of how this first clause of verse 24 relates to the next clause, 'that he should eat and drink and get satisfaction in his labor.' Leupold translates it as 'It is not a good thing inherent in man that he is able to eat and drink and get satisfaction in his toil.'[19] Such a translation does not indicate that mankind is inherently wicked; it merely speaks to the inability of people to enjoy the fruit of

---

19. Leupold, *Ecclesiastes*, 74.

their labor. As Leupold says, 'What the author seeks to indicate is merely this, that even the simplest forms of enjoyment cannot be made to yield satisfaction by man himself.'[20] Translators and commentators who take verse 24 as a comparative sentence ('nothing better than') normally assume a corruption of the Hebrew text and then modify the text to fit their assumption – not an advisable treatment of the text.[21]

Enjoyment of life is a gift from God. God-given enjoyment does not give approval to hedonism (the pursuit of and devotion to pleasure wherever and whenever one finds it). A great contrast exists between the person who is 'good' in God's sight and the sinner (v. 26). Solomon's appraisal of the world agrees with John's: 'all that is in the world, the lust of the flesh and the lust of the eyes and the boastful pride of life, is not from the Father, but is from the world. The world is passing away, and *also* its lusts' (1 John 2:16-17). According to Wright, 'One could hardly find a better statement than this of the whole theme of Ecclesiastes (e.g., 2:1-11; 5:10). Life in the world has significance only when man remembers his Creator (12:1).'[22] Life in this world can only have significance and provide enjoyment for the believer. Indeed, because the unbeliever cannot reckon with his or her sin and rebellion, life turns out to be a bitter disappointment and its joys empty and fleeting.[23]

Study Questions

1. How can you balance work and recreation to the glory of God?

2. What does Scripture say about a person's work/ employment?

3. Describe the wisdom that pleases God.

4. What distinguishes the death of the wise from the death of the foolish?

5. What characterizes a godly attitude toward possessions?

---

20. Ibid., 76.
21. 'But in view of similar expressions in 3:12, 22; 8:15, and with support from some of the Versions (Pesh., Vulg., and some MSS of LXX), the commentators are almost unanimous in supposing that a *mēm* (signifying 'than') has dropped out by haplography' (Whybray, *Ecclesiastes*, 63).
22. 'Ecclesiastes,' 5:1146.
23. Kelley, *The Burden of God*, 80.

6. What are the keys to a good night's sleep?

7. What hinders a person from fully appreciating the good things in life 'under the sun'?

8. List God's gifts that 2:24-26 reveal.

3

The Hours, Days, and Years of Our Lives

From observation, *the Preacher* learned
that God has a design for all
things *(3:1–5:20)*, Part I

In our Christian faith we often focus on heaven – the sweet by and by and how what we have in Christ prepares us for that future. However, our faith also equips us for living in what someone once called 'the nasty now and now.' Time spent in this life involves significant experiences stemming from both the sinfulness of man and the mercy of God. Life also provides opportunities for living out our faith in our service for God. Life experience itself reminds each person that God designed it all. Every area of life contains the imprint of divine care and provision. The Creator is the Controller.

Most people in the English-speaking world know of Ecclesiastes 3 through its familiar declaration that 'there is a time for every event under heaven' (v. 1). Although readers tend to apply the series of paired statements to their own lives and some commentators insist that verses 1-8 speak only to 'the brevity and impermanence of human activity,'[1] the text focuses on God's perspective. He ordains each and every event in a person's life. The first clue occurs in verse 1 with the words 'under heaven.'

---

1. Garrett, *Proverbs, Ecclesiastes, Song of Songs*, 297 footnote 64.

In Ecclesiastes, 'under the sun' provides the most common expression for limiting the viewpoint to man's perspective. Another phrase, 'under heaven,' occurs only three times in the book (1:13; 2:3; 3:1). Longman takes the phrase as an alternative expression for 'under the sun.'[2] However, in all three occurrences it appears that Solomon speaks indirectly of God's involvement. In 1:13 Solomon utilizes his God-given wisdom to examine all that human beings do in the tasks that God gives to them. At 2:3 Solomon again engages his God-given mind to investigate pleasure in order to see what God has prepared people to do during their lifetimes. Now, in 3:1, Solomon looks at God's appointed times, because time is in heaven's control, not mankind's control.

This text does not prescribe (it does not tell people how to order their activities or when to perform the listed events); instead it describes these events as part of existence.[3] What is the point of this description of time-oriented events? It is that nothing happens haphazardly. No chance, no fate governs the things that happen in the lives of God's people. He controls all events. This text challenges unbelievers, because people without a relationship to God seek to be gods themselves. Unregenerate mankind engages in a crusade to control time in order to gain an escape from individual responsibility and to obtain what they think will provide peace and security.

Just as the cycles of terrestrial climate (sun, wind, clouds, rain) continue their incessant recurrences, so time inexorably moves along, oscillating from one event to another – even its opposite event. In what Brown calls 'The Poetry of Polarity,' each activity possesses 'its relative worth and suitability, "its place" in the grand providential scheme.'[4] Each event performs its own role in God's grand design.

A Poem on Time (3:1-8)
No one can say for certain whether Solomon penned this poem or merely quotes the work of another poet. In his day, Solomon was the wisest man on earth. His accomplishments include proverbs and love songs, wisdom and poetry. Being

---

2. Longman, *Ecclesiastes*, 114.
3. Kelley, *The Burden of God*, 83.
4. Brown, *Ecclesiastes*, 41.

skilled in the employment of language, he had the ability to take one concept and develop it in amazing ways. Therefore, he could have composed this poetic masterpiece. However, even Solomon could not write such a poem on his own. The eternal and omniscient God, the Creator of heaven and earth, granted him the wisdom that he applies to this task. God controls events from outside of time. He superintends Solomon's composition, leaving His mark on it through His chosen human instrument.

Verse 1 forms a chiasm:

> **A**   for everything
> > > **B**   an appointed time
> > > **B'** a time
> > **A'** for every event

This is just the opening statement – its chiasm focuses on time and introduces the remainder of the poem, which contains a far more intricate chiastic structure. The poem exhibits a structure that reminds one of Ezekiel's 'wheels within wheels.' Here, instead of wheels, pairs of opposites oscillate, rotate, and invert in a carefully woven design:

verse 2	+ giving birth	>	– dying
	+ planting	>	– uprooting
verse 3	– killing	<	+ healing
	– tearing down	<	+ building up
verse 4	– weeping	<	+ laughing
	– mourning	<	+ dancing
verse 5	+ throwing stones	>	– gathering stones
	+ embracing	>	– refraining from embracing
verse 6	+ searching	>	– giving up searching
	+ keeping	>	– throwing away
verse 7	– tearing apart	<	+ sewing together
	– being silent	<	+ speaking
verse 8	+ loving	>	– hating
	– making war	<	+ making peace

Each half of verse 2 starts with the positive (favorable) element, while each half of verse 7 begins with the negative (unfavorable) element. Those first two initial positives (v. 2) are followed by four initial negatives (vv. 3-4) and then by initial positives (vv. 5-6). In verses 3-4, the outer pairs are more intense (*killing/ healing* and *mourning/ dancing*) than the inner pairs (*tearing down/ building up* and *weeping/laughing*). Verses 5-6 begin and end (the outer pairs) with *throwing* paralleled by *gathering/keeping*. The inner pairs both involve *giving up* or *refraining from something*.

The pattern of verses 2-7 is 2/4/4/2. The final verse displays a mirror image arrangement: + / – / – / +. The central elements of the chiasm are the negatives *hating* and *making war* bracketed by *loving* and *making peace*. The first negative element in verse 2 (*dying*) parallels the final negative element of the concluding verse (v. 8, *making war*). Verse 8 acts as a summary.

What does this intricate structure in verses 1-8 indicate? The structure provides organization for the theme of time. The two chiastic verses (vv. 1 and 8) enclose the two inverted series of parallels (vv. 2-7). It is possible that the negative aspects of verses 2 and 7 reflect Solomon's own situation near the end of his life (see 1 Kings 11:11-43). His own time is running down and he spends the final years of his life occupied with adversaries, war (v. 8b), and the uprooting (v. 2b) and tearing apart (v. 7a) of his kingdom. Although his own name speaks of peace, there will be no peace (v. 8b) – he can only hope that it will come someday for his descendants. Life will go on and the normal activities of living will take place, but Solomon faces eternity (see v. 11).

The central focus of verse 1 falls on two different words for time. In its six other occurrences, Scripture employs the first word with the idea of appointed time (cf. Ezra 10:14; Neh. 2:6; 10:35; 13:31; Esther 9:27, 31). Post-exilic Hebrew provides the normal provenance for the usage of the word, with the possible exception of Ecclesiastes. The term has an older history than post-exilic Hebrew. It appears also in Akkadian and reflects an ancient etymology. The second word occurs 296 times in the Hebrew Bible (including 29 times in this poem and 11 more times in Ecclesiastes).

Time operates under God's creative fiat. He ordained the sun, moon, and stars in their courses for the purpose of measuring off seasons, months, days, and years (Gen. 1:14). The orderliness of time reflects the Creator's orderliness. He created all things and deemed them 'good' (Gen. 1:18, 31). Sometimes we tend to think of creation only in terms of the universe, the solar system, our planet, plants, animals, and mankind. However, divine creation extends beyond the visible to include gravity, the speed of light, planetary orbits, lunar tides, combustion, photosynthesis, meiosis, reproduction, digestion, emotions, thought processes, blood clotting, etc. Some commentators argue against the poem being a reflection of divine sovereignty and control. Instead, they argue that all except birth and death represent activities under human control and dependent upon human choice.[5] Verse 11, however, responds effectively to that viewpoint, since Solomon specifically declares that God 'has made everything appropriate in its time.'[6]

Of all the verses, verse 5 provides the most difficult situations to understand. This difficulty has led to a number of interpretations or explanations. A traditional Jewish interpretation identifies the actions as sexual intercourse and sexual restraint. The pattern seems to indicate that 'throwing stones' should be a positive, while 'gathering stones' should be the negative. That favors a reference for the former as removing stones from a field (cp. Isa. 5:2) to prepare it for cultivation and the latter as gathering stones for ruining a field. Or, the casting of stones might refer to the destruction of a field in a time of war by strewing it with stones (cp. 2 Kings 3:19, 25). Some even take these references to stones as the accumulation of wealth (e.g., valuable gems) and the distribution of that wealth.[7] On balance, removing stones refers to preparation for cultivating and gathering stones refers to ruining a field.

Verse 7 might represent activities associated with mourning.[8] The tearing of garments illustrates grief (cp. Gen. 37:29) while sewing up torn garments might indicate an end to a period of grief. As illustrated in the account of Job's suffering and the visit of his three friends, silence can represent grief and speaking the ending of grief.

---

5. Bartholomew, *Ecclesiastes*, 162.
6. Cf. Leupold, *Ecclesiastes*, 81.
7. Provan, *Ecclesiastes, Song of Songs*, 88.
8. Garrett, *Proverbs, Ecclesiastes, Song of Songs*, 298.

The Poem's Message (3:9-22)

Though quite well-known, verse 11 presents an interpretive problem. Does 'eternity' correctly translate the Hebrew word *'olam*? Options proposed by various interpreters include 'world,' 'eternity,' and 'ignorance.'[9] Contextual factors argue for the meaning 'eternity.' First, the poem is about time. Secondly, verse 14 repeats the same term with the obvious meaning of 'forever' or 'eternity.' 'He has made everything appropriate in its time' – some translations have 'beautiful' instead of 'appropriate' – refers to God's governance of the timing of events at the right, or appropriate, time. In addition, the Creator made human beings and placed eternity within them. As Estes notes, 'humans are bound by time, but they are wired for eternity. They intuitively know that there must be meaning somewhere, and that they were made for more than vain toil.'[10]

Human beings, in and of themselves, cannot satisfy their desire to know the divine design for life and its events. Our Creator made us with an innate inquisitiveness and need to observe, research, and contemplate His creation and our own existence. He has even placed us within His created universe on the most conducive observation platform from which to see our celestial neighbors, our solar system, our galaxy, and our corner of the universe.[11]

Solomon's double 'I know' (vv. 12, 14) appears to contrast with the three occurrences of 'I have seen' (vv. 10, 16, 22). Whereas the seeing comes from observation and experience, the knowing might represent intuitive knowledge or prior theological presuppositions. The enigmas of existence can make people frustrated and fretful. Instead of fretting, however, we need to accept our limitations and enjoy those things which God has so graciously provided for us – those good things that He intends that we enjoy (vv. 12-13). 'The key to this enjoyment is that God himself has given these activities as

---

9. Longman, *Ecclesiastes*, 120.

10. Estes, *Handbook on the Wisdom Books*, 313.

11. 'As we learn more about the seemingly accidental features of our atmosphere and Solar System, we begin to recognize a trend. The Earth system offers not only a habitat but also a great viewing platform for its inhabitants.' – Guillermo Gonzalez and Jay W. Richards, *The Privileged Planet: How Our Place in the Cosmos Is Designed for Discovery* (Washington, D.C.: Regnery Publishing, 2004), 79.

gifts.'[12] More than the need to enjoy the gifts of God, we need to develop a correct relationship to our Creator. Brown writes that 'For Qoheleth, an awareness of the systemic limitations of human existence is fundamental to cultivating awe of God.'[13] The fact that a man or a woman cannot change what God has purposed, designed, or brought about generates a proper fear of God (v. 14).

Fearing God is the beginning of knowledge (Prov. 1:7). Solomon's spiritual journey of discovery produces the fear of God that had been absent during the time of his apostasy. The wisest man of his day finally wises up.

Ecclesiastes 3:15, like 1:9, announces the conclusion of Solomon's reflections: nothing changes. The final clause of the verse ('for God seeks what has passed by') might refer to God's control over past events. God not only controls those events – He repeats them over and over again until we finally understand what He desires to teach us through them. Charles Swindoll explains it in the following fashion:

> We are the ones to pass it by. We are the ones who walk away, so God brings us back to the same lesson to learn it again. And he doesn't give up when we pass it by. He brings us back again and again to learn our lesson well. We get weary of learning the lesson and we run from it. We turn it off. Yet He repeats the same lesson. He repeats it and repeats it and repeats it until finally the light comes on and we learn it. Why? Because God seeks what you and I try to escape. God pursues what you and I turn off. God makes a permanent lesson out of what you think is a temporary and passing experience.[14]

Solomon had attempted to escape, but God would not let him go. His Creator kept bombarding him with reality – God's created reality. Solomon, in his old age, was running out of his God-appointed time. Thinking of his own death, Solomon realizes that his desire to know more about what happens following death is a desire God had implanted in the soul of every man and woman. His search for happiness must switch from pursuing wisdom and pleasure 'under the sun' to 'looking for the city which has foundations, whose architect

---

12. Estes, *Handbook on the Wisdom Books*, 315.
13. Brown, *Ecclesiastes*, 45.
14. Swindoll, *Living on the Ragged Edge*, 90.

and builder is God' (Heb. 11:10). Like Abraham before him, Solomon must look for a heavenly city (Heb. 11:16) beyond the sun.

It might seem strange to move from the topic of time to the topic of injustice and oppression (v. 16). Yet the point that Solomon makes involves his observation that a person often spends his time on earth suffering in one way or another. Since God controls all things and everything is in His time, He must also have a time to set right the wrongs, to bring justice where there is injustice. Knowing that God has a time for judging injustice provides hope for human beings (v. 17). 'A time for every matter and for every deed' includes the righting of wrongs and the establishment of divine justice. The 'there' at the end of verse 17 might carry an eschatological sense – referring to either the time and place of future judgment, the grave, or heaven (cp. Ps. 14:5).[15] On the other hand, it might refer to the circumstances of life (even in the perverted courts of the land) in which God is at work to bring about His will.[16] The reference of 'there' remains a problem, but the difficulty does not disrupt the general concept that God controls all matters of timing in the past, the present, and the future. However, mention of 'every matter' and 'every deed' favors a future (eschatological) concept as the reference for 'there'.

Some commentators contend that the speaker's complaint about injustice argues against Solomonic authorship of the book. After all, Solomon was king, and kings acted as judges. If he saw injustice, would it not be in his own court over which he has jurisdiction?[17] However, kings did appoint judges. Jehoshaphat, king of Judah, for example, appointed judges and instructed them to judge righteously and with impartiality in the fear of the Lord (2 Chron. 19:6-7). Solomon speaks generically – he refers to injustice performed in many courts in many lands. He understands that it is characteristic of mankind – even that he himself might commit an injustice in any given case that might be set before him for his decision.

Simian-Yofre appears to ignore the way that Solomon introduces his statement in verse 18: 'The injustice suffered by

---

15. Garrett, *Proverbs, Ecclesiastes, Song of Songs*, 302-03.
16. Eaton, *Ecclesiastes*, 85.
17. E.g., Longman, *Ecclesiastes*, 127.

the oppressed is one more concrete expression of the general meaninglessness of life, which equates the lot of human beings with that of animals (3:18). The absence of a comforter is an expression of God's silence in the midst of human life.'[18] Solomon introduces the next set of verses (vv. 17-21) with the words 'I said to myself' (literally, 'I said in my heart'). He accurately and honestly records his own thinking. That does not mean that his thought equates with divine truth. Just because Scripture reports the human statement, does not indicate that God approves of that statement. When a person gets as far away from the Lord as Solomon did, he or she will turn their back on the clear truths of Scripture and ignore God's revelation. The creation account in Genesis 1–3 plainly explains key differences between animals and human beings. Solomon was not ignorant of that text – he refers back to it again and again in Ecclesiastes. God created human beings in His image (Gen. 1:26-28). Adam named the animals (Gen. 2:19-20) – the animals did not name Adam. God gave Adam and Eve dominion over the animals. Due to his spiritual crisis and lack of discernment, however, Solomon experiences temporary Scripture amnesia and concludes that human beings are no better off than animals. Cynicism confuses Solomon – and it can do so to any believer whose sins have broken their fellowship with their heavenly Father. Cynicism 'angers us emotionally. It numbs us spiritually. It leaves us scarred, bitter, disillusioned, and, for sure, feeling distant from God. That aptly describes Solomon at this phase of his journey.'[19]

Normal observation without taking into account biblical revelation leads to the impression that mankind and animals both die the same way and go to the same grave. Prior revelation, however, clearly identifies a distinction in that God made only mankind in His image (Gen. 1:26-27). Solomon later reveals that he does recognize a distinct difference between the death of a human being and the death of an animal. In 12:7 he mentions that the human spirit returns to God, its Creator.

---

18. H. Simian-Yofre, 'נחם,' in *Theological Dictionary of the Old Testament*, 16 vols., ed. by G. Johannes Botterweck, Helmer Ringgren, and Heinz-Josef Fabry, trans. by David E. Green (Grand Rapids, Mich.: William B. Eerdmans Publishing Company, 1998), 9:353.

19. Swindoll, *Living on the Ragged Edge*, 103.

Of course, in the Old Testament the examples of Enoch, Elijah, and Moses all predate Ecclesiastes and provide unimpeachable evidence for life after death and for the human soul's return to God, the Creator.

The focus on death reflects a consistency with the manner in which the poem in verses 1-8 had begun ('A time to give birth and a time to die,' v. 2). Verse 20 indicates that Solomon was aware of the truth of Genesis 3:19 – that mankind returns to the dust out of which God had created Adam. Duane Garrett observes that Ecclesiastes 3:18-21 does not deny the existence of an afterlife, but does 'force the reader to take death seriously'[20] (cp. v. 18, 'God has surely tested them in order for them to see that they are but beasts' – i.e., destined to die).

Verse 21 offers yet another interpretive problem. Some commentaries treat it as a question[21] while others treat it as a declaration.[22] The introductory phrase ('Who knows') commonly occurs to introduce a statement regarding potentiality. For example, in 2 Samuel 12:22 ('Who knows, the LORD may be gracious to me, that the child may live'). In other words, it almost has the force of 'it is possible that.' The same usage appears again in Ecclesiastes 3:21 on virtually the identical matter. In other words, the reader can conclude that Solomon indicates it is possible for man's spirit to ascend to God at death while the spirit of the animal somehow returns to the earth. His uncertainty is more about the animal's spirit than about the man's.

Verse 22 echoes 2:24 and 3:12 by expressing once again the need for satisfaction with what God has given. Why fret over our lack of control over the timing of events, our failure to eradicate injustice, and our inability to avoid death? God has better things for us to do than to spend our time fretting over things that we cannot control. But, God has revealed what we ought to do in the *carpe diem* passages.[23] Ecclesiastes 3 states that God's intervention and personal attention to mankind in the world is not random or disorganized or aimless, regardless of appearances. Our Creator is in control and

---

20. Garrett, *Proverbs, Ecclesiastes, Song of Songs*, 305.

21. Eaton, *Ecclesiastes*, 88-89; Hengstenberg, *Ecclesiastes*, 119-20; Leupold, *Ecclesiastes*, 97-100, Kaiser, *Ecclesiastes*, 70-71.

22. Longman, *Ecclesiastes*, 131; Garrett, *Proverbs, Ecclesiastes, Song of Songs*, 303-4; Murphy, *Ecclesiastes*, 31.

23. Ecclesiastes 2:24-26; 3:12-13; 5:18-20; 8:15; 9:7-9; 11:7-10.

makes known His will for His people. We are not to pour more effort into understanding our frustrating and uncontrollable circumstances. Nor ought we to spend our time comparing our lot in life with another's. We ought not indulge in retaliation, resentment, bitterness, or disappear into a fantasy world. Reject these reactions to life's difficult circumstances and intrinsic injustices. Abandon self-pity and despair. Identify the advantage to your disadvantage. Thank God that He uses such circumstances to humble you, to make you more dependent upon Him, and to be thankful for what He has given you to enjoy. Your joy of God's gifts grows greater in the light of your trials while you live 'under the sun.'[24]

STUDY QUESTIONS

1. What should be the Christian's view of time?

2. How do people demonstrate the 'eternity' that God has set in their hearts?

3. What does it mean to fear God?

4. Why does Solomon use injustice and death to deal with the issue of time?

5. What is the purpose of the final question in Ecclesiastes 3:22?

6. What advantage(s) have you gained from your chief disadvantage?

---

24. My thoughts in this paragraph have been shaped by the wonderful insights of Swindoll, *Living on the Ragged Edge*, 103-09.

4

Two by Two

From observation, *the Preacher* learned
that God has a design for all
things *(3:1–5:20)*, Part 2

As Eaton explains, 'Between 4:1 and 10:20 Ecclesiastes resem-
bles the Book of Proverbs, with short epigrams dealing
with various aspects of life.'[1] In fact, this section cites a number of
proverbs and its teachings parallel a number of texts contained
in the Book of Proverbs. These connections add to the argument
in favor of supporting Solomon as the author of Ecclesiastes.

The fourth chapter of Ecclesiastes confronts four major
problems in everyday life 'under the sun:'

- the existence of unrelieved oppression (vv. 1-3),

- unsatisfied jealousy (vv. 4-6),

- unmitigated loneliness (vv. 7-12), and

- the uncertainty of political power
  and popularity (vv. 13-16).

The author mentions observing these problems (vv. 1, 4, 7, 15),
letting us know that he is an eyewitness of these situations.
The numeral 'two' plays a major role in this chapter, occurring
eight times (vv. 3, 6 [dual form], 8, 9, 10, 11, 12, 15). Two[2] gives

---

1. Eaton, *Ecclesiastes*, 90.
2. The NASU translates 'two' with 'both,' 'dependent,' 'another,' and 'second'.

coherence to the text unit and offers an implied solution for the isolation experienced by the lone individual. 'One' occurs five times (vv. 8, 9, 10 *bis*, 11, 12) and the text implies it at least once (v. 6, 'one hand'). 'Three' makes its appearance once (v. 12) – in an illustration demonstrating that three are even better than two.

Observing Oppression (4:1-3)

Four elements in verse 1 accentuate the text's emotional intensity:

1. the root word for 'oppress' occurs three times, indicating a major theme of the passage;

2. 'behold' lends a dramatic effect;

3. 'tears' and 'comfort' highlight the emotional side of the situation; and,

4. the repetition of 'no one to comfort'[3] emphasizes the hopeless condition of the oppressed individual.

The writer does not approach this section dispassionately; he personally identifies with the reality of oppression and with the abuse of power.

Solomon employs the root word for 'oppress' only two other times in the book (5:8 and 7:7). Elsewhere he uses the root five times (Ps. 72:4; Prov. 14:31; 22:16; 28:3, 17), demonstrating that he possessed knowledge of oppressive rulers and their oppressed subjects. Thus, scholars should hesitate to rule Solomon out as the author of Ecclesiastes, just because it speaks of oppression. In Solomon's time, as throughout human history, possessors of power perpetrated oppression ('on the side of their oppressors was power,' v. 1). Although Solomon does not seem to have suffered from oppression himself, he must have been aware of his father's history under Saul. The text declares that he observes the 'tears of the oppressed,' revealing his sympathy for them. He also noted that oppressed persons feel helpless and hopeless, because they have 'no one to comfort *them*' (stated twice for emphasis). He might realize that his

---

3. See these elements identified by Whybray, *Ecclesiastes*, 81.

descendants will face oppression following the division of his kingdom (see 1 Kings 11).

Similar declarations occur in Job (16:2; 21:34; 30:28) and five times in Lamentations 1 (vv. 2, 9, 16, 17, 21) as well as Psalm 69:20, Isaiah 54:11, and Zechariah 10:2, in order to emphasize a pathetic condition. The repetition sets the stage for the later discussion of loneliness and companionship (vv. 7-12). Readers of the New Testament cannot help but be reminded that God's people receive comfort from all three Persons of the Godhead (Acts 9:31; 2 Cor. 1:3-7). God champions the cause of the oppressed (Pss. 9:9; 10:17-18; 103:6; 146:7).

Solomon congratulates (or, praises) the dead for being better off than the oppressed who cannot enjoy their life under the sun (v. 2; cp. Job 3:3-5, 11-19; Jer. 20:14-18). In 3:15-17 the writer advances future divine justice as the resolution of oppression. Here (4:1-3), however, death itself (even before the time of divine vindication and establishment of justice) offers a better alternative. This is consistent with the logical development of the text, since Solomon introduces a discussion of death in the intervening section (3:18-22).[4] Even better off is the individual who never existed, who had never been born (4:3). Such 'better (than)' axioms occur twenty-three times in Ecclesiastes.[5] The form also characterizes many of the wisdom statements contained in the central sections of the Book of Proverbs, where they appear twenty-four times.[6]

Should we characterize Solomon's attitude as cynical or skeptical in regard to the preference of death or non-existence to experiencing oppression? Leupold answers, 'There is nothing skeptical or cynical about such an attitude. It is the only permissible estimate that can be put upon earthly values apart from the heavenly.'[7] Long ago, Franz Delitzsch commented on the statement that death or non-existence is better than living with oppression: 'so long as the central point of man's

---

4. Garrett, *Proverbs, Ecclesiastes, Song of Songs*, 306.

5. 2:24; 3:12, 22; 4:3, 6, 9, 13; 5:5; 6:3, 5, 9; 7:1 (2×), 2, 3, 5, 8 (2×), 10; 9:4, 16, 17, 18.

6. 3:14 (2×); 8:11, 19 (2×); 12:9; 15:16, 17; 16:8, 16, 19, 32; 17:1; 19:1, 22; 21:9, 19; 22:1; 25:7, 24; 25:24; 27:5, 10; 28:6.

7. Leupold, *Ecclesiastes*, 104. Kelley, *The Burden of God*, 91-92 agrees: 'His attitude is not one of cynical resignation; he merely reflects soberly on what is inescapable for man in his rebellion against God.'

existence lies in the present life, and this is not viewed as the fore-court of eternity, there is no enduring consolation to lift us above the miseries of this present world.'[8] Solomon's earlier assertion that God has 'set eternity' (3:11) in the hearts of human beings supplies a source for hope in the midst of the negative experiences of life.

For those who deny Solomonic authorship for Ecclesiastes, the text's discussion of oppression appears 'awkward when attributed to the mind of Solomon. Not only could Solomon have done something about oppression, but he, according to the historical books, contributed heavily to it in the last days of his life (1 Kings 11).'[9] Such an approach ignores the depth of Solomon's God-given wisdom, the breadth of his international relationships, the extent of his access to the situations in many neighboring lands, and the variety of his personal experiences.

Scripture condemns the abuse of power. God consistently reminds His people of the sins of exploitation and oppression (Exod. 22:21; 23:9; Lev. 19:13; Deut. 24:14; Ps. 62:10; Zech. 7:10; Mal. 3:5). The godly not only refrain from oppressing others, they actively seek justice for the oppressed (Deut. 16:19-20; Ps. 106:3; Prov. 21:3, 15; Isa. 1:17; Micah 6:8; cp. Matt. 23:23; Col. 4:1).

Observing Jealousy (4:4-6)

Envy, jealousy, covetousness, and greed all serve to motivate people to work with fervor for long hours. Jealousy carries with it a positive connotation only in regard to the relationship between God and His people and the marital relationship.[10] Jealousy or envy divides families (Gen. 30:1; 37:11), kills (Job 5:2), harasses (Isa. 11:13), and produces anger (Prov. 6:34), 'rottenness to the bones' (perhaps illness, Prov. 14:30), and hatred (Ezek. 35:11). One should not envy a violent person (Prov. 3:31) or sinners (Prov. 23:17). No wonder the Scripture describes this sort of labor or work as 'evil' (Eccles. 4:3). Such activity displays a dog-eat-dog attitude wherein a person

---

8. Delitzsch, *Song of Songs and Ecclesiastes*, 274.
9. Longman, *Ecclesiastes*, 132ff..
10. Bartholomew, *Ecclesiastes*, 187. See Exod. 20:5; 34:14; Num. 5:14-30; 25:11, 13; Song of Solomon 8:6; Zech. 1:14; 8:2; cp. 2 Cor. 11:2.

seeks to get ahead, even if he or she must step on colleagues in their climb to the top of the corporate ladder. In Walter Kaiser's examination of this passage, he acknowledges that 'men can be as cruel and inhuman to each other in unnecessary competition as they can be in oppression.'[11] Envy destroys others just as certainly as the exercise of oppressive power. It is more popular to criticize corporate greed and political oppression than to recognize that such great injustices originate with the envy and jealousy that too often motivates a person in his or her own drive to succeed at any cost.

Solomon constructs a contrast between verses 4 and 5. The avaricious individual of verse 4 displays too much ambition and too little contentment, whereas the indolent individual of verse 5 exhibits too little ambition and excessive contentment.[12] Folding the hands appears elsewhere in Proverbs 6:10 and 24:33 depicting the slumber of a lazy person. Lying on their beds, they fold their hands over their chest or bosom as they sleep. Biblical wisdom writers condemn laziness and associate the characteristic with fools (Prov. 6:9; 10:26; 12:27; 13:4; 15:19; 19:15, 24; 20:4; 21:25; 22:13; 24:30; 26:14, 16; cp. Matt. 25:24-30). Commentators understand 'consumes his own flesh' (v. 5) in at least three different ways: (1) self-cannibalism speaking metaphorically of self-destruction,[13] (2) 'still has his meat to eat,'[14] (meaning that the fool does nothing, but still has food to eat), and (3) reducing oneself to poverty.[15] The first of these appears to be most consistent with the imagery and the context.

By means of yet another proverb, the writer of Ecclesiastes expresses the truth that contentment can exist where the individual actually possesses fewer material goods, but finds satisfying rest (v. 6). 'Fists' consists of a word that indicates the cupping of the hands to be able 'to take as much as possible'[16] (see Exod. 9:8; Lev. 16:12; Prov. 30:4; Ezek. 10:2, 7). In other words, preoccupation with the pursuit of wealth is as evil as laziness. Solomon declared in Psalm 127:2:

---

11. Kaiser, *Ecclesiastes*, 72.
12. Estes, *Handbook on the Wisdom Books*, 322.
13. Gordis, *Koheleth*, 241.
14. Murphy, *Ecclesiastes*, 31.
15. Rankin and Atkins, 'The Book of Ecclesiastes,' 5:54; Barton, *Ecclesiastes*, 114.
16. Eaton, *Ecclesiastes*, 93; Barton, *Ecclesiastes*, 115.

It is vain for you to rise up early,
To retire late,
To eat the bread of painful labors;
For He gives to His beloved *even in his* sleep.

Elsewhere, he binds contentment to the believer's relationship to the Lord (Prov. 15:16; 16:8) and to harmonious and loving relationships with others (Prov. 15:17) – the opposite effect to that of envy and jealousy.

Observing Loneliness (4:7-12)

In the third reference to observation (v. 7), Solomon gets directly to the usual summary declaration of 'vanity' ahead of reporting his observations. In verse 3 his summary omits the word, but depicts non-existence as preferable to oppression. Then, in verse 4, he brings the summary forward ('This too is vanity and striving after wind') after briefly describing what he had observed. Whereas verses 1-3 speak of no comforter and verses 4-6 imply no rest, verses 7-12 dwell on the concept of no companion.[17]

An exact rendering of the opening words of verse 8 reveals both the concise nature of the statement and the usage of two numbers: 'There is one and there is not a second.' Thus the writer introduces a discussion of loneliness (the one alone) and companionship (the one with a second). In case the reader might think that Solomon speaks of marriage, he next qualifies what he means by 'not a second:' 'neither a son nor a brother.' Even David needs a Jonathan or a Joab. An individual who isolates himself or herself from companionship fails to experience community and its God-ordained blessings. Remember, God Himself declared of the perfect man in his unfallen state, 'It is not good for the man to be alone' (Gen. 2:18). God advocates companionship over solitary lives.

Self-made hermits tend to be selfish and focused on the riches they hope their labor will bring to them. 'Indeed, his eyes were not satisfied with riches' (v. 8) reminds the reader of the earlier proverb in 1:8. A third mention arises in 5:10 where the writer offers further clarification: 'He who loves money will not be satisfied with money, nor he who loves abundance

---

17. Kaiser, *Ecclesiastes*, 73.

with its income.' Why do people end up alone? According to Craig Bartholomew,

> There are various reasons a person like this ends up alone. We can speculate as to why, and his workaholism may provide a clue. It is more likely that for circumstantial reasons this person has found himself alone, and in this rough situation, he has sought meaning in work and wealth. But they fail to provide the meaning he seeks.[18]

Note that the translators of NASU have placed '*and he never asked*' (v. 8) in italics. The phrase does not occur in the original language. However, the following question implies this transition at least in thought. Does Solomon himself ask the question, or is this just a general hypothetical illustration? Some commentators find in verses 7-8 a situation involving the absence of an heir, while verses 9-12 involve the absence of a companion, and verses 13-16, the absence of a successor.[19] Garrett offers a pithy and apropos synopsis: 'Money is their only kin.'[20] Preoccupied with climbing the corporate ladder, a man often tells himself that he does so in order to take care of his family, but, in reality, he is caught up in his projects to make a name for himself. His family soon becomes a casualty due to his neglect for their real welfare.

Do you know someone who fits the illuminating examples that you read about here in Ecclesiastes? By keeping the descriptions general, Solomon invites all readers 'to think of their own acquaintances and say, in effect, "I know somebody like that."'[21] He identifies three examples of solitary existence in contrast to companionship in order to make his point. All three might arise from the experience of travel in the ancient Near East. The first might refer to falling into a pit or a ravine (v. 10), the second might describe attempts to keep warm outdoors during the cold of night (v. 11; cp. 1 Kings 1:1-4), and the third might refer to highwaymen or robbers encountered along the road (v. 12). The lessons should not be restricted to travel, however. A helper, a comforter, and a defender all apply to many life settings.

---

18. Bartholomew, *Ecclesiastes*, 189.
19. Murphy, *Ecclesiastes*, 41.
20. Garrett, *Proverbs, Ecclesiastes, Song of Songs*, 307.
21. Longman, *Ecclesiastes*, 139.

References to a three-strand or three-ply rope (cord) occur in ancient Sumerian and Akkadian texts. In the Sumerian story of Gilgamesh's encounter with Humbaba, guardian of the Cedar Forest, Gilgamesh exhorts his friend Enkidu not to abandon his quest. He says, 'Two men will not die; the towed rope will not sink. A towrope of three strands cannot be cut. You help me and I will help you.'[22] This mention of the three-strand rope concludes the section dealing with pairs of people. Such a numeric arrangement reflects the pattern $x +$ $(x + 1)$, which occurs in a number of Old Testament passages. The Old Testament reveals the following patterns: one/two (Ezra 10:13), two/three (Deut. 17:16; Prov. 30:15; Amos 4:8), three/four (Prov. 30:15, 18, 21, 29; Amos 1:3, 6, 9, 11, 13; 2:1, 4, 6), four/five (Isa. 17:6), five/six (2 Kings 13:19), six/seven (Job 5:19; Prov. 6:16), and seven/eight (Eccles. 11:2; Micah 5:5). Such a pattern normally implies fullness or a full measure.

Compare Jesus' statement in Matthew 18:20: 'For where two or three have gathered together in My name, I am there in their midst.' Indeed, since two are better than one, how much better might it be to have three people. And, how much better to have with those two or three the Lord Himself present!

Observing Politics (4:13-16)

Besides the theme of political power and popularity, these verses contrast generations. Sometimes the aged lack wisdom and act foolishly (Job 12:20). On the other hand, the younger may be wiser than their elders (Ps. 119:100). Old Testament writers employ the word 'lad' (*yeled*, v. 13) for Joseph at the age of seventeen (Gen. 37:30) and for the companions of Rehoboam when he was over the age of forty (1 Kings 12:8; cp. the first use of the term in Gen. 4:23), as well as utilizing the term to describe children of a very young age (Gen. 21:8; Exod. 2:9). Therefore, the contrast focuses on relative ages, not on someone who is very young.

Although many scholars have sought to identify this situation in history, they have failed to prove any satisfactory identification. Suggestions include Joseph (see v. 14, 'he has come out

---

22. John Day, 'Foreign Semitic Influence on the Wisdom of Israel and Its Appropriation in the Book of Proverbs,' in *Wisdom in Ancient Israel*, ed. by John Day et al. (Cambridge, England: Cambridge University Press, 1998), 61. Cp. Longman, *Ecclesiastes*, 143.

of prison') and Pharaoh as well as Saul and David. Another incident involves Solomon's son Rehoboam who ignored the advice of his counselors (1 Kings 12:1-19). Henry Morris speculates that the entire story stems from the Lord's revelation given to Solomon in 1 Kings 11:11-13. Solomon himself had become foolish and one of his servants whom Solomon had driven into exile in Egypt (1 Kings 11:26-40) would supplant his son, Rehoboam (1 Kings 12:1-24), though Rehoboam would still retain power over one tribe.[23] The revelation that the Lord had given to Solomon was confirmed by the prophet Ahijah whom God sent to Jeroboam (1 Kings 11:29-39). If the illustration in Ecclesiastes 4:13-16 actually possesses a historical precedent, the prophetic announcements to Solomon and Jeroboam would seem to fit the best. However, insufficient evidence exists to enable a dogmatic identification. Even in the modern era, former political prisoners or exiled leaders occasionally replace a foolish regime. William Brown cites Iran, Nicaragua, South Africa, and South Korea as examples and notes that such replacements might be for good or for ill.[24]

Prisons in the ancient Near East did not house only criminals and traitors. Often the prisons were filled with individuals unable to pay their debts or to fulfill their financial obligations.[25] (cp. Matt. 5:26; Luke 12:59). Thus, the text also mentions that the second king was poor as well as the fact that he was born in poverty (Eccles. 4:13-14).

An underlying lesson within this historical or fictitious illustration applies to the wisdom of accepting advice and counsel. The king proves to be foolish when he 'no longer knows *how* to receive instruction' (v. 13). The term used for 'instruction' might also be translated 'admonition' or even 'warning.' In essence, the aged king was acting as a loner, refusing to listen to his counselors. Proverbs identifies wise counsel as characteristic of the best plans and decisions (11:14; 15:22; 20:18; 21:5; 24:6; cp. Luke 14:31). Of course, the best counsel comes from God Himself (Prov. 16:1, 3, 9; 19:21). The old king ignores this reality, choosing to act on his own.

---

23. Morris, *The Remarkable Wisdom of Solomon*, 200-01.
24. Brown, *Ecclesiastes*, 54.
25. Estes, *Handbook on the Wisdom Books*, 325-26.

When the writer says, 'I have seen' (v. 15), this does not exclude Solomon from the authorship of the book. In one sense, if the reference is to Solomon, Jeroboam, and Rehoboam, Solomon has already seen it by the revelation God granted him as recorded in 1 Kings 11. If those three are not the royal personages in view, Solomon lives long enough, experiences enough interaction with fellow royals throughout the Near East, and gathers enough information from his ships' voyages as far abroad as India and Africa to learn of such a situation in another land. In brief, wisdom, age, power, youth, political astuteness, and popularity all fail to guarantee political success or longevity. In the end, subsequent generations of citizens will forget both the wise and the foolish, the aged and the young, the popular and the unpopular.

Conclusion

Humankind constantly dreams of some sort of utopia on earth. Over and over again, generation after generation, political regime after political regime, people seek solutions to the problems of humanity in both the social and moral realms. They expend great wealth and power on attempting to right society's wrongs. Frustratingly, however, every attempt meets failure. All solutions prove to be temporary, at best. Every 'Great Society' comes to a time when it all collapses and the advances of decades disappear in the dust of another depression, another war, or another natural disaster. Derek Kidner's keen observation about 4:1-3 provides a potential association between the oppression in verses 1-3 and the political inconsistencies of verses 13-16. He notes the paradox that a transfer of power to promote change actually 'limits the possibility of reform itself, because the more control the reformer wields, the more it tends to tyranny.'[26]

The all-inclusive fallen condition of humanity defies self-restoration. As Michael Kelley observes, 'The masses willingly support revolution because they cannot believe that the fault lies in them."[27] The indelible sinful nature of fallen mankind prevents the success of setting up the kingdom of God apart

---

26. Kidner, *A Time to Mourn*, 44. While the observation on vv. 1-3 is Kidner's, he fails, at least in this source, to make the link to vv. 13-16.

27. Kelley, *The Burden of God*, 94.

from the return of Jesus Christ. Ideal social justice must await the Righteous One Himself.

STUDY QUESTIONS

1. Why are oppressed people hopeless and helpless?

2. What motivates you to work with fervor for many hours?

3. Why does Ecclesiastes condemn people who are lazy?

4. In what ways does envy lead to a loss of companionship?

5. Who are the believers' companions?

6. Why should believers listen to wise advice and counsel?

7. Why do political solutions for society's problems fail?

5

Beyond the Sun

From observation, *the Preacher* learned
that God has a design for all
things *(3:1–5:20)*, Part 3

Consumed by his search for meaning in life 'under the sun,' Solomon first notes that God had 'set eternity' in the human heart (3:11). Then he indicates that God will right the wrongs and provide justice (3:17). Throughout chapter 4 the author focuses on the ongoing issues of everyday life: unrelieved oppression (4:1-3), unsatisfied jealousy and envy (4:4-6), unmitigated loneliness (4:7-12), and the uncertainty of political power and popularity (4:13-16). These four situations demonstrate that, individually and corporately, people cannot resolve their most persistent problems – and these do not rise to the level of death itself, the chief problem (cp. 2:14-16 and 3:19-21).

Solomon's investigations lead him to a consideration of mankind's relationship to God. Swindoll opens his examination of Ecclesiastes 5 with the following thought:

> So many of Solomon's ideas and observations are horizontal musings … the bitter, barren, boring side of life seen through disillusioned eyes. But on a few, rare occasions the man breaks out of his cynical syndrome. At those times his comments contain a remarkable vertical perspective that scrapes away the veneer of empty religion and takes us back to the bedrock of a meaningful relationship with the living Lord.[1]

---

1. Swindoll, *Living on the Ragged Edge*, 146.

Each individual must realize that God's involvement in his or her life consists of more than afflicting people with 'a grievous task' (1:13; cp. 3:10) and providing work, food, enjoyment, wisdom, and knowledge (2:24-26). God makes a distinction between the good person and the sinner (2:26). Indeed, the difference in one's status in God's sight will manifest itself in a future judgment (3:17). One's relationship to God includes one's awareness and pursuit of eternity (3:11).

After death the spirit of the individual ascends to God (3:21; cp. 12:7). Therefore, each person 'under the sun' must anticipate an encounter with the eternal God beyond the sun. What does that look like? How does one prepare for life beyond the sun? Solomon takes up the topics of attitude and behavior in worship (5:1-3), vows (5:4-6), the fear of God (5:7), justice (5:8), and wealth (5:10-17). Each topic reveals something about one's relationship to God, who provides the greater companionship that every person needs in life (cp. 4:7-12).[2]

Approaching the Presence of God (5:1-3)

Solomon, as a keen observer of people and their habits and practices, offers constructive criticism. Those who heed his critiques will benefit from his advice. Solomon observes that too many of God's covenant people approach worship with a lackadaisical attitude. He notes a lack of true reverence for the holy, and for the Holy One Himself. Each act of superficial worship reveals this truth – whether it is an individual's mannerisms and attitude upon entering the place of worship, or the type of obedience he manifests, or the sacrifice he brings, or the prayer he offers, or the vows of service to which he commits himself. According to Hubbard,

> the Preacher wanted to remind his hearers of the greatness of God who could see through any extravagance in prayer. Wild promises, unguarded commitments, vain repetition were all to be avoided. Poise, control, measured speech and action were considered expressions of sound conduct by the wise.'[3]

---

2. 'We stand in need of an altogether greater companionship' (Eaton, *Ecclesiastes*, 97.

3. Hubbard, *Ecclesiastes, Song of Solomon*, 131.

Verses 1-3 contain a series of four commands: 'Guard your steps' (v. 1a),[4] 'draw near to listen' (v. 1b), 'Do not be hasty' in word or thought (v. 2a), and 'let your words be few' (v. 2b).

Guarding Our Steps (5:1a)

'Guard your steps [lit., feet] as you go' might mean that the worshiper should prepare for worship by his or her obedience to God beforehand (Ps. 17:4-5; Prov. 4:20-27). Gathering for public worship must not be taken lightly. Garrett states that it refers to entering the Temple with reverence.[5] The instruction might also concern not going astray into paths of disobedience on the way to the place of worship, regardless of the temptations one might encounter (cp. Prov. 1:15). The first understanding forms the most likely meaning – if for no other reason than that it finds company in the phraseology of biblical wisdom literature.[6] Barton presents the following paraphrase: 'Do not run to the place of worship thoughtlessly, or because it is the fashion to go frequently, but consider the nature of the place and thy purpose in going.'[7] Although his paraphrase differs somewhat with the meaning, it plucks the same string. As in Christ's statement in John 4:23-24, we ought not to approach worship lightly nor without intentional preparation in heart, head, and hand (or, foot!) – we must worship in spirit and in truth.

What is 'the house of God'? The phrase occurs throughout the Old Testament in reference to a place of worship. Jacob first uses the phrase to identify the site of his dream about a ladder to heaven (Gen. 28:17). He even names the place Bethel, which means 'house of God' (Gen. 28:19). Next, Scripture designates the Tabernacle as 'the house of God' (Judg. 18:31; 1 Chron. 6:48). The Temple of Solomon also bears this title

---

4. The English versions' 5:1 is 4:17 in the Hebrew text. Thus, the numbering throughout chapter 5 differs between the two (e.g., the English 5:2 is the Hebrew's 5:1, etc.).

5. Garrett, *Proverbs, Ecclesiastes, Song of Songs*, 310.

6. It might also be pointed out that, if one takes Solomon as author of Ecclesiastes, the similarity of Prov. 4:20-27 offers much by way of comparison. It is axiomatic that writers tend to employ vocabulary and phraseology characteristic of their communications. Though some might argue that the similarities support the current popular view of some later individual taking upon himself the persona of Solomon, and thus utilizing Solomon's speech and thought patterns to heighten that impression, it represents a less than straightforward reading and understanding of the text.

7. Barton, *Ecclesiastes*, 122.

(1 Chron. 22:2; 2 Chron. 3:3). Most commentators who date the Book of Ecclesiastes to the post-exilic period identify the 'house of God' in 5:1 with Zerubbabel's Temple,[8] but those who hold to a pre-exilic date, as I do, understand it to be the Temple that Solomon constructed. Any who are tempted to make the synagogue the reference must, of necessity, take the following reference to sacrifices as figurative, since the Jews did not offer sacrifices at synagogues.

The gathering of the saints for public worship in our own day equates well with the setting in Ecclesiastes. Obedience to the Word of God in private life prepares the believer for participation in public worship. What a sweet spirit of praise will prevail in our churches, if we all arrive thus prepared.

Drawing Near to Listen (5:1b)

Solomon instructs those who worship in the Temple to listen when they come to the Temple for worship. Listening pre-supposes a spoken word. Therefore, the worshiper should come to hear God's Word spoken by God Himself or by His chosen spokesman. Listening alone, however, does not exhaust the intent of the text. As Kelley points out, 'To listen is to obey. To state the matter thus is to specify who is to have authority over man's life. It is to be God, and God alone.'[9] Listening and obeying the Word of God take place only through submission to Him as the Sovereign Lord of one's life. 'Draw near to listen' echoes 'Go near and hear' in Deuteronomy 5:27, which specifically identi-fies God as the speaker and the commitment of the hearer to 'do it.' Thus far the concept that rises to prominence is that worship is theocentric (God-centered). Derek Tidball stresses the same truth when he writes, 'Worship is about entering the presence of almighty God.'[10]

In contrast, someone might pursue the alternative by offer-ing 'the sacrifice of fools' (v. 1). This might refer to bringing a sacrificial animal that does not qualify for sacrifice or to offering a sacrifice without the correct heart attitude (cp. 1 Sam. 15:22; Prov. 15:8; 28:9; Heb. 11:4). In context, it appears to depict someone going through the motions of offering a sacrifice

---

8. Ibid., 64. Barton dates Ecclesiastes to the second century b.c. (ibid., 62).
9. Kelley, *The Burden of God*, 95.
10. Tidball, *That's Just the Way It Is*, 78.

while spewing a torrent of empty words, but not possessing any awareness of God. Whybray associates this attitude with the sacrificer's belief that their sacrifice 'will automatically cancel out their sins without the need for repentance.'[11] If this represents the intent of the passage, then Matthew 6:7-8 offers a similar critique of wordy worship. Kelley suggests that the reference is to an unruly, noisy, hasty, and self-centered irreverence that refuses to submit to God's word.[12] Perhaps Solomon, in keeping with a context dealing with speech, intends to offer a contrast to 'the sacrifice of praise' (Heb. 13:15). Later, Hosea 14:2 would speak to the same situation:

> Take words with you and return to the LORD.
> Say to Him, 'Take away all iniquity
> And receive *us* graciously,
> That we may present the fruit of our lips.'

'Fool' occurs three times in this chapter (vv. 1, 3, 4). In all three appearances, the Hebrew word is $k^e sil$. As the most frequently occurring word for 'fool' in the Old Testament (seventy times), the word denotes 'one who is dull and obstinate' and normally refers to a person's 'chosen outlook, rather than his mental equipment.'[13] As indicated in the Book of Proverbs, this 'fool' (1) does not engage in a pursuit of wisdom (Prov. 17:16), (2) manifests a spiritual, rather than mental, problem (Prov. 1:29), (3) enjoys his folly (Prov. 26:11), (4) has no reverence for truth (Prov. 14:8), and (5) is a menace in society (Prov. 13:20; 17:12; 18:6).[14] 'Fool' and 'folly' stand out as key words throughout Ecclesiastes.[15] Solomon's use of the term in Ecclesiastes echoes all that has been indicated by Proverbs.

Commentators take a variety of approaches to the final clause of verse 1 ('for they do not know they are doing evil'). Barton translates it, 'for they do not know (except) to do evil,' and explains that it means that 'They go from their sacrifices

---

11. Whybray, *Ecclesiastes*, 93.
12. Kelley, *The Burden of God*, 96.
13. Kidner, *The Wisdom of Proverbs, Job & Ecclesiastes*, 40.
14. Ibid.
15. The translations 'fool' and 'folly' represent 32 occurrences of words derived from two different Hebrew roots (19× *ksl* and 13× *skl*) – 1:17 (*skl*); 2:3 (*skl*), 12 (*skl*), 13 (*skl*), 14 (*ksl*), 15 (*ksl*), 16 (2x, *ksl*), 19 (*skl*); 4:5 (*ksl*), 13 (*ksl*); 5:1 (*ksl*), 3 (*ksl*), 4 (*ksl*); 6:8 (*ksl*); 7:4 (*ksl*), 5 (*ksl*), 6 (*ksl*), 9 (*ksl*), 17 (*skl*), 25 (2×, *ksl, skl*); 9:17 (*ksl*); 10:1 (*skl*), 2 (*ksl*), 3 (2×, *skl*), 6 (*skl*), 12 (*ksl*), 13 (*skl*), 14 (*skl*), 15 (*ksl*).

with an easy conscience to plunge again into evil.'[16] This is similar to Leupold's 'for they do not know, and so they do wrong.'[17] Berkeley's translation, 'for they do not know when they do wrong,' approximates Eaton's preference, 'for they do not know in doing wrong.'[18] Provan goes with NEB's translation, 'who sin without a thought.'[19] Similarly, Longman argues that it means 'that they are so foolish that they are not even aware that their sacrifices are evil, an offense to God.'[20] Ginsburg, on the other hand, understands the phrase as a statement about true worshipers: 'they who obey know not how to do evil'.[21] This is most certainly wrong. The best translation is the simplest: 'they do not know that they are doing evil' (NASU, RSV, NKJV, ESV, NIV). In other words, they are so dull of spiritual understanding that they actually think that they are doing something good and acceptable.

Avoiding Hastiness (5:2a)
The first caution against haste addresses the mouth, but the second one addresses the heart (literally, 'do not let your heart hurry to cause a word to go out before God'). Wisdom literature warns against hasty words and actions (Eccles. 7:9, 'eager'; 8:3; Prov. 10:19; 20:21; 21:5; 25:8; 28:20, 22; 29:20; Ps. 115:3). James Rosscup describes hastiness in prayer as 'without sincerity' and that such prayer 'devalues God as just someone to be used at the impulse of lust to gratify one's own ends. This cheapens God, is a slam at His honor, wants Him only as a "grab-bag," not as God.'[22] Hastiness begins in the thoughts, then proceeds to the mouth. Solomon exhorts worshipers to discipline their minds as well as their mouths. God's presence is everywhere, so the worshiper is always in His presence, even when he is not in the sanctuary.

Limiting Our Words (5:2b-3)
By declaring that 'God is in heaven,' Solomon indicates the dwelling-place of God. However, the statement refers to

---

16. Barton, *Ecclesiastes*, 122, 123.
17. Leupold, *Ecclesiastes*, 116, 118.
18. Eaton, *Ecclesiastes*, 98.
19. Provan, *Ecclesiastes, Song of Songs*, 116.
20. Longman, *Ecclesiastes*, 151.
21. Ginsburg, *The Song of Songs and Coheleth*, 2:335.
22. Rosscup, *An Exposition on Prayer in the Bible*, 1065.

perspective more than to distance.[23] God is above and beyond this world – beyond the sun. His greatness, knowledge, and power exceeds anything this world has to offer. God cannot be manipulated in the way idolaters attempt to manipulate their deities with sacrifices and empty promises. Biblical prayer does not seek to manipulate God. Prayer provides the believer with the opportunity to speak openly and sincerely with the Sovereign Lord of all creation. Such prayer, as Jesus taught His disciples, likewise refers to God being in heaven (Matt. 6:9).

The 'dream' might be nothing more than 'day-dreams, reducing worship to verbal doodling,' according to Derek Kidner.[24] 'Much effort' (v. 3) identifies what distracts an individual from the proper exercise of worship and causes the increase of hasty words. A quick prayer or an under-pressure promise due to being overly busy both exemplify speaking in haste. Context indicates that the meaning probably involves the thought that 'many have delusions of their competence before God and acceptability to him.'[25] The reader of the New Testament cannot but be reminded of James 1:19: '*This* you know, my beloved brethren. But everyone must be quick to hear, slow to speak *and* slow to anger.'

Apprehending Promises to God (5:4-7)

In this next section, the commands include: 'do not be late' in fulfilling the vow (v. 4), 'Pay what you vow' (v. 4), 'Do not let your speech cause you to sin' (v. 6), 'do not say … that it was a mistake' (v. 6), and 'fear God' (v. 7). These verses address the matter of making vows.

According to the New Testament, Christians make vows (Acts 21:23). Even the apostle Paul himself took a vow (Acts 18:18). Jesus taught His disciples about unconditional integrity and truthfulness in Matthew 5:33-37. A Christian must maintain a life of integrity. He must not be manipulative or deceitful. If a Christian decides to make a vow, he or she must fulfill it in order to maintain integrity of life and

---

23. *Contra* Longman, *Ecclesiastes*, 151: 'We take this statement not as an assertion of divine power, but of divine distance, perhaps even of indifference.'

24. Kidner, *A Time to Mourn*, 53.

25. Garrett, *Proverbs, Ecclesiastes, Song of Songs*, 311 footnote 119.

word in God's presence. Exhibit 'A' in the matter of insincere or deceptive promises has to be the case of Ananias and Sapphira in Acts 5:1-11.

In the Old Testament, one of the best known examples of a rash vow is the one that Jephthah made in Judges 11. The following points aid our understanding of what was involved in his situation:

- Since Scripture records the incident, we ought to learn from it, because all Scripture is 'profitable.'

- It reveals the seriousness of vows to God (Num. 30:2; Deut. 23:21-23; Eccles. 5:4-5).

- It teaches about the folly of rash vows (Prov. 20:25).

- It teaches the need to control our tongues before God and man (Eccles. 5:2).

- Jephthah is more interested in himself than either Israel or his family (note the 'I/my/ me' references in Judges 11:30-31).

- Jephthah's intent has nothing to do with human sacrifice, because evidently he is thinking of animals, not people. His thinking lacks clarity – something else for us to learn from.

- Jephthah is either ignorant of or arrogantly ignores the Mosaic law that allows him to redeem his vow and preserve his daughter's life by making compensation to the priest at the Tabernacle (Lev. 27:1-8).

- Jephthah focuses so much on the present and the advantage he hopes to gain for himself, that he sacrifices his future.

- The text leaves Jephthah as a tragic figure who began well and had exhibited faith (cp. Heb. 11:32), but who ends on the ash heap of history because he fails to live out his faith to the end of his life.

- Scripture does not commend Jephthah for his actions in this matter.

Rash vows consist of hastily made promises and commitments, especially to God. Proverbs 20:25 speaks to the same problem (cp. Deut. 23:21-23).

Vows in the Old Testament primarily involved dedicating or giving things to the Lord, not in limiting oneself to a humanly-produced representation of God's will and way. One vowed to give oneself (Num. 6:2), a child (1 Sam. 1:11), animals (Mal. 1:14), or sacrifices (Deut. 12:11). Rash vows most often involve declaring that something must be treated as 'holy' (Prov. 20:25) when they probably should not be considered as such – perhaps it was not their own possession or it was something unclean or it was something outright sinful (1 Sam. 28:10; Jer. 44:25). Rash vows by women could be reversed by their husbands, if they heard the vow and reacted to nullify it (Num. 30:6-8). If a person could overturn rash vows, any rash vow might be overturned by the one with the power or authority to do so when it is seen to be rash. Since the New Testament believer is a priest of God (1 Pet. 2:9), he (or she) has the spiritual authority to nullify rash vows. Indeed, it is incumbent upon the believer to remove all foolishness from his or her life and to make their speech wholesome (Eph. 4:29) and their thoughts honest, pure, and excellent (Phil. 4:8). Are you guilty of making a rash promise to God? Determine not to make such vows again.

Fulfilling Commitments (5:4-5)
The message of these two verses stands out clearly. Believers should keep their promises to God – without delay. Only a fool makes promises that he cannot or should not have made. Resist making vows in times of trial. If, however, you do make a vow, know that God expects you to fulfill it.

Meaning What We Say (5:6)
Who is 'the messenger' who might come to a person in order to remind him or her about their vow? Potential identifications include the angel of the LORD, a prophet (cp. Hag. 1:13; Mal. 3:1), a priest (Mal. 2:7), or a messenger sent by a priest. Eaton believes the answer can be either of the last two options.[26] In ancient Israel, the believers would inform the priests of such promises

---

26. Eaton, *Ecclesiastes*, 100.

and the priests (or agents for the priests) would make the effort to remind the individual and to receive payment (especially if sacrifices were promised).

The individual about whom Solomon writes tells the messenger that it was all 'a mistake.' The term indicates an inadvertent error (cp. Lev. 4:22-35; Num. 15:22-31). Vows should be intentional, not unintentional. God finds no pleasure in such foolish promises. Claiming an error in such a situation is tantamount to admitting that the promise was made in haste. The results, when God judges or disciplines such foolish people, can be catastrophic – even resulting in the destruction of the work of one's hands.

Fearing God (5:7)

The 'many dreams' and the 'many words' fall into the category of empty things – things with no purpose, no value, or no meaning. Vows made on the basis of such dreams (or personal illusions and fantasies) and words result in purposeless, empty conversation, prayer, or vow before God.

Many Christians find it difficult to describe what it means to 'fear God.' Does it mean to be afraid, to have reverential awe, or to mortify the flesh or crucify self? The more one reads commentaries, theologies, and devotionals, the more one finds that few have a clear concept of what 'the fear of the Lord' involves. If we cannot define it, then how can we exercise it or claim to fear God? Since 'the fear of the Lord is the beginning of knowledge' (Prov. 1:7), our knowledge faces a severe deficit without that fear. Likewise, no wisdom exists apart from 'the fear of the Lord' (Ps. 111:10; Job 28:28). In addition, Scripture associates blessing with the fear of God (Pss. 112:1; 115:13; 128:1, 4). Without 'the fear of the Lord,' therefore, an individual lacks knowledge, wisdom, and blessing.

God reveals in His Word exactly what comprises 'the fear of the Lord.' Biblically, the fear of God includes the following six elements:

- First, one must trust God completely (Ps. 115:11).

- Second, one must experience God's forgiveness in reality (Ps. 130:4).

- Third, one must sincerely delight in God's Word (Ps. 112:1).

- Fourth, one must go beyond delighting in God's Word by actually keeping (obeying) it (Ps. 119:63; Eccles. 12:13).

- Fifth, one must sincerely and consistently hate evil (Prov. 8:13).

- Sixth, one must steadfastly hope in God's loyal love (Ps. 147:11).

The second of these six elements identifies true believers as the only individuals who are able to rightly fear God (cp. Acts 2:38; 10:43; 26:18; Eph. 1:7).

Understanding the Role of Rulers (5:8-9)

Ecclesiastes 5:8-20 focuses on the issue of money. One of the section's key words is 'eat' (or 'consume' – vv. 11, 12, 17, 18, 19).[27] Solomon uses 'eat/consume' to refer to the consumption of goods or of 'one's attempt to survive or make a living.'[28] Verse 11 implies that 'those who consume' the 'good things' exhibit greediness. The mention of rulers and the oppression they sometimes practice relates directly to wealth or, more properly, to the lack of wealth. The rich and powerful often oppress the poor, because the poor cannot afford to defend themselves. For the poor, justice grinds too slowly, costing them an increasingly higher amount of money. They cannot afford to wait in their situation and cannot afford financially to speed up the process.

The successive tiers and levels of bureaucracy result in officials watching out for one another (v. 8). Sometimes such watching involves checks and balances that enable government to operate efficiently and justly. However, all too often those successive levels of government provide a means of sharing bribes that are distributed up the chain by the original recipient, who keeps but a small part of it for himself. Mutual protection makes it difficult to root out corruption.[29] The point Solomon

---

27. Provan, *Ecclesiastes, Song of Songs*, 126.
28. Seow, *Ecclesiastes*, 208.
29. Garrett, *Proverbs, Ecclesiastes, Song of Songs*, 312.

makes is that a person ought not to be shocked that such things exist within the bureaucracy – it is merely the outcome of fallen human nature. Government comes with a price. It is exactly what Samuel warned Israel about when they requested a king for themselves 'like all the nations' (1 Sam. 8:5). Samuel revealed that the 'procedure of the king' would involve pressing many citizens into royal service, the seizing of property, and taxation of crops and livestock. In the end, the people cry out to God because of the oppressive reign of their kings (1 Sam. 8:10-18).

Verse 9 contains multiple interpretive issues. The entire verse is riddled with multiple choices for meaning. 'After all' (NASU) appears in other English versions as 'all things considered' (NRSV), 'in all' (RSV), 'for all' (NKJV), 'in every way' (ESV), and 'by all' (HCSB, NIV, NET). Gordis identifies the next issue as an 'insuperable crux.'[30] What is the relationship of the king to the cultivated field? Eaton believes that the text conveys the fact that 'bureaucratic officialdom does not totally override the value of kingly authority.'[31] In other words, despite the presence of oppression and corruption in a government, there is yet an advantage in having a king. Therefore, citizens ought not be too hasty about overthrowing him. As Kidner puts it, 'even tyranny is better than anarchy.'[32]

With a slightly different take on the text, Kaiser takes the view that it refers to ruler and people being 'happiest when they both realize that they are served by the farmed fields.'[33] Provan offers the following paraphrase, 'In the end, the only "gain" from hard work in the fields is the monarchy, which flourishes in the soil of the workers' labor.'[34] Basically, this view echoes 1 Samuel 8:10-18. Others, like Hubbard, take it as an excuse for bureaucracy voiced by corrupt officials: 'There is profit to the land in all this; after all the king has a right to the tilled field.'[35]

Three views represent the best options for interpreting verse 9: (1) The problem of injustice permeates society to the extent that even the king is corrupt (note Amos 7:1 as a parallel); (2)

---

30. Gordis, Koheleth, 250.
31. Eaton, Ecclesiastes, 101.
32. Kidner, A Time to Mourn, 55.
33. Kaiser, Ecclesiastes, 76.
34. Provan, Ecclesiastes, Song of Songs, 126.
35. Hubbard, Ecclesiastes, Song of Solomon, 136.

regardless of injustice and corruption, the king and his government provide some gain or profit for the nation; and, (3) society benefits from a king under whose reign private owners might profitably cultivate the land rather than the king seizing it for royal use (cp. Prov. 29:4). The king ensures that justice prevails and that the boundaries of one's field remain in force. In other words, a text like Proverbs 23:10-11 deals with matters within the king's authority.[36] The third option makes the best sense.

One of the major questions involved in this interpretive problem involves whether the text confirms or supports those who believe that Ecclesiastes presents a 'negative view of leadership.'[37] Many commentators believe that such a view of leadership makes it awkward for Solomon to be the author. On the one hand, could he be critical of kings? On the other hand, would it not be consistent with the God-given wisdom that Solomon possesses and exercises? Every great ruler should indulge in introspection and be capable of evaluating his own governing, the governing of other kings with whom he has contact politically, and the government administered by various higher officials within his government. After all, the Scripture charges believers to engage in self-examination (cp. 1 Cor. 11:28; 2 Cor. 13:5; Gal. 6:4) – and this despite the fact that Paul speaks of not examining himself, but allowing the Lord to do so (1 Cor. 4:3-4). No contradiction exists in these two seemingly different instructions. Individuals must recognize their inability to fully evaluate themselves and their works – only God can do that. However, when we look into the 'mirror' of God's Word (James 1:23), we see and compare ourselves to God's demands. Besides, Solomon certainly realizes what had transpired between the people of Israel, Samuel, and God in 1 Samuel 8. He also knows what God demands of kings as revealed by Moses in Deuteronomy 17. God Himself establishes the standards for administrative justice and reveals them to Moses to pass on to future kings even before a king had taken the throne over Israel.

Dealing with the Pursuit of Wealth (5:10-17)

Money leaves human covetousness unsatisfied (v. 10), attracts hangers-on as self-styled dependents, and presents opportuni-

---

36. Bartholomew, *Ecclesiastes*, 218.
37. Longman, *Ecclesiastes*, 159.

ties for gaining more wealth (v. 11), disturbs one's peace (v. 12), places an individual in greater jeopardy because of the potential for experiencing a greater loss (vv. 13-15), and fails to help anyone avoid death (vv. 16-17). Solomon employs three different terms for wealth in verse 10: 'money' (*keseph*, which also means 'silver'), 'abundance' (*hamon*, the goods and possessions equivalent with material prosperity), and 'income' (*tebu'ah*, income, gain). The threefold identification certifies the significance of the topic. Solomon employs a chain of proverbs to speak of money and the impact it has upon people's lives.

Salary raises and bonuses produce more income, but increased income draws the attention of family and friends whose greed drives them to participate in its consumption (v. 11). The more the income, the bigger the celebration and list of invitees – thus, the increase in spending. Of course, as long as government levies taxes, an increase in income also results in an increase in taxes. An increase in wealth can also bring about increased responsibility in growing the business – channeling the profits back into the growth of the business by adding equipment, employees, employee benefits, increased marketing, building expansion, etc. The truth is, we always manage to live up to our income – and beyond. It is never enough.

Two biographical samples highlight the contrast between having riches and not having riches (v. 12). The poor working-class individual sleeps soundly even on beans and rice, but insomnia afflicts the wealthy even on a full stomach. The word for 'full stomach' in verse 12 comes from the same root as the word for 'satisfied' in verse 10. One would think that the banquet of the rich would bring some degree of satisfaction. The irony of it is that it does not bring satisfaction – instead, the rich person's full stomach will keep him awake, disturbing his rest.

Some people tend to hoard their financial gains, never investing them in the lives of others or themselves (v. 13). Others engage in risky investments that result in leaving their families without adequate support (v. 14). Most biblically literate people recognize verse 15 as one of the more familiar verses in Scripture when it comes to the topic of wealth. No one takes their wealth with them when they die – they all go empty-handed (cp. Ps. 49). Paul cites this concept indirectly in

1 Timothy 6:7 where the context commends godly contentment and warns against the love of material wealth (vv. 6-10).

Since a person enters this world without any material wealth and leaves this world in the same condition, why should anyone labor for and gather material possessions and wealth (Eccles. 5:16)? 'Vexation, sickness and anger' accompany the wealthy while they eat in darkness (v. 17). First, vexation refers to the burdensome cares of this life. Second, sickness indicates the physical toll on the laborer. Lastly, anger identifies the emotional outcome of the frustration of ambitions. These include becoming the target of other ambitious people, and the failure of one's plans to come to fruition due to economic downturns, governmental interference, cruel competitors, and industrial spies.

Concluding Thoughts Regarding Wealth (5:18-20)

Although the experiences Solomon describes in verses 8-12 produce a sense of hopelessness and frustration, a remedy exists. The key word in this section is 'God.' All of those experiences take place 'under the sun' apart from God. Solomon observes individuals who include God in their worldview and how that impacts their enjoyment of life, despite its ups and downs, its times of want and times of abundance. God desires that people enjoy His gifts, whether as a poor individual (v. 18) or as a wealthy person (v. 19). Such people do not spend their time bewailing lost ventures or joylessly hoarding their gains – they occupy themselves with matters of the heart, especially God-given and animated gladness (v. 20). According to Daniel Estes, 'When humans enjoy life as God's gift, they remain aware of their mortality, but they are not oppressed by the thought of it. This enjoyment enables humans to keep life and death in the proper perspective.'[38]

'To eat, to drink and enjoy oneself' involves sharing the enjoyment of fellowship and being satisfied with that which God gives, regardless of the amount. 'Here it is the symbol of a contented and happy life,' according to Eaton.[39] The historian identifies the same aspects of life in his description of the glory days of Solomon's reign (1 Kings 4:20, 'Judah and Israel *were* as numerous as the sand that is on the seashore

---

38. Estes, *Handbook on the Wisdom Books*, 334.
39. Eaton, *Ecclesiastes*, 103.

in abundance; *they* were eating and drinking and rejoicing'). During those early years of Solomonic splendor, power, affluence, and influence, the nation prospered. Its citizens were contented and happy. Things were so good because Solomon was still serving the Lord and honoring Him in all that he did. Perhaps Solomon remembers those years with nostalgia and writes of them in Ecclesiastes 5:18-20. Verse 19 makes it clear that the problem does not rest with wealth itself. As Paul writes, it is 'the love of money [that] is a root of all sorts of evil' (1 Tim. 6:10). Elsewhere, the apostle addresses the matter of living with a contented attitude whether in want or in prosperity (Phil. 4:12; see also Matt. 6:19-24).

In his book *Business for the Glory of God*, Wayne Grudem states that

> In fact, *money is fundamentally good* because it is a human invention that sets us apart from the animal kingdom and enables us to subdue the earth by producing from the earth goods and services that bring benefit to others. Money enables all of mankind to be productive and enjoy the fruits of that productivity thousands of times more extensively than we could if no human being had money, and we just had to barter with each other.[40]

Consider the following factors that describe money:

- It is more widely accepted than bartered goods of any kind (including food).
- It lasts longer than most goods.
- It is more transportable than other goods.
- Everyone is willing to exchange goods for money.
- It stores value until exchanged or spent.
- It 'makes voluntary exchanges more fair, less wasteful, and far more extensive.'[41]

As good stewards of our finances, we acquire the opportunity to employ money to glorify God. Whenever we give to the Lord's work or to those who are in need, we exercise a rulership over the things of this world (cp. Gen. 1:28). In giving to

---

40. Grudem, *Business for the Glory of God*, 47.
41. Ibid., 49.

others we imitate God's mercy and love. By our wealth we can expand and strengthen gospel ministries worldwide in order to bring others to salvation in Christ.

What Solomon teaches in Ecclesiastes 5 matches Paul's teaching in his epistles. Both Old and New Testaments agree that contentment and joy accompany those who think and live with a perspective beyond the sun, rather than limiting themselves to what is 'under the sun.' As Eaton so aptly asserts, 'Secular man may live a life of drudgery, but for the God-centred man it will be otherwise.'[42] Ecclesiastes does not exude skepticism and pessimism. Instead, it proclaims a need for godly satisfaction with that which God gives. The apostle Paul makes the same observations and proclaims the same teachings – confirming the accuracy of Solomon's observations and the integrity of his conclusions.

The closing verse of this chapter declares that God will keep a person 'occupied with the gladness of his heart' (v. 20). 'Occupied' represents the same word translated 'afflicted' in 1:13 and 'occupy' in 3:10. Here the usage appears to be more positive by context. There might even be a hint of a play on words. The same word can also be translated 'answer.' This God-given joy is His *answer* to the *affliction* of the endless exercise of labor by which a person ekes out a living 'under the sun.' David's prayer in Psalm 4 leaps to mind as a fitting conclusion for the study of Ecclesiastes 5:

> 5 Offer the sacrifices of righteousness,
> And trust in the LORD.
>
> 6 Many are saying, 'Who will show us *any* good?'
> Lift up the light of Your countenance upon us, O LORD!
>
> 7 You have put gladness in my heart,
> More than when their grain and new wine abound.
>
> 8 In peace I will both lie down and sleep,
> For You alone, O LORD, make me to dwell in safety.

STUDY QUESTIONS

1. How can we prepare ourselves for worship on Sunday mornings?

---

42. Eaton, *Ecclesiastes*, 104.

2. What causes us to sometimes speak or act too hastily?

3. What kinds of vows would be legitimate for New Testament believers?

4. In what ways is Solomon qualified in writing a critique of a monarchy?

5. Why is the love of money a root of all sorts of evil?

6. What good qualities does money possess?

7. What produces godly contentment?

8. What can you do this week to enhance the gladness of your heart?

6

Possessing Everything, But Enjoying Nothing

By application, *the Preacher* found the explanation for apparent inequalities in divine providence *(6:1–8:17)*, Part 1

After discussing the role of wealth in one's life (5:10-17), Solomon explains that people can enjoy God's gifts of possessions and wealth (5:18-19). Such enjoyment provides relief from the toil and trouble of mortal life under the sun (5:20). With these thoughts in mind, Solomon moves on to address an apparent inequity: someone can possess wealth but be unable to enjoy it. Life's manifold mysteries confound even a man as wise as Solomon. Mere mortals cannot adequately understand all that occurs in God's world. How is it possible for a person to gain all that his or her heart desires (gold, wealth, honor, family, long life, and education), yet never find any joy in those attainments? Thus, Solomon presents

- An evaluation of man's outward fortunes (6:1–7:15).

- An evaluation of man's character (7:16-29).

- A consideration of the role of government (8:1-14).

Case History #1: A Full Treasury (6:1-2)

By experience and by observation, Solomon comes to the conclusion that *prosperity is not always as good as it might appear.*[1] 'There is' (v. 1) involves a common formula in Ecclesiastes (2:21;

---

1. Estes, *Handbook on the Wisdom Books*, 334.

4:8; 5:13; 6:1, 11; 7:15; 8:14; 10:5) introducing specific examples or cases that the author employs to formulate his argumentation. He clearly identifies the viewpoint of the discussion: 'under the sun.' Mere mortal beings who conduct their lives without God in this life will face enigmas without finding any solution. An individual who lives by faith in the Creator and Sovereign of all things may experience the same enigmas, but God's sovereign control provides the means for enjoying His gifts in spite of the difficulties and discouragements.

Note the two contrasts between 5:18-19 and 6:1-2:

'Here is what I have seen to be good and fitting' (5:18)	vs.	'There is an evil which I have seen' (6:1)
'every man to whom God has given riches and wealth' (5:19)	vs.	'a man to whom God has given riches and wealth and honor' (6:2).

Those good things that God gives look, in at least one situation, as though they bring nothing but evil, calamity, or trouble upon a person. How can this be? James 5:1-6 reveals one of the key causes of such a turn of events: the individual thus gifted spends his or her wealth on wanton pleasure while oppressing the poor. His heart is not right with God. To be sure, a wicked heart and wanton life style are not the only causes for gold's loss of glitter. The righteous individual also might lack the opportunity to enjoy possessions and wealth. God controls both the giving and the enjoying – note that 'God has not empowered him to eat from them' (Eccles. 6:2).

The author of 2 Chronicles 1:11-12 also mentions 'riches and wealth and honor' (Eccles. 6:2) as gifts from God to Solomon (cp. Eccles. 2:1-8). Perhaps Solomon speaks of his own experience. The question that arises from the text concerns the identity of the 'foreigner' (or, 'stranger') who enjoys what God gives. The stranger might be someone outside the family. In 2:21 Solomon describes someone who did not work for what he receives. He might have Jeroboam in mind (see previous discussion of 4:13-16). The truth of the matter, according to Brown, involves the fact that 'Ownership is, thus, a misnomer. One's possessions are exclusively gifts of God, and as easily as God gives, so God takes away to give to others. The givenness of material possessions is a two-edged sword.'[2] In other words, there are no guarantees in life when it comes to one's possessions and wealth.

Case History #2: A Full Quiver (6:3-5)

Another apparent inequity occurs in real life: someone who has 'a hundred *children* and lives many years' (v. 3) may live an unsatisfying life (enjoying neither children nor wealth) and not even receive a proper burial. Scripture depicts numerous offspring as a significant blessing (Ps. 127:3-5). Obviously, Solomon might match this particular description of many children, given the number of his wives and concubines. However, other biblical personages also fathered large numbers of children. Gideon's many wives bore him seventy sons (Judg. 8:30). Ahab also produced seventy sons (2 Kings 10:1). Rehoboam, Solomon's son, sired twenty-eight sons and sixty daughters (2 Chron. 11:21) – a total of eighty-eight offspring. The individual about whom Solomon speaks sired ten times as many children as Job before his troubles began (Job 1:21).

Ironically, Solomon declares that a miscarriage (stillbirth or unborn fetus) is better off than this man with 100 children (Eccles. 6:3). A reference to a 'miscarriage' occurs also in Job 3:16 where Job opines that he would have been better off as a miscarried infant rather than to have suffered the loss of all of his children and all of his possessions, as well as his health. In Psalm 58:8 David uses the condition of a miscarriage to describe how wicked and violent men should be removed from life. Such comparisons to a miscarriage focus on the quality of life rather than the duration of life. No one lives a shorter time than a miscarriage. Solomon characterizes the state of the miscarried infant as 'futility' and 'obscurity' (Eccles. 6:4). Indeed, the last portion of verse 4 indicates that no memory remains of the miscarriage either because no one gave it a name or because no one recognizes the name since the individual never entered the sphere of their existence. Still, the unborn infant enjoys a better circumstance (v. 5) than someone who has brought 100 children into the world and whose home is filled with their love, yet cannot enjoy his life or find satisfaction and rest.

The miscarriage 'knows' nothing of the frustrations, disappointments, and enigmas of life under the sun. 'It is better

2. Brown, *Ecclesiastes*, 65.

off than he' should be translated more literally, 'more rest has this one than that one' (NASU margin). Interestingly, mention of such things as 'rest,' someone living twice 1,000 years (v. 6), and names (vv. 4, 10) brings to mind Genesis 5:28-29 with the naming of Noah (derived from the root for 'rest') in a time when longevity could be just under 1,000 years. Solomon refers to 'rest' in 4:6 ('one hand full of rest is better than two fists full of labor'), so this is not the first time that the concept makes its appearance in Ecclesiastes. The comparison between the miscarriage and the man who had 100 children and lived many years reminds the reader of Solomon's words in 4:2 – 'So I congratulated the dead who are already dead more than the living who are still living.'

Old Testament writers consider burial (6:3) as a significant responsibility that the living must fulfill for the dead (cp. 1 Sam. 31:11-13). Improper treatment of a corpse (such as exposure to the elements) comprises dishonor and is emblematic of being cursed (cp. 1 Kings 14:10-11; 2 Kings 9:33-37; Isa. 14:19-20; Jer. 16:4; 22:18-19).

The familiar spiritual, 'This World Is Not My Home,' addresses the reason for a lack of satisfying rest 'under the sun:'

> This world is not my home, I'm just a passing through;
> My treasures are laid up somewhere beyond the blue.
> The angels beckon me from Heaven's open door,
> And I can't feel at home, in this world anymore.[3]

Individuals who seek to make this world their focus tends to lay up treasures here and to place too much emphasis upon what one possesses and experiences in this life (cp. Matt. 6:19-21). Their fallen nature fails to include God in their worldview. A miscarriage might not experience any life under the sun, pass into obscurity, and remain unknown, but he or she will experience the grace of God and will be at rest with Him.

Case History #3: A Full Life Span (6:6)
Literally, verse 6 reads, 'Even if he lives a thousand years twice and does not see good.' Two thousand years doubles the life

---

3. Jessie R. Baxter, Jr. (Stamps-Baxter Music and Printing Co., 1946). The second line of the second stanza asks, 'If Heaven's not my home, then Lord what will I do?'

span of Methuselah, who lived 969 years (Gen. 5:26-27). Adam himself lived 930 years (Gen. 5:5). According to the Ten Commandments, a long life comes as a divine blessing to those who honor their parents (cf. Exod. 20:12; Ps. 91:16; Prov. 3:16). Thus, the miscarriage (Eccles. 6:3), who lives such a short time, still has greater enjoyment than someone who lives twice as long as Methuselah. Having in his possession all that some people count as blessings, a person 'can still depart unnoticed, unlamented and unfulfilled.'[4]

The Elusiveness of Satisfaction and Rest (6:7-9)

From verses 3-6 the reader comprehends that 'Despite family, longevity and fame, life may so miscarry as to incur life-long dissatisfaction and an unmourned death.'[5] Like verse 6, Proverbs 16:26 also mentions both 'mouth' (translated 'hunger') and 'appetite' (literally 'soul') in its description of a worker. Solomon already addressed lack of satisfaction in 1:8; 4:8; 5:10; and 6:3, so this proverb in 6:7 merely repeats the truth within the context of the previous three case histories. Each of the situations depicts a lack of satisfaction. The term translated 'satisfied' actually means 'filled,' the same word used parallel to 'satisfied' in 1:8. The proverb teaches that a person living as a mere human being without God in his or her life can never find satisfaction in the quantity of possessions, wealth, children, or years of life.

Verse 8 expresses a second proverb containing two rhetorical questions. Translating and interpreting verse 8 has produced much scholarly wringing of hands.[6] In spite of the difficulty in translating the verse, it is clear that both questions demand the same negative answer: 'There is no advantage.' Neither the wise man nor the fool has an advantage when it comes to satisfaction. A wise man might gain a temporary advantage over a fool. Indeed, a fool might have a temporary advantage in knowing how to live without wealth and power. However, neither one can gain any advantage over death or over God (see 2:12-17).

---

4. Kidner, *A Time to Mourn*, 59.
5. Eaton, *Ecclesiastes*, 105. See, also, Kaiser, *Ecclesiastes*, 80.
6. Hubbard, *Ecclesiastes, Song of Solomon*, 154.

The third proverb (v. 9a) presents an equivalent to 'A bird in the hand is better than two in the bush.' Dreaming about something does not bring it to pass or bring it into one's possession. Take what you have – what you can see – and do not count on your desires being fulfilled. In other words, better to be content with what I have than to waste my life desiring what I do not have.

'This too is futility [*hebel*] and a striving after wind' (v. 9b) wraps up the three case histories with the same summation Solomon offers again and again throughout the book (1:14, 17; 2:11, 17, 26; 4:4, 6, 16; 5:16). In fact, the author does not employ the phrase again in the rest of the book. The very next verse (v. 10) marks the middle of the Hebrew text of Ecclesiastes. Therefore, the first half of the book comes to a close with this phrase. The next three verses set up the remainder of the book and introduce the theme for the second half.

A Sovereign Lord (6:10-12)

In effect, verses 10-12 comprise Solomon's reflection upon the Fall.[7] The passive 'been named' (v. 10) infers that God is the actual agent – a so-called divine passive. Ancient Near Eastern peoples regarded giving a name to something or someone as an act appointing its, his, or her character (cp. Gen. 2:19-20).[8] Naming displays authority. The Creator established His authority over creation by naming the day, the night, the expanse, the waters, the land, the seas, and man (Gen. 1). Likewise, He revealed His authority over the stars by naming them (cf. Isa. 40:26). Such naming consists of more than pronouncing a title that others might use to designate something or someone – it involves the very existence of something or someone. God named the first human being 'man' (*'adam*), a word that comes from the word for earth (*'adamah*, Gen. 2:7; 3:19; Eccles. 3:20; 12:7). Thus, man has been properly named. He is earthly – made of earth and tied to the earth. That name puts all mankind in their proper place (cp. Eccles. 5:1).[9]

7. Garrett, *Proverbs, Ecclesiastes, Song of Songs*, 317.
8. John Gray, *The Legacy of Canaan: The Ras Shamra Texts and Their Relevance to the Old Testament* (Leiden, The Netherlands: E. J. Brill, 1957), 207.
9. Hengstenberg, *Ecclesiastes*, 143.

Mankind's position is on earth and 'him who is stronger than he is' probably refers to God, who is in heaven (cp. Eccles. 5:2; 1 Cor. 10:22). Swindoll summarizes verse 10 in this way: 'So long as I fight the hand of God, I do not learn the lessons He is attempting to place before me.'[10] The Sovereign Creator controls all things – including the circumstances of life that we face as human beings. We can talk about life and speak about having control, but only God can determine what happens. Thus, the emptiness and enigma of multiplying words once again comes to the forefront of Solomon's discourse (v. 11; cp. 5:1-3). Elihu reaches a similar conclusion in Job 35:16 ('So Job opens his mouth emptily; he multiplies words without knowledge'). In Isaiah 45:9-12 the prophet employs the figure of a potter and his clay pot to explain the futility of someone quarreling with his Maker.

Verse 12 opens with a question that implies that God 'knows what is good for a man during *his* lifetime.' 'Good' also serves as a verbal bridge to what follows in chapter 7. A brief statement to emphasize the brevity of a person's life follows: 'He will spend them like a shadow.' 'Shadow' depicts the ephemeral nature of human existence (Eccles. 8:13; 1 Chron. 29:15; Job 8:9; 14:12; Pss. 102:11; 109:23; 144:4). Then Solomon's second question has the same implication as the first question: only God can reveal to a person what will happen 'under the sun.' This verse supplies a fitting wisdom summary for the thematic elements in both Ecclesiastes 1–6 and Isaiah 40–46.

According to Roland Murphy, 'The uncertainty of life tomorrow is as bad, if not worse, than the uncertainty of "life" after death.'[11] The ultimate message is that human beings do not exercise control over the present or the future. God alone possesses the power to determine what happens in our lives. The apostle Paul asks, 'Who are you, O man, who answers back to God? The thing molded will not say to the molder, "Why did you make me like this," will it?' (Rom. 9:20). Solomon carefully demolishes every question and every observation that mere mortals might offer in the process of questioning their Creator's wisdom. Point by point Solomon draws the reader to the conclusion that only God can control one's destiny. The reason

10. Swindoll, *Living on the Ragged Edge*, 192.
11. Murphy, *Ecclesiastes*, 59.

things are as they are is due to the fact that the Sovereign Lord of creation does it that way for His own purposes.

The gist of Solomon's discourse in chapter 6 exceeds the superficial topics of satisfaction, enjoyment of God's gifts, labor, and advantage. Solomon systematically removes every rationale that a person might offer for the existence of inequalities in life 'under the sun.' He places the creature in contrast with his Creator to exhibit mankind's weakness in the presence of the Almighty God. As Eaton puts it, 'Like the Mosaic law (*cf.* Gal. 3:22), the Preacher is slamming every door except the door of faith.'[12]

Hubbard aptly summarizes Ecclesiastes 6 with a series of truths the reader must acknowledge:

- Contentment is more satisfying than wealth.

- Doing God's will is more important than gaining goods.

- Doing God's will brings the highest wealth of all.[13]

In Mark 10:29-30 Jesus speaks clearly to this matter of not finding satisfaction in possessions, family, and longevity:

> Truly I say to you, there is no one who has left house or brothers or sisters or mother or father or children or farms, for My sake and for the gospel's sake, but that he will receive a hundred times as much now in the present age, houses and brothers and sisters and mothers and children and farms, along with persecutions; and in the age to come, eternal life.

May we learn these lessons well and continue to look up, beyond the sun, to our Creator. Satisfaction comes only through obedience to His will and in accepting with thanksgiving and joy all things He grants to us.

STUDY QUESTIONS

1. Why do gold and silver fail to guarantee life or happiness?

2. What are the essentials for enjoying a satisfied or contented life?

---

12. Eaton, *Ecclesiastes*, 108.
13. Hubbard, *Ecclesiastes, Song of Solomon*, 156-57.

3. Why are some people unmourned in their death?

4. Why do large families (many children) sometimes fail to provide satisfaction and joy?

5. What are some of the disadvantages of a very long life?

6. In what ways does God reveal His sovereignty in a person's life?

7

Life Is Complicated: Live with Care

By application, *the Preacher* found the
explanation for apparent inequalities in
divine providence *(6:1–8:17)*, Part 2

The smell of death, the crackling of thorns in a fire, nostalgia
for yesteryear, something bent that cannot be straightened,
the whispering of servants, and the hardened hearts of fallen
mankind – these are some of the images Solomon summons in
Ecclesiastes 7. At the mid-point of the book,[1] he returns to the
themes with which he had commenced his spiritual journal
(see 1:2-3, 15). Life is transitory. The phrases of 6:12, at the end
of the first half of the book, emphasize the fact: 'lifetime,' 'the
few years,' 'his futile [*hebel*, or fleeting] life,' 'like a shadow,'
and 'after him' – life is transitory. What advantage do people
have in life? In 6:10-12 Solomon depicts death as the reigning
king in every individual's life. He moves on in chapter 7 to
examine this topic more diversely and deeply. First, he pulls
the reader aside to invite him or her to a funeral. There they
will listen in as the mourners discuss the deaths of friends
and loved ones. Readers will observe how such an experience
affects the lives of those who have witnessed the state of the
deceased person's affairs.

---

1. The exact middle of Ecclesiastes actually comes at 6:10. Ancient Jewish
tradition divided the book into four *sedarim* (weekly liturgical readings for completing
the reading of the Hebrew Bible every three years): 1:1–3:12, 3:13–6:12; 7:1–9:6,
and 9:7–12:14.

Theological tension permeates the chapter. How can a sovereign God still be in control of creation when death interrupts the good life He so graciously grants to a man or a woman? Solomon's reflection on the Fall of mankind in 6:10-12 comes to the fore again at the end of chapter 7 (v. 29). Life under the sun continues with all of the baggage of Adam's disobedience. This is a fallen, corrupted world. Mankind chose the life they now live – a life outside the Garden of Eden.

Throughout chapter 7 a variety of topics, propositional truths, phrases, and words hark back to Genesis 1–3. They include naming (v. 1; Gen. 1:26), death (v. 1; Gen. 2:17; 3:19), thorn bushes (v. 6; Gen. 3:18), beginning (v. 8; Gen. 1:1), good (*tov* – 13× in Eccles. 7; 15× in Gen. 1–3), the work of God (v. 13; Gen. 2:2-3), 'God has made' (v. 14; Gen. 1:7, 16, 25, 31), cursing (using different Hebrew words – vv. 21, 22; Gen. 3:14, 17), woman (vv. 26, 28; Gen. 2:22-23), man (v. 28; Gen. 2:5, 7, 8, 15), and 'God made men' (v. 29; Gen. 1:26).

In Ecclesiastes 7:1's proverb, 'A good name is better than a good ointment,' the adjective 'good' operates as a verbal bridge between chapters 6 and 7, between the first half of the book and the second half of the book. The author utilizes the phrase 'better than' (literally, 'more good than') to offer a series of contrasts that argue for the superiority of wisdom over foolishness, of righteousness over wickedness:

- In life or death a good reputation is better than smelling good (v. 1a).

- One's dying day is better than the day of his or her birth (v. 1b).

- A funeral is better than a festival (v. 2).

- Grief is better than laughter (v. 3).

- A wise man's rebuke is better than a fool's song (v. 5).

- The end of something is better than its beginning (v. 8a).

- Patience is better than pride (v. 8b).

- Realism about the present and occupation with the future are better than nostalgia over the past (v. 10).

The wise person will choose that which is better over that which is not; the foolish person will pursue the opposite course of action. The upshot of it all is that Solomon has learned that the truly godly individual takes life and death seriously. Remembering that he must stand before the righteous and eternal God to give an account of himself, a person lives to please God, rather than to please himself.[2]

Proverbial wisdom occupies a significant portion of the final half of Ecclesiastes. Solomonic parallels abound. For 7:1-14 alone, readers will observe the following echoes of the Book of Proverbs:

	Ecclesiastes		Proverbs
7:1a	A good name is better than a good ointment,	22:1	A *good* name is to be more desired than great wealth, Favor is better than silver and gold.
7:3[3]	Sorrow is better than laughter, For when a face is sad a heart may be happy.	14:13	Even in laughter the heart may be in pain, And the end of joy may be grief.
7:5	It is better to listen to the rebuke of a wise man Than for one to listen to the song of fools.	13:1 15:31	A wise son *accepts his* father's discipline, But a scoffer does not listen to rebuke. He whose ear listens to the life-giving reproof Will dwell among the wise.
7:7	For oppression makes a man mad, And a bribe corrupts the heart.	15:27	He who profits illicitly troubles his own house, But he who hates bribes will live.
7:8b	Patience of spirit is better than haughtiness of spirit.	14:29 16:32a	He who is slow to anger has great understanding, But he who is quick-tempered exalts folly. He who is slow to anger is better than the mighty,

---

2. Kelley, *The Burden of God*, 113-14.
3. The Ecclesiastes text is the reverse of the Proverbs text.

	Ecclesiastes		Proverbs
7:9	Do not be eager in your heart to be angry, For anger resides in the bosom of fools.	14:17a 14:29	A quick-tempered man acts foolishly, ... [See above.]
7:12b	But the advantage of knowledge is that wisdom preserves the lives of its possessors.	3:2 3:16a	For length of days and years of life And peace they will add to you. Long life is in her right hand;

Two more collections of proverbs are found in 9:17–10:4 and 10:8–11:4. Solomon employs these proverbs to advance his observation that an individual's life is all too brief and filled with a multitude of enigmas and contradictions. In other words, life is complicated, therefore we must learn to live it with great care.

The two sections of chapter 7 examine a person's circumstances (vv. 1-14) and character (vv. 15-29). Solomon looks at the first in the light of eternity and the second in the light of divine revelation. Both sections together proclaim, 'Life Is the Time to Serve the Lord' – the title of one of Isaac Watts' hymns based upon Ecclesiastes.

A Person's Present Conditions in the Light of Eternity (7:1-14)

Mature individuals facing their final cycle of years on the planet realize that their bodies are deteriorating rapidly. Increased pain, arthritis, weakness, and medical issues relative to the aging process all mark the transition. Eventually, if the deterioration affects the quality of one's life significantly, the aging person begins to long for the relief that will come with death. Just as severely oppressed people might look to being freed from their torturous circumstances by death (4:1-3), so too, even the godliest individuals endure the ravages of time with the hope that passing from this life will bring a desirable release from the effects of the Fall.

God does not limit the release from suffering, pain, and sorrow to the aged. All too late in life, we come to the realization that an infant's death might well display God's mercy in delivering that child from a traumatic, painful, and sorrow-filled existence (6:3-6; cp. 2 Kings 22:18-20; Isa. 57:1-2). Only the omniscient and sovereign God of the universe knows such things and makes such judgments. The power of death is in His hand.

Eaton notes that Ecclesiastes 7:1-14 appears to follow up on 'the theme of Ecclesiastes as a whole with the question: Will the life of faith survive hard and troublesome times when the "good old days" have gone and the "days of adversity" come?'[4] Solomon's answer declares that life remains worth living,[5] even in this fallen existence, until our Sovereign Lord determines that the proper time has come for us to make our final exit. With these thoughts in mind, what *is* good for a person in life?

Death Is Good (7:1-4)

Solomon initiates his response to the question he voiced at the start of 6:12 ('For who knows what is good for a man during *his* lifetime...?') by mentioning two good things: a good repu-tation and the day of one's death. Naming comprises one of the topics shared with Genesis 1–3. At creation, God displayed His authority by giving names to individual entities like light and darkness, the expanse, the dry land and the collection of waters, and man (Gen. 1:5, 9, 10, 26). The man (Adam), in turn, named the animals and woman (Gen. 2:19, 20, 23; 3:20). Parents continue to this day to name their children at or shortly after birth. The naming displays a certain degree of authority by which human beings demonstrate their God-given rulership. However, no matter what name a person receives at birth, his or her reputation at the time of death becomes far more signi-ficant. Their reputation testifies to the success or lack of success with which they meet life's challenges.

Solomon's poetic skill emerges from a reading of the Hebrew text of verse 1a. The Hebrew exhibits an inverted play on words: *tov shem mishshemen tov*. 'Good' (*tov*) appears at the beginning and the end of the statement. This inclusion brackets the pro-verb with attention to the governing theme. Between the two

---

4. Eaton, *Ecclesiastes*, 108.
5. Stuart Olyott highlights this concept in the title of his study of Ecclesiastes and the Song of Solomon, *A Life Worth Living and A Lord Worth Loving*.

uses of 'good' the author clusters 'name' (*shem*) and 'oil' (*shemen*), separated only by the comparative 'than' (a preposition pre-fixed on *shemen*). The poetic nature of the proverb makes it memorable. At its center are the two entities that produce the visual (and auditory) imagery. Indeed, good does occur in a lifetime. At the beginning of one's life, an individual receives a name. Throughout one's lifetime, that name obtains either a good reputation or a bad one – preferably a good one. In fact, one's name accrues value and has the potential of being more valuable at death than at birth. The good, therefore, comes at death.

The 'good ointment' might make reference to any of a number of normal situations in ancient Israel's culture: (1) the bathing of an infant in oil at birth (cp. Ezek. 16:4),[6] (2) refreshing the body to provide relief from body odor, muscle soreness, dry skin, and other conditions,[7] (3) a luxury provided by the possession of significant wealth,[8] or (4) the preparation of a corpse for burial, since the context speaks of 'the day of *one's* death' (v. 1b) and 'a house of mourning' (vv. 2, 4).[9] The immediately preceding context also discusses matters of death and burial (5:15-16; 6:3, 6). Fredericks astutely observes that 'Ten verses earlier, even a burial plot was in question, much less the attending ointments for a respectable ceremony.'[10] Given the flow of the context and the topic of death, the fourth situation provides the best setting for the proverb.

The second half of 7:1 continues to elevate one's death above one's birth. Birth commences a temporary existence 'under the sun' on this planet. Death, however, propels a person into an existence in infinite time. Birth pales in the light of death in both time and significance. Paul summed up the concept beautifully for the people of God: 'To die is gain.... I am hard-pressed from both *directions*, having the desire to depart and be with Christ, for *that* is very much better' (Phil. 1:21, 23).

Verses 2 and 4 form a proverbial pair sandwiching verse 3:

---

6. Gordis, *Koheleth*, 267.
7. Ryken, *Ecclesiastes*,150.
8. Whybray, *Ecclesiastes*, 113.
9. Fredericks, 'Ecclesiastes,' 166.
10. Ibid.

the house of mourning vs. the house of feasting (v. 2)
sorrow and laughter
sadness and goodness[11]
the house of mourning vs. the house of pleasure (v. 4)

'The house of mourning' refers to the home of the deceased, where the family mourns the departure of their loved one. Jacob's family observed a seven-day period of mourning, a practice still continued among the Jews.[12] Solomon explains that death 'is the end of every man, and the living takes *it* to heart' (7:2c,d). Everyone will face the day of their death (cp. Rom. 6:23) – the few who read this page are among the few who have not yet died, but they too will go the way of all flesh. At 'the house of mourning' the living person takes this end to heart. Sadly, people do not always give due consideration to the significance of death. During the prophetic ministry of Isaiah, he made the observation that people in that day were not laying it to heart when they saw the righteous die (Isa. 57:1). What does an individual gain from visiting a family in mourning, standing beside the open casket and gazing upon the lifeless form of the deceased, or listening to an account or eulogy regarding the life of the dead person? The benefits include:

- Understanding more clearly the ultimate result of the Fall.

- Giving proper consideration to the brevity of life, indeed, the transitory nature of our own existence.

- Being reminded that how we live does count – what have I done with my life thus far?

- Recommitting ourselves to live life in the light of eternity.

- Preparing to die.

---

11. See the later discussion of v. 3 and the translation of its final phrase.

12. See Ecclesiasticus 22:12: 'Mourning for the dead lasts seven days, but for a fool or an ungodly man it lasts all his life;' Bruce M. Metzger, ed., *The Apocrypha of the Old Testament, Revised Standard Version*, Oxford Annotated Apocrypha (New York: Oxford University Press, 1977), 156. When Moses and Aaron died, Israel mourned for thirty days (Num. 20:29; Deut. 34:8). Jewish practice often observes seven days of greater mourning followed by 23 days of lesser mourning (Delitzsch, *Song of Songs and Ecclesiastes*, 314).

- Learning the value of comfort and being comforted – the great benefit of the believing family and believing community.

- Knowing that no one lives to herself and no one dies to himself – a life, as well as a death, impacts the lives of others.

In other words, 'Every funeral anticipates our own,' according to Eaton's laconic summary.[13] Only when an individual takes the seriousness (the finality) of death to heart, does he or she benefit from the life-lessons that a funeral imparts.

Interrupting the two parallel proverbs of verses 2 and 4, verse 3 specifies why a visit to a funeral proves beneficial. Returning to his meditation on the futility of pleasure, Solomon converts 2:2 ('I said of laughter, "It is madness," and of pleasure, "What does it accomplish?"') into a concise axiom: 'Sorrow is better than laughter.' The reason for the axiom's truth is that the sadness which shows in the face results in a better[14] heart, a spiritually healthy heart.

Why does verse 3 appear to contradict the wisdom expressed in Proverbs 14:13? Some interpreters think that the writer of Ecclesiastes challenges traditional (biblical) wisdom like that found elsewhere in Scripture.[15] This apparent contradiction with Proverbs provides seemingly conflicting opinions in wisdom literature with which the author of Ecclesiastes must wrestle. His search for ultimate wisdom immerses him in the complexities of life by flooding his study with new questions in an ever-increasing web of arguments and counter-arguments. Estes explains this apparent contradiction between Proverbs and Ecclesiastes as the presentation of additional insights in order to bring about 'a more comprehensive understanding of how life functions.'[16] Ecclesiastes supplements Proverbs as Solomon casts his net more widely in his search for the true meaning of life. After all, no proverb can synthesize the totality of life or its meaning. Life is not simple; it is complicated. Even

---

13. Eaton, *Ecclesiastes*, 109.
14. The translations of NIV, NET, KJV, and NKJV represent the Hebrew better than those translations employing 'happy' or 'glad.'
15. Seow, *Ecclesiastes*, 246.
16. Estes, *Handbook on the Wisdom Books*, 342.

the wisest man in history struggles to grasp the full picture and to distill it to an understandable description.

Verse 4 provides the transition from verses 1-3 and 5-7 by acknowledging the connection to wisdom by means of the characteristic pairing of 'the wise' and 'the fools.' Biblical wisdom literature majors on the contrasting natures, paths, and destinies of these two types of people. Ecclesiastes first contrasts them in 2:14-19. A wise youth and a foolish old king depict the dissimilarity in 4:13. In 4:5 and 17, as well as in 5:1-4, Solomon identifies laziness, careless sacrifice, verbosity, and failure to fulfill a vow as the follies of fools. Both the wise and the fool experience the equality of death (6:8). References to fools and foolishness occur seven times in chapter 7 (vv. 4, 5, 6, 9, 17, 25 [2×]), while references to the wise and wisdom appear thirteen times (vv. 4, 5, 7, 10, 11, 12 [2×], 16, 19 [2×], 23 [2×], 25). Despite the introduction of this opposition in verse 4, the verse still belongs to the preceding context because of the role it plays in the literary sandwich establishing the contrast between houses of mourning and feasting. The connection can also be noted in the repetition of 'heart' (vv. 2, 3, 4 [2×]). The literary sandwich announces that the heart of a wise person improves its spiritual health at a funeral. The fool dulls the sharp interruption of death by directing his heart to revelry and hilarity.

The Superiority of Wisdom (7:5-12)

Receiving rebuke with humility, patience, and a willingness to change marks the wise (7:5). Many people prefer foolish humor to shrug off the rebuke and to excuse bad behavior and poor attitudes (7:6). Solomon enlists a pun to drive the point home in verses 5 and 6. He contrasts 'the song [shir] of fools' with the 'crackling of thorn bushes [sirah] under a pot [sir].' Thorn bushes crackle pleasantly in the fire, but the flames quickly consume them without any enduring heat with which to heat a pot of water or food. The heat produced is temporary. The humor and laughter of fools possesses an equally fleeting benefit. Indeed, their merriment is hebel, transitory and insubstantial. Verse 6 ends with 'futility.' The previous uses of this word came at the close of the first half of the book (6:9, 11, 12). In this way Solomon contrasts the good that comes from wisdom with the transitory and insubstantial results of folly.

Ryken's exposition of verses 5 and 6 summarizes the message of Ecclesiastes as it relates to the edification that comes from criticism and friendly reproof:

> Wise people will say all of the things that Ecclesiastes says. They will tell us that living for pleasure and working for selfish gain are striving after wind. They will tell us that God has a time for everything, including a time to be born and a time to die. They will tell us that two are better than one in facing all of the toils and trials of life. They will tell us that because God is in Heaven and we are on earth, we should be careful what we say. They will tell us that money will never satisfy our souls. In short, they will teach us not to live for today but to live for eternity.[17]

We become that to which we listen. The ear can be a Golden Gate for wisdom, knowledge, holiness, righteousness, and grace to enter, or it can become the Dung Gate for foolishness, ignorance, impurity, iniquity, and crudity. Solomon declares that the better path is the former, even if a rebuke appeals less than a song even to the saint's ear. Instead of drowning out the realities of life and death with music, humor, and feasting, the believer would do well to sit at the feet of a wise counselor who will not be reluctant to offer heart-strengthening admonition.

In a fallen world true biblical wisdom attracts persecution. An accurate translation presents a better opportunity to rightly interpret verse 7: 'Surely oppression makes the wise foolish' (v. 7a, NRSV). Life's complexities include the deleterious effects of oppression on even a wise person's stability of mind.[18] Readers might choose between three approaches to the meaning of verse 7. The first approach explains that the text refers to persecution possessing the power to pressure the wise into speaking or acting as fools – in other words, contrary to the faith they espouse. A second, and slightly different, interpretation understands the text to speak of the subversion of a wise person by means of corruption – everyone has his or her price.[19]

---

17. Ryken, *Ecclesiastes:*, 156.
18. Eaton, *Ecclesiastes*, 110-11;
19. Estes, *Handbook on the Wisdom Books*, 343. Bartholomew, *Ecclesiastes*, 249, writes, 'Even the wise person buckles under oppression and is susceptible to a bribe, and bribery and corruption destroy the heart.'

A third approach takes the wise person as the oppressor rather than being oppressed: 'Even the wise can sin (7:20) and stoop to intimidating another person physically, emotionally, legally or even ecclesiastically.'[20] Of the three approaches to verse 7, the first two appear more solidly based upon a straightforward reading of the text.

The second half of the verse continues the effects of corruption in the realm of influence and power. Bribery can do to the upright in heart (cp. Exod. 23:8) what oppression can do to the wise of heart. When innocent victims behold the public humiliation of their wise counselor (who is made to look like a fool) and the corruption of previously honest witnesses, they lose heart. Injustice appears to prevail and life becomes even more complicated.

Verse 8 transitions from verses 5-7 to verses 9-12. 'Living for the End in the Now'[21] labels 7:8-12 in Brown's commentary. The contrast of beginning and ending closely parallels the opening of the chapter with the acknowledgment of birth and death (the beginning and ending of a single life). How can the end of a matter be better than the beginning? Bartholomew points to verse 5 for one example: 'the rebuke of a wise person may be unpleasant, but its end or result may be good.'[22] According to Estes, a race nicely illustrates the point, since 'the only measure that counts is the finish line, and in life it often takes considerable time until the wise course is vindicated.'[23] Anyone who has run a marathon might readily admit that the end of a marathon is better than its start.

'Patience of spirit is better than haughtiness of spirit' in the second half of verse 8 literally reads, 'Better is length of spirit than height of spirit.' 'Length of spirit' refers to patient endurance – being slow to anger (cp. Prov. 14:29; 15:18; 16:32 – all three proverbs use 'length of anger' to mean 'slow to anger'). 'Height of spirit' occurs also in Proverb 16:18 with the meaning of 'a haughty spirit.' In other words, Solomon indicates that patience and humility enable a person to wait for the outcome of a matter and actually to witness the truth

20. Fredericks, 'Ecclesiastes,' 169.
21. Brown, *Ecclesiastes*, 76.
22. Bartholomew, *Ecclesiastes*, 249.
23. Estes, *Handbook on the Wisdom Books*, 343.

that the end is better than the beginning. Without these two attributes, a man or woman will not discover what time can do to improve a situation.

Anger finds fuel for its fire in impatience and pride. Thus, verse 9 follows logically on the heels of verse 8. The catchword 'spirit' (twice in v. 8 and once in v. 9 – translated sometimes as 'heart' in the latter verse) ties the two verses together conceptually. 'Fool' comprises another word linking this verse to its preceding context. The heart of a fool seeks pleasure (v. 4), his song lacks wisdom (v. 5), his laughter lasts momentarily (v. 6), and he harbors anger (v. 9). Kidner describes this fool as obstinate, with no patience to seek wisdom, and possessing no reverence for truth.[24]

The lack of wisdom on the part of fools promotes an unhealthy and irrational nostalgia for the past (v. 10). The fool wishes for a return to the past when things surely were better than they are in the present. In reality, the fool exercises selective memory. Dreamers of bygone days reveal ignorance of history, false theology regarding the sinfulness of man and fallen condition of the world, blindness to opportunities existing in the present, and impatience regarding the future. In short, this way of thinking 'is not from wisdom.'

Extremes in attitudes characterize the fallen person's approach to daily life. They swing between a pessimistic outlook for the future (v. 8) and an unrealistic and nostalgic view of the past (v. 10). Dealing with disaster, disappointment, discouragement, and death creates friction with patience, pride, and personal plans. But what do we really know about the future? Who does know the future? Difficult times require a person to wait patiently on God. He will bring about all that He has designed for us by the trial. His best for us is yet ahead. We must humbly submit to our Lord's sovereign providence in order to gain the spiritual maturity to handle life's many complications.

Verses 10, 11, and 12 all employ the catchword 'wisdom.' Solomon builds on his earlier references to the wise of heart (v. 4), the rebuke of the wise (v. 5), and the oppression of the wise (v. 7). The wise value a funeral above a feast (v. 4) and a rebuke above a song (v. 5), but wisdom has its price (v. 7; cp. 1:18). Life is not only brief, it is filled with trouble (cp. Job 5:7). How then can someone

---

24. Kidner, *The Wisdom of Proverbs, Job & Ecclesiastes*, 40.

experience good (Eccles. 6:12)? Individuals who possess wisdom and who also receive an inheritance, do experience good (7:11). After all, there is an advantage to having an inheritance – an advantage that can be enjoyed only in this life by 'those who see the sun.' Seeing the sun implies pleasantness and enjoyment (11:7; 12:1-2) as well as making reference to life on earth (Ps. 58:8). The vicissitudes of life can bring pain and loss, but sometimes even the loss results in a gain. Inheritances come to a person as the result of the death of someone near and dear (Prov. 19:14; cp. Heb. 9:16-17). Good and godly people seek to leave an inheritance for their children and grandchildren (Prov. 13:22). On the contrary, the fool, like the prodigal son, squanders his or her inheritance (Eccles. 2:18-19, 21; cp. Luke 15:12-13). The texts dealing with this issue imply that a wise person will not waste an inheritance, but will appreciate it and, if possible, even multiply it for his descendants.

An inheritance together with wisdom is good because both provide protection (v. 12; literally, 'because in the shadow of that wisdom is in the shadow of that silver'). A shadow might appear a bit unusual as a figure for protection in this context, since 6:12 appropriates the figure to emphasize the brevity of life. However, a shadow also symbolizes protection (as from the heat of the sun; Judg. 9:15; Ps. 17:8; Isa. 4:6). Both money and wisdom provide only temporary shelter, however, when it comes to preserving life. No matter how much wisdom a person possesses and exercises, he will yet die. No matter how much money a person expends for comfort and medical care, she will eventually die. The fact that neither wisdom nor wealth can prevent death does not make these things worthless, bad, or a disadvantage. Wisdom and money enable the wise to handle life's complications well, so that a person might enjoy his or her God-given life for the short time it lasts. This approach to life countermands the axiom 'Eat and drink for tomorrow we die,' because it demands biblical wisdom involving *right teaching* (from Scripture) that produces *right thinking* resulting in *right choices* that make for *right living*.

The Sovereign God Is in Control (7:13-14)

Bringing this section (7:1-14) to a close, Solomon calls upon his readers to think about their present conditions in the light of eternity. How does God figure in their situation? How do they relate to His will? Literally, the author's imperative reads, 'See the work of God' (v. 13). The imperative 'see' occurs twice at the conclusion of 7:1-14 (vv. 13, 14) and twice at the end of 7:15-29 (vv. 27, 29).[25] English translations use a variety of verbs for the same Hebrew root (e.g., 'see,' 'observe,' 'consider,' 'enjoy,' 'tell,' 'look'). A survey of all occurrences in Ecclesiastes reveals the scope of human observation, experience, enjoyment, and consideration:

Meaning of 'See'	Objects of 'See'
Observing	everything done 'under the sun' (1:14) that everything comes from God (2:24b) the task God gives to mankind (3:10; 8:16a) injustice and wickedness (3:16) what is good for mankind (3:22a; 5:17a) oppression (4:1; 5:7) competition or rivalry (4:4) 'vanity (*hebel*) under the sun' (4:7) popularity (4:15) greed (5:12) not enjoying the fruit of one's labor (6:1-2) everything (7:15; 8:9) death (8:10) time and chance (9:11) wisdom (9:13) life's inequities (10:5-7)
Searching	for satisfaction (1:8) for something new (1:10) through all wealth and knowledge (1:16) through all wisdom and folly (2:12-13)
Seeing	the sun (7:11; 11:7; *not seeing*, 6:5) what has been discovered (7:27, 29) anything (12:3)
Experiencing	good (3:13) evil (*not experiencing*, 4:3) sleep (*not experiencing*, 8:16b)

---

25. The imperative appears prior to chapter 7 in 1:10 and 2:1 and following chapter 7 only in 9:9.

Meaning of 'See'	Objects of 'See'
Enjoying	good (2:1, 3, 24a; *not enjoying*, 6:6) labor/work (5:17b) a wife/married life (9:9)
Knowing	the future (3:22b)
Understanding	that humans are like beasts (3:18)
Watching	clouds (11:4)
Considering	God's work (7:13, 14; 8:17)

After listing some of the good, beneficial, and advantageous aspects of life (7:1-12), Solomon turns the reader's attention Godward. 'Consider the work of God' (v. 13) expresses the focus on God in this section. He implies that God possesses the solution to the issues of both life and death that trouble mortal mankind. God's work cannot be altered (v. 13). To express the concept, Solomon revisits what he has already mentioned back in 1:15 and 3:14. Some things in life must be accepted in the way they come, because God has appointed both the good (the straight) and the bad (the bent or crooked). Life is not a matter of mere 'fate,' because a personal God who really cares for His people controls life's ever-changing events. Mortals cannot alter the work of the immortal God.

Job voices his trusting acceptance of this very fact of human existence when he says, 'Shall we indeed accept good from God and not accept adversity?' (Job 2:10). Such will always be the faith of the godly. God controls all events in their lives and designs them for their good (Rom. 8:28). They should accept everything with thanksgiving (1 Thess. 5:18), being content in every circumstance (Phil. 4:11-12). In fact, both James (James 1:2) and Peter (1 Pet. 1:6) exhort believers to count it a joy to pass through times of trouble and trial. The Spirit of God, who superintends Solomon as he writes, intends this instruction (Eccles. 7:13-14) 'to build confidence and define boundaries within which one can act wisely.'[26]

---

26. Fredericks, 'Ecclesiastes,' 173.

Verse 14 contains two uses of the word for 'good.' 'In the day of prosperity be happy' literally reads, 'In a good day be in good' (v. 14a). Solomon encourages readers to take advantage of the enjoyment of the days of good, prosperity, health, and happiness. The English idiom 'be in the moment' approximates the meaning Solomon intends. In other words, do not miss the enjoyment of the good times. Savor them and treasure them – build memories to sustain hope during the more difficult times of life.

Next, Solomon turns to the 'day of adversity' (v. 14b). For the second time in two verses, he exhorts the reader to 'consider' the work of God in bringing about both kinds of days in a person's life (v. 14b-c). Human beings cannot predict which kind of day tomorrow (or even today) might be (v. 14d). In fact, the fluctuations of life's extremes exhibit no regularity and the changes come with astonishing speed. God's people must learn to trust Him, because He alone knows the purpose of those fluctuations.[27] Estes observes that, 'What appears on the surface as adversity may in truth be a severe mercy of the sovereign God that leads to a more profound and substantial blessing'[28] (read again Isa. 57:1-2 and 2 Kings 22:18-20). Whether these changes are economic (prosperity vs. recession or depression), physical (health and life vs. illness and death, peace vs. war, environmental stability vs. earthquake or flood), or social (support and acceptance vs. rejection and persecution), we must find our peace and confidence in knowing that God remains at the helm.

'Discover' (v. 14d) may also be translated 'find.' This word occurs only once in the first half of the book (3:11), but sixteen times in the second half, half of them in 7:14-29. What does the author mean by 'anything *that will be* after him' (v. 14d; cf. 10:14)? Does it refer to the future here on earth or does it refer to the afterlife? Some interpreters conclude that it cannot be the afterlife, since they find no references to the afterlife elsewhere in the book.[29] Thus, the text may speak only of the future, ongoing cycle of life and death after a person has

---

27. Eaton, *Ecclesiastes*, 113.
28. Estes, *Handbook on the Wisdom Books*, 346.
29. E.g., Longman, *Ecclesiastes*, 192.

departed from 'under the sun.' Only God knows the future (2 Sam. 7:19; Isa. 46:9-11; 48:3-5; Dan. 2:45).

A Person's Character in the Light of Revelation (7:15-29)
Two qualities of personal character dominate 7:15-29: wisdom and righteousness. Indeed, biblical wisdom displays a steady choice of right in accord with God's written Word. Thus, biblical wisdom finds expression in how a person lives his or her life. After a careful reading of Ecclesiastes, Charles Swindoll identifies those practical implications in his definition of wisdom: 'Wisdom is the God-given ability to see life with rare objectivity and to handle life with rare stability.'[30]

Attempts to interpret or translate Ecclesiastes face severe challenges in 7:15-24. As Murphy declares, 'It is hard to be satisfied with any commentary on this section; it is very difficult to understand.'[31]

Balanced Living (7:15-18)
Wisdom and righteousness characterize the lives of those who 'fear God.' However, exhibiting those characteristics requires balance in how a person spends his or her life. Solomon comes to this conclusion through careful observation. Verse 15 marks the eleventh time Solomon has used the phrase 'I have seen.'[32] These comments remind the reader that Ecclesiastes records a thorough examination of life 'under the sun.' Indeed, the writer speaks of observations about his own life, a life he characterizes as 'my lifetime of futility' (literally, 'in the days of my futility' or 'in my fleeting days'). The same combination of *hebel* and 'days' occurs also in Job 7:16 ('my days are *but* a breath'), Psalm 78:33 ('So He brought their days to an end in futility'), Ecclesiastes 6:12 ('the few years [lit., days] of his futile life'), and 9:9 ('all the days of your fleeting life'). Although life has passed Solomon faster than he could imagine, he manages to make some observations related to its brevity. First, he notices that a righteous person's life might end while he is still living righteously. Second, he observes that a wicked person might experience an extended life in

---

30. Swindoll, *Living on the Ragged Edge*, 220.
31. Murphy, *Ecclesiastes*, 72.
32. See 1:14; 2:24; 3:10, 16, 22; 4:4, 15; 5:13, 18; 6:1; 7:15; 8:9, 10; 10:5, 7.

spite of his continual wickedness. In other words, the length of a person's life does not depend upon his or her spirituality.

Solomon's observations of real life appear to contradict the teaching of both biblical law (e.g., Deut. 4:40; 5:16; 30:17-18; compare 1 Kings 3:14) and wisdom (e.g., Prov. 10:27; 12:21). Law and wisdom announce principles and proclaim the ideal. While the law promises blessing for righteous, obedient living, the wisdom of Proverbs builds on those principles, establishing general truths. In fact, individual proverbs 'present life in the form of *paradigms*, patterns, and stereotypical generalizations.'[33] They were not intended to cover all circumstances. Instead, the 'proverb is limited to the specific slice of reality that it portrays.'[34]

Righteous living (obedience to the Word of God) prolongs a person's life, while the opposite (disobedience and wicked living) shortens an individual's life. This does not mean that the righteous will live longer than the average person's lifespan, or that the wicked will live a shorter time than the average. Only God knows what the lifespan is for each individual (Job 14:5; Eccles. 3:1-2). On the one hand, God extends the lives of some righteous individuals for their godliness, but they might still die younger than some of the wicked people among whom they live. On the other hand, God shortens the lives of some wicked people by 'the debilitating effects of their lifestyle and the judicial actions'[35] which He will take against them. However, those same wicked persons might live longer than the righteous who live among them.

Does Solomon refer merely to physical life and death in his observation of these contrasting circumstances? Rather than referring to the concepts of physical life and death (i.e., clinical death), the text might speak of 'abundant life in fellowship with God, a living relationship that is never envisioned as ending in clinical death in contrast to the wicked's eternal death.'[36] Thus,

---

33. Ted A. Hildebrandt, 'Proverb,' in *Cracking Old Testament Codes: Interpreting the Literary Genres of the Old Testament*, ed. by D. Brent Sandy and Ronald L. Giese, Jr. (Nashville, Tenn.: Broadman & Holman Publishers, 1995), 235 (emphasis is Hildebrandt's).

34. Ibid., 249.

35. Steveson, *A Commentary on Proverbs* (Greenville, S.C.: BJU Press, 2001),

36. Waltke, *The Book of Proverbs: Chapters 1–15*, 105.

Proverbs depicts the wicked spending their time in darkness (2:13; 4:19; 20:20) rather than in light. In Ecclesiastes, Solomon repeats the description of the unrighteous and foolish who are living in darkness (2:14). Statements like Proverbs 12:28 cannot possibly mean that the righteous person will not die, so the text might refer to an abundant life rather than a life governed by death and darkness.

Few verses have stimulated more discussion and investigation than 7:16-18 with their seeming contradiction to biblical norms of behavior. Interpreters who have already placed Ecclesiastes in the Hellenistic era and associated the book with Greek philosophy, identify the 'Golden Mean' with these verses.[37] The concept of moderation alone, however, fails to do justice to the text. Verses 16 and 17 seem to recommend a response to the observation recorded in verse 15. Since being righteous or being wicked does not guarantee a longer or shorter life in comparison with other individuals, it is wise not to go to extremes in either righteousness or wickedness. The former will not guarantee living longer than anyone else and the latter will not guarantee dying sooner than anyone else.

Kaiser rightly observes that people sometimes delude themselves, as well as family and friends,

> through a multiplicity of pseudoreligious acts of sanctimoniousness; ostentatious showmanship in the act of worship; a spirit of hypercriticism against minor deviations from one's own cultural norms, which are equated with God's righteousness; and a disgusting conceit and supercilious, holier-than-thou attitude veneered over the whole mess.[38]

In 2:15 Solomon asks why he has been 'extremely wise,' since both the wise and the fool meet the same fate (death). Both that text and the present verses encounter the same issue. The real delusion occurs when some think they can either forestall or hasten their own deaths by engaging in more extreme forms of religious or irreligious living. They are not in control of their deaths – God is!

---

37. E.g., Gordis, *Koheleth*, 275-76. See response in Brindle, 'Righteousness and Wickedness in Ecclesiastes 7:15-18,' 302.

38. Kaiser, *Ecclesiastes*, 85-86.

Resuming his examination of what is good in life 'under the sun,' Solomon observes that (1) it is a good thing to both enjoy life while one has it and (2) to pursue godliness (v. 18). The one who fears God (see 3:14 and 5:7) maintains both pursuits.[39] Fearing God includes, in this context, a sense of dependence upon Him for one's security.[40] God gives the good things in life and He controls the time of one's death.

Wisdom Rather Than Perfection (7:19-22)

Next, Solomon turns to an illustration that describes the great value of wisdom (v. 19). He compares an individual's benefits from wisdom to the benefits a city experiences by having ten rulers to take care of the needs of her citizens. Eaton concludes that the illustration teaches that 'wisdom in the fear of God may be greater than the collective wisdom of a group of experienced leaders.'[41] The thought fits the instruction found in Proverbs 24:5-6 and anticipates a more expanded illustration in Ecclesiastes 9:13-16.[42]

Verses 20-22 return to a thought brought up earlier in verse 7. Even the wise and the righteous manifest the effects of a fallen nature. No one can claim to be free of sin during his or her lifetime 'under the sun.' That flaw in the human character prevents anyone from being able to depend on their own wisdom or righteousness to provide them with the enjoyment of God's good gifts. Verse 20 sounds Pauline (cp. Rom. 3:9-20, esp. v. 10, the only potential New Testament quotation of Ecclesiastes). Interestingly, Paul chooses to cite passages from the Old Testament in order to prove the sinfulness of mankind. The doctrine of total depravity originated in the Old Testament. This very verse appears to be an expansion of a briefer statement Solomon made at his dedication of the Temple: 'When they sin against You (for there is no man who does not sin) …' (1 Kings 8:46).

In Romans 6:23 the apostle Paul declares that 'the wages of sin is death.' Although Solomon does not refer to wages in this way, he speaks of the labor of mankind and the fact that

---

39. Garrett, *Proverbs, Ecclesiastes, Song of Songs,* 324.
40. Estes, *Handbook on the Wisdom Books,* 347.
41. Eaton, *Ecclesiastes,* 115.
42. Compare these illustrations with the historical example of a wise woman in 2 Sam. 20:15-22.

labor does not succeed in gaining an escape from death. [43]
Paul continues his proclamation with a contrast, 'but the gift
of God is eternal life.' Solomon expresses a similar thought by
focusing on the gifts that one receives from God in this life and
the fact that He has set 'eternity in their heart' (3:11-13). When
the reader connects Ecclesiastes 7:20 with 7:15-18, he learns
that no amount of righteous living can prevent the sin that
so easily assails every person. Both sin and death are certain
– neither can be avoided completely. Thus, the question that
remains involves how a person can be delivered from sin and
death. How can an individual experience life beyond the sun?
The answer has already been revealed with the imperative in
5:7 ('fear God') and the advice in 7:18 ('the one who fears God
comes forth with both of them').

Some might question Solomon's assertion that everyone is
an unrighteous sinner. Anticipating just such an objection, Solomon directs the reader to consider the tongue (see James 3:2-12).
Each individual fails in act and in speech (Eccles. 7:20-22). Everyone has spoken ill of another outside that person's presence
(see 10:20). On the one hand, overly righteous (self-righteous)
individuals might hold a grudge over what someone else has
said about them behind their backs. On the other hand, overly
wicked persons respond in kind with cutting speech against
those whom they believe have defamed them. The individual
who is acutely aware of his or her own sinfulness will more
readily shrug off the foolish and unkind remarks of others.
Solomon knows that his major point involves demonstrating
that everyone sins – something they must know before they
can rightly prepare for life beyond the sun. However, he also
takes the opportunity to offer instruction as to how a wise and
righteous person ought to behave while yet 'under the sun.'

The Search for an Explanation (7:23-29)
The final section of chapter 7 (vv. 23-29) continues the focus
on wisdom. Solomon confesses that he lacks the wisdom
which offers the capability of answering life's tough questions
– especially questions about the inequities of life and the
inevitability of death. The failure lies partly in the fact that

---

43. Note the use of the word (Hebrew *yithron*) translated variously as 'gain,'
'advantage,' and 'profit' in 1:3; 2:11, 13; 3:9; 5:8, 15; 7:12; 10:10, 11.

he relies upon his own desire and will to be wise (v. 23). True wisdom comes only from God. How can Solomon make such a statement about the failure of his wisdom, when God had granted him an abundance of wisdom (1 Kings 3:9-12)? According to the historical account, God gave Solomon wisdom primarily to discern and administer justice. As he writes Ecclesiastes, however, Solomon realizes that even his God-given wisdom has limits. Only God is all-wise. No human being possesses the capacity to fully understand God's plan and program. Solomon's search for that kind of wisdom brings him to the same questions and the same conclusion as those Job reached (see Job 28:12-13, 23). Ultimate wisdom does not reside 'in the land of the living' (Job 28:13), but God knows its place (Job 28:23). Yes, such wisdom 'is remote and exceedingly mysterious. Who can discover it?' (Eccles. 7:24). As for the answer to entering life beyond the sun, Job speaks of a Redeemer (Job 19:25-27; cp. 33:23-28). Does Solomon know about a Redeemer? To what conclusion will his observations lead him?

Solomon himself set out to discover ultimate wisdom. 'I directed my mind' (literally, 'I and my heart looked around,' v. 25) stresses Solomon's determined purpose. The threefold description of his goal ('to know, to investigate, and to seek') summarizes his previous declarations concerning his search for wisdom (1:13, 17; 2:3). 'Explanation' translates a Hebrew word first occurring in Ecclesiastes at 7:25. It occurs three times in verses 25-29 and a final time in 9:10. According to Estes, the writer 'indicates that he endeavored to make an intellectual accounting of the events in the universe.'[44] When Solomon adds up all he has learned, what is the outcome? Before revealing the outcome, he further qualifies the scope of his search: it includes seeking knowledge about the wickedness and delusion of foolishness (v. 25; see 1:17; 2:3, 12).

His finding amounts to what he concludes as early as 3:11 – 'man will not find out the work which God has done from the beginning even to the end.' As recently as 7:14, Solomon makes a similar observation ('man will not discover anything *that will be* after him'). In verse 24 he poses a rhetorical question, 'Who

---

44. Estes, *Handbook on the Wisdom Books*, 349.

can discover it?' Obviously, no one can – not even someone with the wisdom of Solomon.

However, the reader is in for a shock. Solomon not only repeats the impossibility of success in his search, he associates his discovery with his relationship to a seductress. Commentators disagree on the identification of this woman and the significance of concluding the search in such a fashion. Garrett argues that the text teaches that 'because of sin, married life will be a war instead of a joy.'[45] He bases his interpretation on his understanding of Genesis 3:16. He claims that God grants a loving wife rather than 'a human trap' to a righteous man.[46]

A better interpretation, however, takes the woman to be a figurative representation of folly (compare Prov. 9:1-6, 13-18).[47] Wisdom and folly permeate the immediate context of verse 26, so this interpretation makes a good deal of sense. Even the figurative references to folly, both in Proverbs and here, provoke readers to remember Solomon's many wives and concubines. Consider the type of women with whom Solomon had the closest acquaintance. One thousand harem-wives and concubines only turned the king's heart away from God (1 Kings 11:1-8). If any man knew what effect a seductress might have on a man, Solomon did. He instructs his sons accordingly, warning them of the evil woman. Since he depicts wisdom as a woman (Prov. 1:20-33) and speaks highly of a number of good women (Eccles. 9:9; Prov. 18:22; 31:10-31), the reader dare not take Solomon's statement as a universal truth regarding all women.

So, what does Solomon mean when he declares, 'I have found one man among a thousand, but I have not found a woman among all these' (v. 28)? He utilizes a hyperbole ('one among a thousand')[48] to express the uniqueness of one individual (cp. Job 33:23). Gender wars and an over-emphasis on political correctness encourage modern readers to accuse the author of chauvinism and sexism.[49] Solomon did tend to marry pagan women of influence who were beneficial to him politically. What godly woman would place herself willingly in the

45. Garrett, *Proverbs, Ecclesiastes, Song of Songs*, 325.
46. Ibid.
47. Estes, *Handbook on the Wisdom Books*, 272.
48. Whybray, *Ecclesiastes*, 127.
49. Longman, *Ecclesiastes*, 204.

midst of the jealousies, ungodliness, and politics of Solomon's royal harem?[50] Although Solomon has 1,000 wives, there is no guarantee that this 'thousand' refers only to them – certainly they may be included, at least some of them. It is just a large rounded figure to express the rarity of a wise person, be that person male or female. Bartholomew summarizes the message of verse 26 with 'Flee folly!'[51] If one's folly involves love of money, flee! If one's folly is lust, flee! – whether the person representing that folly is male or female.

Verse 27 returns to the 'explanation' (v. 25) toward which he has systematically worked. He still seeks it (v. 28), because it has eluded his search. Among 1,000, Solomon has found one man, but not one woman. Remember the discussion above – Scripture characterizes Solomon's experience with women quantitatively, not qualitatively. No wonder he could not find a wise woman – those who dominated his life drew him into idolatry and a departure from God and His Law. The writer interprets verse 28 with verse 29: 'Behold, I have found only this, that God made men upright, but they have sought out many devices.' God is not to blame for the absence of wisdom – mankind is. From the Fall to the present, people have turned away from God and away from wisdom. They have all walked the path of folly. Isaiah penned the same truth by means of a different metaphor: 'All of us like sheep have gone astray, each of us has turned to his own way' (Isa. 53:6). Thus, the chapter concludes with the observation that people pervert the right way of God – they bend that which He has created straight. The irony of this leaps off the page, since no human being can 'straighten what He has bent' (v. 13). The wording augments the enigma of mankind's existence and his pursuit of wisdom.

At the conclusion of his exposition of chapter 7, Swindoll asks three questions that every believer ought to ponder after studying 7:15-29. Each question concerns one of the products of God-given wisdom:

---

50. Esther 2:1-19 provides an account of the type of process involved in being chosen to join a royal harem in ancient near eastern cultures. Ahasuerus conducted a beauty pageant including sleep-overs so the candidates could demonstrate their qualifications to be his wife and queen.

51. Bartholomew, *Ecclesiastes*, 267.

1. Regarding *balance:* Is wisdom guarding us from extremes?

2. Regarding *strength:* Is wisdom keeping us stable?

3. Regarding *insight:* Is wisdom clearing our minds?[52]

STUDY QUESTIONS

1. What have I done with my life thus far?

2. Am I prepared to leave this life?

3. In what ways do people seek to escape life's complications?

4. How can we properly enjoy and treasure life complications?

5. What is there about God that causes us to trust Him in life's trials?

6. What helps you to resolve the seeming contradictions between what you see in life and what the Word of God promises?

7. How do enjoying life and pursuing godliness sometimes come into conflict?

8. What is the connection between life 'under the sun' and life beyond the sun?

9. Why do some interpreters so readily accuse Solomon of chauvinism?

---

52. Swindoll, *Living on the Ragged Edge*, 231 (emphasis his).

8

Wisdom Has Its Limits

By application, *the Preacher* found the
explanation for apparent inequalities
in divine providence *(6:1–8:17)*, Part 3

The topic of wisdom, so evident in the preceding chapter, brackets chapter 8 with two declarations about 'the wise man' (vv. 1, 17). Verse 1 speaks again of the rarity of the truly wise person (see 7:27-28); verse 17 announces the frustration of the wise person who says, 'I know,' but cannot comprehend all the work of God 'under the sun.' Wisdom, indeed, has its benefits (v. 1b), but it also has its limits (v. 17).

Wisdom in Situations beyond a Person's Control (8:1-9)
The first verse of chapter 8 serves as a transition between chapters 7 and 8. Some commentators take it as the conclusion to the previous chapter since it focuses on the topic of wisdom which dominates 7:15-29.[1] Whether it concludes the seventh chapter or commences the eighth, the verse serves as a 'hinge'[2] between the two. Rhetorical questions like those in the first half of verse 1 normally receive a negative answer. The questions anticipate 'no one knows' (v. 7) and the reference to those who think they know, but have not come to a full comprehension of all that God does (v. 17).[3] However, in the second half of

---

1. Whybray, *Ecclesiastes*, 128.
2. Cp. Estes, *Handbook on the Wisdom Books*, 351.
3. Seow, *Ecclesiastes*, 290.

the verse Solomon answers this pair of rhetorical questions by indicating that such individuals do exist – despite their extreme rarity (7:28).

A wise person possesses the ability to interpret[4] a matter, and the resulting calm assurance produces a radiant visage (v. 1b). Similar terminology occurs in the Aaronic blessing: 'The LORD make His face shine on you, and be gracious to you' (Num. 6:25). Psalm 4:6 also attributes a radiant countenance to the LORD. When such a countenance belongs to God, the context indicates that the shining face refers to God's favor, grace, and mercy (Ps. 67:1). Proverbs 16:15 applies the metaphor to human beings ('In the light of a king's face is life, And his favor is like a cloud with the spring rain') in a way that parallels Ecclesiastes 8:1, which shows up in a context discussing kings. Verse 1 concludes with the statement that a person's wisdom 'causes his stern face to beam' (literally, 'the strength of his face changes'). Wisdom softens one's face as a reflection of the softened heart (cp. Prov. 15:13). In other words, that individual becomes more gracious, merciful, and forgiving.[5]

In a context of wisdom (7:15-29) Solomon exhorts his readers to be forgiving of those who have spoken ill of them (v. 21). Now, in 8:1, he offers a fuller explanation of what transpires in the manifestation of such a forgiving spirit. Since the contexts of both chapters 7 and 8 depict wisdom as something desirable and positive, Longman's view of 8:1 'as a sarcastic exclamation of frustration'[6] finds no objective basis in the text itself – although 7:23, 24 seem to conclude that wisdom is unattainable.[7] Even Longman notes that such an interpretation is 'hypothetical because it is the context, rather than anything explicit in the text, that signals the sarcastic tone.'[8]

---

4. The Hebrew word for 'interpretation' (*pesher*) occurs only here in the Hebrew Bible, but it appears often in the Dead Sea scrolls.

5. Eaton, *Ecclesiastes*, 117; Bartholomew, *Ecclesiastes*, 280. Garrett, on the other hand, considers 'his face' a reference to the king, mentioned in the following verse (Garrett, *Proverbs, Ecclesiastes, Song of Songs*, 326, footnotes 183 and 184). However, this view strains the context and runs counter to the straightforward reading of the text, which takes the antecedent of 'his' to be the wise man. Verse 5 in the following context reiterates the wise person's actions in his submission to the king.

6. Longman, *Ecclesiastes*, 208.

7. Ibid., 209.

8. Ibid.

Some commentators question Solomonic authorship of Ecclesiastes in view of the instruction regarding kings in 8:2-9.[9] The verses seem to present royal authority in a negative light. Would King Solomon speak of kings (and thus his own authority) in such a manner? In response, one could ask, who better to expound on practical politics in the royal court than a king? Not only has Solomon reigned over a kingdom, but he has interacted with the sovereigns of a number of nations. His advice resounds with credibility gained from firsthand experience. As Fredericks notes, the royal perspective pervades Ecclesiastes and both exilic and post-exilic periods of Israel's history provide very little opportunity for applying wise instruction regarding the monarchy's operations. 'There was no monarchy!' [10] Thus, Solomonic authorship contributes to the authenticity and integrity of these instructions and observations. Would doubters of Solomonic authorship argue that a king could not possibly compose such advice and ask readers to also reject royal involvement (Solomon, Hezekiah, and Lemuel) in the Book of Proverbs, because it too contains extensive advice for behavior in the royal court?

Being Wise in a King's Throne Room (8:2-6)
First, the writer of Ecclesiastes advises his readers to submit to the king (v. 2). Who is the king? Does Solomon refer to a human monarch or to the divine King? Leupold claims that every reference to the king in verses 1-8 'fits the heavenly Monarch, in fact, applies to Him more aptly than it does to an earthly ruler.'[11] While such an interpretation might nullify one argument wielded against Solomonic authorship,[12] it does not do justice to the language and context of the text itself. Many parallels with Proverbs reinforce wisdom connections with behavior in a king's presence. Opening the instruction with 'I say' (literally, 'I' – no verb[13]) echoes 6:3 ('I say' referring to the writer's comparison of the miscarriage with the man

---

9. Ibid., 6, 209.
10. Fredericks, 'Ecclesiastes, 32.
11. Leupold, *Ecclesiastes*, 180.
12. Leupold, however, does not argue for Solomonic authorship, dating the book to the Persian period; ibid., 11, 183.
13. The unusual wording does not necessitate emendation of the Hebrew text. The following translation depicts the meaning accurately: 'As for me, *the rule is* "Keep the king's command."' Cp. 1 Sam. 12:14: '[do] not rebel against the command of the LORD' (literally, 'the mouth of the LORD').

with many children and an improper burial) and 8:14 ('I say' in reference to inequities in life).

Submission and obedience to royal authority finds its basis in 'the oath of God' (literal translation, v. 2). The construction contains a degree of grammatical ambiguity, since the genitive can mean an oath that God takes or gives (ESV, NJPS),[14] an oath characterized by God ('sacred oath,' RSV, NRSV), or an oath taken to God (NKJV) or before God (NASB, NET, NIV). The last comprises the most likely meaning. With God as witness, subjects make their oath of allegiance to their sovereign. Similar wording in Exodus 22:11, 2 Samuel 21:7, 1 Kings 2:43, and 1 Chronicles 29:24 offers adequate evidence for the validity of this understanding. Solomon exhorts people to be faithful in their sworn allegiance to their king.

Verse 3 continues the exhortation to allegiance and submission. Subjects should not hastily depart from the king's presence. One should wait to be dismissed by the king himself. A person should demonstrate that his or her business does not transcend the king's and that they will adapt their time to his will. Indeed, an individual who makes an untimely exit might lose the opportunity of influencing the king.[15]

Subjects must also beware of getting involved in or entangled with any matter that the king might find displeasing, disagreeable, or contemptible. In other words, they should not engage in a 'bad cause' (NIV, HCSB). Garrett suggests that one should 'not champion an idea the king opposes' (his paraphrastic translation).[16] The king will punish any appearance of evil, lack of submission, lack of respect, rebellion, or improprieties as he sees fit (cf. Prov. 14:35; 24:21-22).

Verse 4 warns about arguing with the king or demanding an explanation for his decisions. The rhetorical question ('who will say to him, "What are you doing?"') demands the negative response, 'No one.' The same question appears in Job's first response to Bildad (Job 9:12) and in Isaiah's discourse on the sovereignty of God as illustrated by the potter's molding

---

14. Ryken, *Ecclesiastes*, 185, believes that the oath refers to God's promise to David that his descendants would sit on the throne of Israel.

15. Garrett, *Proverbs, Ecclesiastes, Song of Songs*, 326-27.

16. Ibid., 327 footnote 188. Longman is of the opinion that the concept 'is probably closer to a 'bad idea' than it is to a full-blown political conspiracy' (*Ecclesiastes*, 212).

of clay (Isa. 45:9). God, king, and potter all exercise similar power over their subjects. Obedience to royal decrees keeps one out of trouble with the king (v. 5a; cf. Prov. 16:14; 19:12; 20:2). A citizen must employ the correct process at the proper time to present any disagreement or grievance (v. 5b).

The mention of a proper time (v. 5) brings to the writer's attention other issues involving timing (vv. 6-8). In verse 6, 'there is a proper time … for every delight' closely reproduces the wording of 3:1, 'a time for every matter.' 'Delight' need not be the translation of the term in the original language. In contexts dealing with time translators tend to render 'delight' as 'matter' (3:1, 17). In contexts speaking of being pleased or delighted, they translate it as 'delight' (5:3). Since 8:6 is close to 3:1 in wording, it would seem more appropriate to translate it as 'matter:' 'For there is a proper time and procedure for every matter.' It fits the context better, because the topic deals with how to live under the authority of a king. The final clause of verse 6 further clarifies the intent: 'though a man's trouble is heavy upon him' (literally, 'though the trouble of that person is plentiful [abundant] upon him'). The phrasing echoes Genesis 6:5 ('the wickedness of man was great'). This might imply that the individual's trouble stems, at least originally, from his own sinfulness (see Eccles. 7:29). No matter how many troubles the royal subject experiences due to the king's decrees, he or she must not rush the matter and commit an error in approaching the king improperly for much needed relief.[17]

Being Wise through Life's Uncertainties (8:7-9)

Next, mention of proper timing and the troubles which people face 'under the sun' brings up mankind's lack of knowledge concerning the future (v. 7). No one knows the future, so no one can explain to someone else what will happen. The identical phrase for 'what will happen' appears also in 1:9 ('that which will be'), 3:22 ('what will occur'), and 10:14 ('what will come'). In 2:18 the only other use of the phrase modifies 'the man' ('who will come'). All speak of an unknown future. Only God has the power to declare the future (see Isa. 46:10-11).

---

17. Eaton, *Ecclesiastes*, 120, identifies this trouble with the general theme of Ecclesiastes – the oppressive burdens of life itself.

Mankind's apparent helplessness with regard to the future relates to other matters 'under the sun' over which no individual has control. Solomon offers four examples of an individual's lack of control over life:

(1) no one can restrain the wind
(v. 8a; cp. Prov. 27:16),

(2) no one can control the day of his or her death
(v. 8b),

(3) no soldier can discharge himself in time of war
(v. 8c), and

(4) wicked deeds can never deliver evil doers[18]
(v. 8d).

Ambiguity creates difficulty in interpreting and translating the first of these examples. 'Wind' (cp. 1:6, 14; 11:4, 5) represents the same Hebrew word (*ruach*) translated 'breath' (cf. 3:19, 21) and 'spirit' (cf. 7:8; 12:7). If the author's intent is 'spirit,' it would mean that no one can prevent the departure of his or her spirit at death.[19] It fits well with the second example dealing with the inability to prevent death.[20] However, taking both of the first two clauses with the same basic reference to death seems to be incongruous with a numerical saying proverb[21] in which the reader would expect four different items.[22] Ryken, taking the first and second as the same basic thought, logically proceeds to make the third and the fourth closely related by relating the wickedness mentioned in the fourth to the battlefield.[23] That strains the

---

18. Literally, 'evil will not deliver its master(s).' Bartholomew, *Ecclesiastes*, 283, observes that the statement depicts a bondage of a person's will to evil.

19. Leupold, *Ecclesiastes*, 189, takes this verse as a reference 'to keeping back a spirit that is about to depart from the earthly tabernacle of this body.' Kidner, *A Time to Mourn*, 76, likewise concludes that the verse speaks of man's 'inability to hold his own spirit captive, or to lord it over death.' However, Bartholomew, *Ecclesiastes*, 279 footnote 13, proposes including both meanings ('wind' and 'spirit'), 'picking up the theme of "striving after wind" as well as our lack of control over death.'

20. Murphy, *Ecclesiastes*, 84.

21. See the earlier discussion of 4:12 and the illustrations of the pattern $x + (x + 1)$.

22. Greidanus, *Preaching Christ from Ecclesiastes*, 213 footnote 27.

23. Ryken, *Ecclesiastes*, 188.

words unnecessarily. It seems better to keep each example distinct.[24]

The final illustration provides an interesting insight. Literally, the text reads, 'wickedness will not deliver its masters.' In other words, those who practice evil or wickedness have mastered its character and actions. Solomon avoids the argument that novices in evil have no power, but that those who excel through long practice might very well pull off a deliverance by means of wickedness. No, even evil's masters remain endangered, helpless, and subject to God's authority. All four of these illustrations add to the point of verse 7 and expand the picture of the inability of human beings to control their circumstances. The realms in the initial statement and the four illustrations include the future, climate, death, war, and salvation. In the most basic sense, all of these realms are outside mankind's control. Only God controls all of these things.

Solomon concludes this first section of chapter 8 by referring to his pursuit of wisdom regarding life 'under the sun' (v. 9). He has given his mind to every deed performed in this life by which people might exercise authority over someone else for ill. That comprises the same issue that he addresses in 7:20 and 29. Fallen humanity perverts the right ways of God and is incapable of true righteousness. Men and women are sinners. They tend to use the authority they do manage to gain in order to do evil against their fellow man. Fallen humanity cannot change, cannot deliver, cannot contravene the decrees of God – and, cannot avoid death. The 'wherein' of some translations (e.g., NASB) actually reads 'a time which' (HCSB, NKJV) or 'while' (RSV, NRSV). It is the same word that appears twenty-nine times in chapter 3 as well as in 8:5 and 6. The duration of life 'under the sun' constitutes a person's 'time' during which he or she might exercise any acquired authority.

From verses 1-8, Charles Swindoll summarizes five characteristics of a wise leader:

---

24. Brown, *Ecclesiastes*, 87, however, understands all four examples as references to the inability to avoid death: 'There is no 'discharge,' or privilege of substitution ... from the battle against death, and wickedness, most certainly, is no defense.' Eaton, *Ecclesiastes*, 120, argues for making each of the four examples distinct. However, the first he assigns the meaning of mastering one's spirit (not a reference to avoiding its departure).

- a clear mind (v. 1a),

- a cheerful disposition (v. 1b),

- a discreet mouth (vv. 2-4),

- keen judgment (vv. 5-7), and

- a humble spirit (v. 8).[25]

Readers wrestling with the interpretation of Ecclesiastes must take the opportunity to learn more about their own spiritual journey. Is Solomon the only individual to face the limitations of his wisdom? Does God expect only Solomon to model godly wisdom?

Being Wise in God's Throne Room (8:10-17)

Some commentators consider verse 10 the most difficult in Ecclesiastes.[26] Solomon speaks again of what he has seen (vv. 9, 10). He has observed wicked people being buried (cp. 7:1, 2). Those same wicked individuals dared to enter the 'holy place' (probably the Temple)[27] where they mingled with believers. They did not live up to the impressions they made while in the holy place. What good did it do them? They are dead, buried, and forgotten.[28] Their works, whether evil or good, appear to count as nothing. This is the ultimate meaning of 'evil will not deliver those who practice it' (v. 8d). They did not obtain a good reputation (7:1; cp. Prov. 10:7) and their fellow citizens (and fellow worshipers) soon forget them. 'This too is futility [hebel],' Solomon declares. This is the

---

25. Swindoll, *Living on the Ragged Edge*, 237-47.

26. Longman, *Ecclesiastes*, 218, 'certainty eludes every honest interpreter, even though the problems are often hidden behind smooth English translations.'

27. Whybray, *Ecclesiastes*, 135. Garrett prefers 'funeral' as a paraphrase for 'holy place;' *Proverbs, Ecclesiastes, Song of Songs*, 328-29 footnote 199; see, also, Gordis, *Koheleth*, 295, who identifies it with the cemetery. Hengstenberg, *Ecclesiastes*, 200, concludes that 'the holy' indicates 'ideal persons' (the righteous).

28. Commentators suggest a number of emendations for 'forgotten' in an attempt to eliminate the difficulty of speaking of the forgetting of the wicked as something negative, when it would seem to be a good thing. Thus, one emendation uses 'praised,' which a reader could more readily take as a cause for the frustration of the righteous; Garrett, *Proverbs, Ecclesiastes, Song of Songs*, 329 footnote 200; Longman, *Ecclesiastes*, 218-19. Another solution retains 'forgotten,' but inserts 'the righteous' as the object; Murphy, *Ecclesiastes*, 85. The contrast then rests between the wicked being buried with honor and the righteous being forgotten.

thirteenth time for this announcement.[29] The final occurrence will come in 8:14.

A well-known axiom asserts that 'the wheels of justice grind slowly.'[30] Because of the extra slow pace of the legal system, the law loses its power to dissuade people from evil. Solomon observes that people give themselves more fully to committing evil deeds when 'the sentence against an evil deed is not executed quickly' (v. 11). Deniers of Solomonic authorship for Ecclesiastes point out that Solomon, as king, had control over the pace of justice. Why complain about something over which he himself had control? First, Solomon did not make every legal decision with regard to every evil deed. Like all kings (and even Moses nearly 500 years earlier), he delegated authority in the lesser cases to administrators, judges, or leaders (see 5:8). Secondly, those leaders did not take an equal interest in expediting justice. Perhaps some were slowed in the process by accepting bribes (cp. 7:7). The lack of a uniform execution of justice provides the reality to which Solomon refers. All such cracks in the façade of justice come about because of the fallen nature of humanity.

In verse 12 Solomon notes that an evil person might have the opportunity to commit an act of evil 100 times (probably hyperbolic – refers to a large number of times) and still be allowed to live a long life. In the light of verse 11, it appears that he attributes to God the same delay in justice that is so evident in human courts of law. It is enough to cause discouragement,[31] but Solomon declares, 'still I know that it will be well for those who fear God, who fear Him openly' (literally, 'who become fearful before Him'). Notice the departure from the writer's usual 'I have seen.' This truth he knows by conviction and holds by faith.[32] As Ryken explains, 'He believes what he cannot see – that one day all will be well for everyone who lives in the fear of God.'[33] A true God-

29. This phrase ('this is *hebel*') occurs in 2:15, 19, 21, 23, 26; 4:4, 8, 16; 5:10 [Heb., 9]; 6:2, 9; 7:6; and 8:14.

30. Originally, the Greek philosopher Sextus Empiricus said, 'the mills of the gods grind slowly, but they grind small.'

31. 'Deferred justice encourages cynicism and moral havoc' (Estes, *Handbook on the Wisdom Books*, 354).

32. Eaton, *Ecclesiastes*, 123.

33. Ryken, *Ecclesiastes*, 196.

fearer lives with a full awareness of the omnipresence of the omniscient and omnipotent God. He or she goes through life more conscious of what God thinks or knows, rather than of what people might think or know.

An evil person's major problem consists in the lack of any fear of God (v. 13). A seeming contradiction focuses the reader's attention on verses 12 and 13. In the former, a sinner 'may lengthen his *life*,' but in the latter, the wicked 'will not lengthen his days.' Kidner, observing this conflict of concepts, implies that the first refers to physical life, but that the latter subtly raises the matter of an afterlife for godly individuals: 'This could mean that whereas the godly man has hope beyond the grave, the ungodly has none: however long postponed, death will be the end for him.'[34] The addition of the comparison, 'like a shadow,' probably refers to the way that shadows become exceedingly long late in the day – they seem to stretch nearly to the horizon. Barton takes that figure to indicate that 'sinners never reach the evening of life.'[35] Malachi 3:13–4:3 replicates these same themes:

- the seeming futility of serving God when the wicked appear to prosper (3:13-15),

- the contrast between those who fear God and those who do not (3:16-18), and

- the future judgment of the wicked (4:1-3).

The double reference to 'futility' (*hebel*) in verse 14 anchors Solomon's recapitulation of the testimony he wrote in 7:15. Life's inequities create an insoluble enigma. What God is doing 'under the sun' remains incomprehensible. Tidball summarizes verse 14 as follows:

> It is bad enough when human beings don't apply justice where they could. But, what is worse, life itself doesn't seem to help. It always seems biased in the wrong direction. Wicked people prosper and live healthily, and righteous people seem burdened and suffer. It's all so unfair! The parcels of retribution and reward have had their labels switched and have been delivered to the

---

34. Kidner, *A Time to Mourn*, 77. He refers to Psalms 49:14-15 and 73:18-20 for the same concept of an afterlife. Likewise, Eaton, *Ecclesiastes*, 123.

35. Barton, *Ecclesiastes*, 154; Longman, *Ecclesiastes*, 220.

wrong addresses. Fortunes and misfortune have been reversed and life has conspired to make it so.[36]

Verse 15 reveals the third *carpe diem* text declaring that life is the gift of God (see 2:24-26 and 5:18-20). The Hebrew word for 'I commended' may carry the meaning 'praise' (e.g., Ps. 63:3, 'my lips will praise You'). Its use conveys the concept of a strong recommendation.[37] Solomon nowhere commends enjoyment of life as an anesthetic to deaden the pain of inequity, injustice, and death. Instead, he focuses on the fact that human beings ought not waste their God-given joys by seeking to usurp the authority and the work of their Creator. Fretting over the brevity and seeming unfairness of life brings no joy, no peace, no rest, and no solution. God's wise bestowment of all things and His benevolent providence stand behind all that happens 'under the sun.' No individual can understand the ultimate reasons for what happens, because even the wisest is but a fool by comparison to the wisdom of God. We should not beat our 'heads against the wall trying to figure out life.'[38] It is pointless to remain continually vexed over our inability to explain injustice or to rid our lives of inequities.[39] Kaiser concludes that 'No God-fearer ought ever, nor does he ever need, to stoop to low means and obtain nothing but anxiety, sweat, and emptiness as a reward for all his work. Enjoyment is still in the hands of man's Creator and Redeemer.'[40] In his comments on verse 15, Wright reminds the believer of the continuity between Solomon's teaching and that of Jesus:

> The verses say much the same as Jesus said in the Sermon on the Mount. Do not let your life be burdened with anxiety; relaxed enjoyment comes through seeking first the kingdom of God and taking food, drink, and clothing from the hands of your Father (Matt. 6:25-34). So the Teacher refers to God-given work, God-given food and drink, and God-given joy. It is the realization of this that he commends.[41]

In the Sermon on the Mount, Jesus spoke of anxiety about the future (Matt. 6:34). Similarly, the Teacher recognizes the

---

36. Tidball, *That's Just the Way It Is*, 137.
37. Bartholomew, *Ecclesiastes*, 291.
38. Estes, *Handbook on the Wisdom Books*, 356.
39. Garrett, *Proverbs, Ecclesiastes, Song of Songs*, 330.
40. Kaiser, *Ecclesiastes*, 79.
41. Wright, 'Ecclesiastes,' 5:1181.

tendency toward worry of people who want to know what lies ahead (vv. 16-17).

Solomon reviews his pursuit of wisdom in verses 16-17 (cp. 1:13). He mentions sleep only twice in the book. The laborer obtains pleasant sleep (5:12 [Heb., 11]), but the search of wisdom could eliminate sleep and still not succeed (8:16). Interestingly, his earlier speech about laboring with wisdom (2:18-23) includes the observation that the mind of the laborer working 'with wisdom' (v. 21) has no rest even at night (v. 23). How much more the sleeplessness of the man pursuing wisdom itself.

The 'work of God' serves as the object of Solomon's observation (8:17; cp. 3:11, 14; 7:13, 29). However, human beings are incapable of discovering all of God's work 'under the sun.' Zophar asked Job a related question: 'Can you discover the depths of God? Can you discover the limits of the Almighty?' (Job 11:7). In the context of Solomon's musings, a substantial element in what the wise person seeks is a knowledge of the future (Eccles. 7:14), but it also involves what has already occurred in the past (7:24). Therefore, whether the search involves God's work in the past or the future, it will elude the searcher. The apostle Paul writes similarly when examining the mercy of God in Romans 11:33-36. 'How unsearchable are His judgments and unfathomable His ways!' (Rom. 11:33b). Paul's statement does not reflect skepticism, neither does Solomon's.[42]

Chapter 8's conclusion reverberates in the words of 1 Corinthians 1:20-25:

> **20** Where is the wise man? Where is the scribe? Where is the debater of this age? Has not God made foolish the wisdom of the world? **21** For since in the wisdom of God the world through its wisdom did not *come to* know God, God was well-pleased through the foolishness of the message preached to save those who believe. **22** For indeed Jews ask for signs and Greeks search for wisdom; **23** but we preach Christ crucified, to Jews a stumbling block and to Gentiles foolishness, **24** but to those who are the called, both Jews and Greeks, Christ the power of God

---

42. *Contra* Longman, *Ecclesiastes*, 223. Longman cites Lauha, *Kohelet*, 162, in identifying lack of divine revelation as the problem for the frustration of the writer of Ecclesiastes. This approach denies the revelatory nature of Ecclesiastes as the Word of God.

and the wisdom of God. **25** Because the foolishness of God is wiser than men, and the weakness of God is stronger than men.

Human wisdom cannot save anyone either from their inability to control their circumstances or from their inherited sinful nature. Only God's wisdom meets this task. God displays His wisdom in a person—the person of the Messiah Himself. The ultimate answer to Solomon's questions comes in the person and work of Jesus Christ. Ecclesiastes removes all claims to the salvific value of human wisdom. This book prepares the human heart for the greater message of redemption. No one can turn to the Redeemer until he or she first recognizes their own inability to do anything for themselves.

People must avoid deciding truth on the basis of experience. As Kelley so keenly observes, 'What God does, not what they experience, is all that matters. Man must set his sights not by his experience, whether good or bad, but by the God of the covenant.'[43] Such is the ultimate lesson Solomon draws from his search and his meditation. Thus the focus falls once again on the work of God, in direct contrast to the work of mankind. The final chapters of Ecclesiastes pick up from the message of 8:16-17 and point the reader toward God, the Maker or Creator, who alone controls life 'under the sun.'[44]

STUDY QUESTIONS

1. What produces greater graciousness and forgiveness in believers?

2. How should believers conduct themselves before government leaders?

3. Over what things in life do we have no control?

4. What are some biblical characteristics of wise leaders? Which of these characteristics does Ecclesiastes mention?

5. How does Solomon 'know' what he knows in verse 12?

6. What does fretting over inequities and injustices and inabilities say about one's relationship to his Creator?

---

43. Kelley, *The Burden of God*, 123.
44. Estes, *Handbook on the Wisdom Books*, 357.

9

Imperatives for Living Wisely

In conclusion, *the Preacher* determined
to fear God, obey God, and
enjoy life *(9:1–12:14)*, Part I

Whereas chapter 8 focuses on the work of God as one of its themes, chapter 9 returns to an emphasis on the human condition. Solomon mentions God only twice in chapter 9 (vv. 1 and 7). However, as Greidanus observes, those occurrences come 'at crucial junctures in his argument.'[1] As to the structure of chapter 9, Gordis distinguishes a literary pattern consisting of an inverted order of literary forms:[2]

- Verses 4-5 = prose
  - o   Verse 6 = rhythmic prose
    - ▪   Verses 7-9a = rhythmic poetry
  - o   Verses 9b-11 = rhythmic prose
- Verse 12 = prose

If this identification proves accurate, one would expect verses 7-9a to be the thematic core of the chapter. In fact, verses 7-9 present the most emphatic of the enjoyment (or, *carpe diem*) passages in the book.

In God's Hand (9:1)

The phraseology, 'I have taken … to my heart' (v. 1), occurs also in 1:13, 17; 8:9, and 16. The distribution demonstrates that

---

1. Greidanus, *Preaching Christ from Ecclesiastes*, 223.
2. Gordis, *Koheleth* , 302.

Solomon opens his discourse with this kind of statement and then repeats it in the second half of the book. The presence of the phraseology in 8:16 and 9:1 indicates a close association that provides a transition from chapter 8 to chapter 9. Similar phraseology appears in 7:2 and a negative form of it in 7:21 ('do not take seriously' literally reads, 'do not give your heart to'). The 'heart' involves his 'total consciousness – not solely intellectual reason, but experiential insight that has been gained through the avenues and alleys of emotional, sensual, physical and spiritual experience.'[3] Thus, Solomon applies more than his brain to his search for an explanation for life's paradoxes. That to which he applies himself in the search consists of 'all this,' which includes what has already been written as well as that which is yet ahead in the book[4] – in other words, the whole gamut of human existence and earthly life.

Nowhere else in the Hebrew Bible does 'explain' translate the Hebrew word Solomon uses in verse 1. The word for 'explanation' in 7:25 and 27 comes from a totally different root word. The word employed here occurs only one other time (3:18, 'tested'). nrsv and esv offer a better translation for 9:1 with 'examining it all, how the righteous and the wise and their deeds are in the hand of God.' Solomon reminds his readers of the reason for examining life in such detail and with such intensity. Yet, he does not focus his search on man apart from God or an awareness of the presence of God, because he recognizes that God is in control of 'the righteous and the wise and their deeds.'

Scripture pairs 'righteous' and 'wise' in only seven texts (Deut. 16:19; Prov. 9:9; 11:30; 23:24; Eccles. 7:16; 9:1; Hosea 14:9). Ecclesiastes 7:16-17 contrasts righteous and wise with wicked and foolish. The three texts in Proverbs juxtapose the two characteristics (righteous and wise) in synonymous parallelism, indicating that those who are righteous are wise and those who are wise are righteous. Such appears to be the understanding in the Law (Deut. 16:19) and in the prophets (Hosea 14:9). By stating that 'their deeds are in the hand of God,' Solomon reveals his conviction that the power of God controls the lives of the righteous/wise. His father, David, employed a similar

---

3. Fredericks, 'Ecclesiastes,' 81.
4. Bartholomew, *Ecclesiastes*, 299.

phraseology when faced with God's inescapable judgment on the nation of Israel: 'Let us now fall into the hand of the LORD for His mercies are great, but do not let me fall into the hand of man' (2 Sam. 24:14). The first enjoyment passage in Ecclesiastes (2:24) speaks of 'the hand of God' as the source of man's enjoyment of food, drink, and labor. Human beings do not exercise total control over their circumstances – they are not sovereign, God is. The righteous/wise, as servants (= slaves) of God, must recognize His Lordship and, like David, rest in His mercies even when facing the end of life 'under the sun' – death.

To what does 'love or hatred' refer in verse 1? Fredericks takes the view that these two actions relate to mankind's actions, not God's. His primary argument relates to the inclusio formed by the two words in verses 1 and 6. Verse 6 adds 'their zeal,' perhaps a reference to jealousy, making the overall reference mankind rather than God.[5] In other words, people have no clue regarding how others might receive them day by day. The wise and righteous encounter love in some situations, but hate in others. They have no prior knowledge of how people will treat them in the future.[6]

A different understanding of the meaning of 'love or hatred' arises with the Old Testament's association of God's love or hate with acceptance or rejection in Deuteronomy 21:15 and Malachi 1:2-3. In the light of such references, Ecclesiastes 9:1 would seem to refer to the unpredictability of God's favor. Such favor might be restricted to some form of prosperity.[7] Indeed, lack of favor usually indicates adversity of some sort. Since the deeds of righteous people 'are in the hand of God,' all His people are subject to Him.[8] With God's control in mind, Solomon speaks of the inability of people to know whether God's love or hate awaits them.[9] After all, divine control dominates the context, making it unlikely that the reference would be to human emotions.[10]

---

5. Fredericks, 'Ecclesiastes,' 206. See, also, Seow, *Ecclesiastes*, 298.

6. Eaton, *Ecclesiastes,* 125.

7. Reichart and Cohen, 'Ecclesiastes,' 2:87.

8. The following commentators opt for the divine view (as opposed to the human view): Bartholomew, *Ecclesiastes*, 299; Kaiser, *Ecclesiastes*, 94; Ryken, *Ecclesiastes*, 204; Longman, *Ecclesiastes*, 227.

9. Bartholomew, *Ecclesiastes*, 296, footnote 6.

10. Murphy, *Ecclesiastes*, 90.

'Anything awaits him' closes this first verse. Literally, the two Hebrew words read, 'the all before them.' The wording is ambiguous. Variety in the English versions reflects the translators' uncertainty:

- 'anything awaits him' (NASU, NASB)
- 'Everything that confronts them' (NRSV)
- 'Everything before them is vanity' (RSV – representing an addition to the text)
- '*by* anything *they see* before them' (NKJV)
- '*by* all *that is* before them' (KJV)
- 'all is before them' (NJPS, JPS, ASV)
- 'both are before him' (ESV)
- 'Everything lies ahead of them' (HCSB)
- 'no one knows what lies ahead' (NET – connecting the phrase more closely with what comes before it; cp. NIV)

Based upon the preceding statement regarding ignorance about whether one will encounter or receive love or hatred, the idea throughout the variety of translations is that the events yet to come in a person's life 'under the sun' remain unknown until they unfold in time. Meanwhile, the righteous and the wise will rest in the confidence that God controls what happens – He is sovereign.

The Reality of Death and the Urgency of Living (9:2-10)

Solomon continues his discourse with yet another very brief and enigmatic declaration, 'It is the same for all' (literally, 'The all just as for the all'). Does verse 2 continue with the thought of encountering love or hate? Should the reader associate verse 2 with verse 3, rather than with verse 1? Coming back-to-back with the close of verse 1, the two statements form a hinge. The repetition of 'the all' brings to mind the refrain that occurs throughout the book: 'All is vanity.'[11] Fredericks understands from this opening that every individual, regardless of their

---

11. See the discussion of the refrain at 1:2.

level of spiritual commitment (or lack thereof), falls prey to the fallen character of mankind.[12] Every individual will someday experience death – that is the universal condition faced by all human beings (v. 2). Solomon lists a number of examples:

- the righteous compared to the wicked
- the good and clean compared to the unclean[13]
- the person with a sacrifice compared to the person without a sacrifice
- the good person compared with the sinner
- the one who vows compared with the person who makes no vow

The last pair presents an interpretive challenge. Eaton understands the first as one who takes an oath by the Lord's name as part of promising allegiance to God's covenant. The opposite would be a person who avoids such loyalty to the divine covenant.[14] On the other side of the matter, Seow takes the first as the person who perjures himself or herself, not taking their oath seriously, while the second has a 'proper reverence for the seriousness of oaths.'[15] Eaton's view offers the better option, since it preserves the order of good before bad throughout all five sets of examples. The point is that everyone without exception faces death. Garrett, in considering the inevitability of death in everyone's life, expressess astonishment that people, knowing death is imminent, still 'fill their lives with the distractions of a thousand passions and squander what little time they have to immediate but insignificant worries.'[16] This is the very thought which Solomon will develop more fully in the coming chapters. He advises that everyone avoid the distractions, focus on what is important, and use the remainder of one's life wisely.

---

12. Fredericks, 'Ecclesiastes,' 207.

13. Provan, *Ecclesiastes, Song of Songs*, 180, mentions that some scholars emend the text here because of the disruption of the neat sets of pairs. Thus, some add 'and bad' to complete the pair begun by 'good.' However, as Provan explains, the combination 'good and clean' might be 'intended to clarify that it is not simply ritual cleanness to which Qohelet refers, but moral cleanness' (ibid.).

14. Eaton, *Ecclesiastes*, 125.

15. Seow, *Ecclesiastes*, 299.

16. Garrett, *Proverbs, Ecclesiastes, Song of Songs*, 331.

According to verse 3, the one fate, death itself, is an 'evil' that awaits everyone. In Hebrew, the meaning of 'evil' in such contexts comes within the semantic scope of 'misery.'[17] As he has in recent chapters, Solomon focuses on the depravity of mankind: 'Furthermore, the hearts of the sons of men are full of evil and insanity is in their hearts throughout their lives.' Malevolence and madness make a morbid mixture. Swindoll identifies this 'insanity' (or madness, cf. 1:17; 2:12; 7:25; 10:13) with the answers people give to 'hard questions, like: "Why did you walk away from your family?" Or, "How can you continue to live like that, knowing that it's wrong and that Scripture stands against such things?"'[18] As though to make certain the reader does not miss the message, Solomon brings the verse to a close by means of an abrupt ending that literally reads, 'and afterwards – to the dead!'[19] Death comes that way – abruptly.

The word 'hope' in verse 4 entails the concept of confidence, trust, or security (Old Testament writers use the same Hebrew root for 'trust' in texts like Ps. 37:3 and Prov. 31:11). This particular noun occurs only here and in 2 Kings 18:19 (parallel to Isa. 36:4). It does not look forward to something or wish for something, it speaks of the certitude one has about something that will happen.[20] Solomon's bold metaphor contrasting a live dog with a dead lion derives from the confidence shown by a lion in his domain (called to mind by 'hope,' better understood as confidence). Cringing and cowering street curs exercise greater confidence than a dead lion. The two animals typify the two extremes of wisdom and folly (Prov. 26:11), power (Prov. 30:30) and weakness, the majestic and the lowly (1 Sam. 17:43).[21] So, one advantage of the living is that they know they will die.[22] Kaiser identifies three objects of the hope mankind possesses while alive: (1) 'hope of preparation for meeting God,' (2) 'hope of living significantly,' and (3) 'hope of doing something to the glory of God before all men personally face Him as 12:14 warns.'[23] In view of the meaning of certitude, a slight alteration

---

17. Provan, *Ecclesiastes, Song of Songs*, 181.
18. Swindoll, *Living on the Ragged Edge*, 280.
19. Whybray, *Ecclesiastes*, 141. See, also, Longman, *Ecclesiastes*, 227.
20. Seow, *Ecclesiastes*, 300.
21. Brown, *Ecclesiastes*, 92.
22. Murphy, *Ecclesiastes*, 92.
23. Kaiser, *Ecclesiastes*, 97.

of Kaiser's three hopes might adhere more closely to the text: (1) the certitude of meeting God, (2) the certitude that it is significant how one lives, and (3) the certitude of God's glory standing as that which each must pursue 'under the sun.'

The dead know nothing of life under the sun and gain no more reward than what they have already gained during life (v. 5). In fact, they are forgotten 'under the sun.' The association of reward with being forgotten incorporates assonance in a word play (or, pun) in the Hebrew. 'Reward' is the word *sakar* while 'memory' is *zeker* from the root *zakar*.[24] The word play may heighten a sense of reversal.[25] The expected reward (or, wages) for a lifetime of labor does not consist of being remembered after one is dead. These verses do not deny the existence of an afterlife. Instead, they insist on the fact that a person can only enjoy God's 'under the sun'-gifts in this life.[26] Now is the time to enjoy the reward of a lifetime of labor.

Everyone's love, hate, and zeal perish from the earth at death (v. 6). Life will continue on without them. Their lot is no longer cast in this world. History will unfold 'under the sun,' but those who are dead no longer appear on its stage. They no longer participate in the events that mark the passing of time and the advancements of the human race. 'Share' or 'portion' in the English translations represents a word used for 'lot' (*cheleq*). It occurs in 2:10 ('reward'), 21 ('legacy'); 3:22 ('lot'); 5:18, 19 ('reward' in both); 9:6 ('share'), 9 ('reward'); and 11:2 ('portion'). A review of its occurrences confirms that one's 'lot/reward/portion' consists of 'the measure of joy and satisfaction that comes through one's daily activities ... found not in self-centred pleasures (2:1-11) but only when taken as the gift of God (3:22; 5:19).'[27] Brown notes that, according to Ecclesiastes, wisdom 'is the awareness of life's ephemeral span ... a knowledge that leads to unpretentious reverence and even resilient joy.'[28] The wise person rightly understands that he or she only lives once. The opportunities and joys of this life will not happen again – and the time is short.

---

24. Gordis, *Koheleth*, 305. Gordis points out that such word plays are not possible in Aramaic, so that argues for the originality of the Hebrew text (ibid.).

25. Watson, *Classical Hebrew Poetry*, 246.

26. Cf. Eaton, *Ecclesiastes*, 126-27.

27. Ibid., 127.

28. Brown, *Ecclesiastes*, 93.

Joy refrains in Ecclesiastes manifest a growing crescendo from the first (2:24-26) to the last (11:7-10). Within this refrain comparison ('nothing better,' 2:24) gives way to command ('eat,' 'drink,' 'enjoy'). The enjoyments include food, drink, work, clothing, oil for comfort, and marriage.[29] From the context, it would appear that Solomon addresses the righteous and wise (vv. 1, 2; cp. 2:26; 3:12; 7:26). He issues 'an urgent summons to action'[30] for the righteous to delight in God's gifts 'under the sun.' The very first command is 'Go!' Greidanus fills out the meaning of this initial imperative by declaring, 'It's a wakeup call. There's no time to waste. Stop your complaining! Stop nursing your anger! Stop brooding about your problems! Get over your anxiety!'[31] After all, as Kaiser asks, 'Why should anyone who truly fears God have the joy of life stolen out from under him because of the unresolved perplexities still remaining in the partially disclosed plan of God?'[32] That which Solomon proposes does not reflect an earth-bound viewpoint characteristic of a pre-Christian approach to spiritual life. His advice coincides with the early church's behavior (Acts 2:46) and the apostle Paul's injunctions (Phil. 4:4; 1 Tim. 4:1-4).

Wearing white garments (v. 8) indicates the attire of celebration and comfort. According to Fredericks, white clothing is cooler.[33] The fragrant oil calls to mind welcome hospitality (Ps. 23:5), unity and blessing (Ps. 133:1-3), and gladness (Isa. 61:3).

Verse 9 enjoins the enjoyment of marital bliss with one's wife (cp. Prov. 5:15-19). Some commentators point out that the translation 'the woman' might obscure the grammar of the Hebrew text, which may be translated 'a woman.' On the basis of this grammatical observation, Fredericks interprets the command as applicable to showing discretion regarding one's choice of companion prior to marriage, rather than life with a woman after marriage.[34] Leupold believes that the absence of the definite article suggests that the writer directs

---

29. Garrett reduces these six areas to three: feasting, marital relationships, and occupation (Garrett, *Proverbs, Ecclesiastes, Song of Songs*, 331).
30. Eaton, *Ecclesiastes*, 127.
31. Greidanus, *Preaching Christ from Ecclesiastes*, 232.
32. Kaiser, *Ecclesiastes*, 100.
33. Fredericks, 'Ecclesiastes,' 209.
34. Ibid.

the instruction to the unmarried who should marry in order to enjoy God's gift.[35] One rabbinic interpretation understands this to mean that a man needs to take advantage of the pleasure of a woman's company. Another rabbinic interpretation, however, insists on the intent of matrimony.[36] Other passages of the Old Testament do use the word 'woman' without the definite article in contexts that demand the meaning of 'wife' (e.g., Gen. 20:12; 21:21; 24:7; Ruth 4:13; 1 Sam. 18:27). Note that the object of 'enjoy' is 'life,' not 'woman.' The phrase 'with a woman' (or, 'with a wife') modifies the verb adverbially, expressing the condition of companionship. A partnership exists through which to enjoy life – that of a man with a woman. Without her, a man cannot experience the fullness of the God-designed life.[37]

Other documents from the ancient Near East echo these same elements of joy in life. Brown constructs a 'synoptic comparison' between the Epic of Gilgamesh (ca. 2000 B.C.) and Ecclesiastes 9:7-10.[38]

Enjoyment	Epic of Gilgamesh	Ecclesiastes 9
Food & Drink in Celebration (Contentment)	Thou, Gilgamesh, let full be thy belly, Make thou merry by day and by night. Of each day make thou a feast of rejoicing, Day and night dance thou and play!	7 Go *then*, eat your bread in happiness and drink your wine with a cheerful heart; for God has already approved your works.
Clothing & Comfort	Let thy garments be sparkling fresh, Thy head be washed; bathe thou in water.	8 Let your clothes be white all the time, and let not oil be lacking on your head.

35. Leupold, *Ecclesiastes*, 215.

36. Reichart and Cohen, 'Ecclesiastes,' 2:91.

37. Fredericks, 'Ecclesiastes,' 210.

38. Brown, *Ecclesiastes*, 94. For the translation of the old Akkadian text, see E. A. Speiser, trans., 'The Epic of Gilgamesh,' in *Ancient Near Eastern Texts*, 2nd ed., ed. by James B. Pritchard (Princeton, N.J.: Princeton University Press, 1955), 90. Eaton identifies the three verses in the following general categories: contentment (v. 7), comfort (v. 8), and companionship (v. 9) (Eaton, *Ecclesiastes*, 129).

Enjoyment	Epic of Gilgamesh	Ecclesiastes 9
Marriage (Companionship)	... Let thy spouse delight in thy bosom! For this is the task of [mankind]!	9 Enjoy life with the woman whom you love all the days of your fleeting life which He has given to you under the sun; for this is your reward in life and in your toil in which you have labored under the sun.

No knowledge of Gilgamesh need be presupposed for poets or sages living in the ancient Near East who might employ a similar or even an identical list. Solomon observes these on his own without the necessity of borrowing from extant literature. The modern interpreter can identify the author's intent in Ecclesiastes without recourse to the Epic of Gilgamesh.[39] Noteworthy for its absence in the Epic of Gilgamesh, man's work or labor stands out in Ecclesiastes. Work forms a significant aspect of God-given joys. Solomon does not treat labor as either a curse or an option. Scripture stresses

- the dignity of labor as part of God's design from creation (Gen. 2:15; Eccles. 9:7)

- the necessity of work in a fallen world (Gen. 3:17-19; Ps. 104:14, 23; 2 Thess. 3:10-12)

- the essentiality of the cycle of work and rest (Exod. 20:9-10; 23:12; Eccles. 5:12)

- the festivity arising from receiving the fruit of one's labors (Exod. 23:16; Deut. 16:13-15; Eccles. 3:13; 9:7-9)

- the spirituality of work guided by the Spirit of God (Exod. 31:3-5; 36:2-8; Rom. 16:3, 6, 9, 12; Eph. 4:12; Col. 3:23)

- the community for which work provides (Deut. 24:19; Prov. 31:10-31; Eccles. 4:9; Acts 20:35; Eph. 4:28)

- the profitability of labor (Prov. 14:23; Luke 10:7)

39. Whybray, *Ecclesiastes*, 144.

- the prosperity that results from labor with God's blessing (Deut. 30:9; Ps. 90:17; Prov. 13:11)

Verse 7 concludes with the thought that God has 'approved' mankind's labors. 'Approved' translates a Hebrew term (*ratsah*) that refers to divine acceptance, divine will, and divine favor. As such, the statement must include the concept that the enjoyment of the divine gifts in life 'under the sun' belongs preeminently to those who do the divine will, who please God, who are recipients of His gracious favor. In other words, 'God approves only that which is in conformity to his will and character.'[40] No one receives a *carte blanche* to pursue any fleshly enjoyment he or she desires. The imperatives in these verses direct the believer to pursue only those things that God identifies as having received His stamp of approval. 'Already' might be taken as 'long ago' – perhaps a reference to creation and God's primeval blessing upon man and the gifts of wife, food, and clothing.[41]

'Enjoy life' (v. 9) reads literally as 'See life' (cp. 2:1 where 'Enjoy yourself' is literally 'See good' and 3:13 where the translation follows a more literal rendering, 'sees good'). 'See,' Whybray points out, sometimes carries 'the sense of "experience" – e.g. "see famine" (Jer. 5:12), "see good" (Job 7:7); and, in this book, "see sleep" (8:16).'[42] Verse 9 continues with words and phrases that characterize the entire Solomonic treatise: 'fleeting life,' 'He has given,' 'under the sun,' 'your reward,' 'in life,' 'your toil,' and 'labored.' Such clustering of concepts draws the reader's attention back to Solomon's original question, 'What advantage does man have in all his work which he does under the sun?' (1:3). The six enjoyments in 9:7-9 represent the advantages. Note, also, the references to the individual's attitude or manner of enjoyment: 'in happiness,' 'with a cheerful heart,' experiencing God's approval, and a woman 'whom you love.'

Verse 10 takes up the thought of verses 4-6 and anticipates the conclusion to Ecclesiastes in 11:1–12:8.[43] Sheol does not offer opportunities for labor, activity, planning, applying knowledge,

---

40. Daniel J. Estes, *Handbook on the Wisdom Books*, 359.

41. Cf. Greidanus, *Preaching Christ from Ecclesiastes*, 233. Provan, *Ecclesiastes, Song of Songs*, 182 footnote 1, declares that the writer says 'that those who eat and drink joyfully may be sure (always) that this is the will of God, for already "God favors what you do."'

42. Whybray, *Ecclesiastes*, 144.

43. Fredericks, 'Ecclesiastes,' 210.

or increasing wisdom. Solomon identifies divine gifts which one can only use or enjoy 'under the sun:' eating and drinking (2:24), wisdom (2:26), knowledge (2:26), joy (2:26), knowledge and search for eternity (3:11), work (3:13), physical life (5:18; 8:15; 9:9), and wealth (5:19). As Tidball remarks, 'Let us use them! If we don't use them here, it is certain that we won't get the opportunity to use them in the hereafter.'[44] Even greater yet is the fact that 'If we do not enjoy God's gifts, we dishonor the Giver.'[45] First Corinthians 10:31 enjoins believers to 'do all to the glory of God,' while eating and drinking – indeed, in 'whatever you do.' The psalmist likewise exhorts believers to 'rejoice and be glad' in the day that God Himself has made (Ps. 118:24).

In this context, Sheol seems to indicate merely the grave and the cessation of all bodily functions characteristic of a living person. Does this indicate that the future life of the righteous beyond the sun does not involve such activities? No. Solomon speaks of what one can do in life 'under the sun.' He does not deny the immortality of mankind nor does he eliminate the existence of the activities of departed spirits, whether in a place of the righteous dead or a place of the unrighteous dead. Solomon focuses on entering into life 'under the sun' wholeheartedly. Life is short; life is fleeting. Do not waste it.

Life's Inescapable Ironies (9:11-12)

Having previously itemized five sets of contrasting individuals in verse 2, Solomon now lists five ironies in verse 11:

- the swift might not win the race

- the warriors might not win the battle

- the wise might not obtain food (or, earn a living)

- the discerning might not gain wealth

- the skilled might not find favor

All such ironies occurring in life 'under the sun' contribute to its unpredictability.[46] Each irony states the negative first, in order to emphasize it. The word for 'swift' (v. 11) occurs only here in

---

44. Tidball, *That's Just the Way It Is*, 157.
45. Greidanus, *Preaching Christ from Ecclesiastes*, 237.
46. Fredericks, 'Ecclesiastes,' 212.

the Hebrew Bible. The term means 'running' or 'race.' In other words, there is no guarantee that the swiftest individual in a race or a chase will be the victor (cp. Amos 2:14-15; see, also, Pss. 33:17; 147:10; Prov. 21:31). Each of the statements emphasizes the same kind of outcome. The thrust of these ironies leads the reader to consider that God is the One in control of all such outcomes. Therefore, Delitzsch cites 1 Samuel 17:47, Psalm 33:16-17, and Romans 9:16 to demonstrate that God alone provides those things that people value: wisdom, victory, food, wealth, favor, influence, and success.[47]

'Time and chance' (v. 11) might express the idea of 'timely events' by means of a hendiadys (using two words to express one concept).[48] 'Chance' represents an unhappy translation,[49] since it refers to 'a happening,' not to anything like luck or fortune. The Hebrew word for 'time' is not the same one highlighted in chapter 3. This word occurs only here and in the Solomonic history at 1 Kings 5:4 (Hebrew, v. 18, 'misfortune' is literally 'evil occurrence'). In both contexts the term 'chance' takes on the negative connotation of something like the English word 'accident.'

Solomon makes the point that no one can know the timing for life's ironic moments (v. 12). People can be trapped by circumstances just like a fish caught by a net or a bird caught by a cleverly designed trap.[50] 'An evil time' seems by context to refer to more than just death – other calamities, disasters, and troubles may be included.[51] Trouble never comes at a good time – neither does death. A frugal man planning for his retirement, can leave life 'under the sun' without the opportunity to enjoy it (cp. Luke 12:16-21). A king can go to battle and become a casualty at a distance by means of an arrow intended for one of his soldiers (2 Chron. 18:33-34). The chores for getting one's house in order before leaving this life might never be completed. Something will always be left incomplete, absent, lost, or never started. Longman concludes that 'human inability drives Paul to divine grace, while

---

47. Delitzsch, *Song of Songs and Ecclesiastes*, 365.

48. Fredericks, 'Ecclesiastes,' 203.

49. Provan, *Ecclesiastes, Song of Songs*, 183 footnote 2, agrees.

50. The Hebrew word for 'snare' (*pach*) displays onomatopoeia, since the word for the snare mimics the sound of the trap snapping shut. See the usage of the same word to climax a threefold series of assonant nouns in Isa. 24:17-18 ('terror' = *pachad*, 'pit' = *pachat*, and 'snare' = *pach*). That final, shortened word resonates with the ultimate finality of the trap snapping shut on the individual – there is no escape from divine judgment.

51. Eaton, *Ecclesiastes*, 130-31.

Qohelet ends up in frustration.'[52] However, Ecclesiastes ultimately reveals that Solomon's frustration at this point in his discourse is a temporary reaction, not a permanent one. His seeming frustration turns to a conscious awareness of the Creator's presence (12:1), the reality of God's future judgment (11:9; 12:14), and the return of man's spirit to God Himself (12:7). The fact that God will judge the good as well as the bad (12:14) indicates that God will make some form of distinction between good and evil beyond the sun.

A Lesson from History (9:13-18)

Wisdom forms the theme of the final section of this chapter. The topic surfaces in verses 1 ('wise men'), 10 ('wisdom'), and 11 ('the wise' – forming an inclusion for vv. 1-11). Then, in verses 13-18 'wise' and 'wisdom' occur a total of seven times. A specific event involving a besieged city and a wise citizen (vv. 14-15) occupies a key role in the section. On the one hand, the outcome follows the pattern of 2:16, 4:13-16, and 9:5 – people will eventually forget the wise and their exploits (cp. Pss. 31:12; 41:5). In this particular case, the city was small (v. 14), making the forgetting of one of its more significant citizens all the more poignant (cp. v. 5).[53] On the other hand, wisdom does produce results, including the saving of lives even during a time of war (cp. 7:12; Prov. 20:18; 21:22; 24:5-6). A similar situation arose at Abel Beth-Maacha where a wise woman succeeded in delivering her city, but her name is unrecorded and unremembered (2 Sam. 20:14-22) – a fitting example for Solomon's point.

'Large siegeworks' (v. 14) represents the same Hebrew word appearing in verse 12 where it is translated 'net.' By using the same word, Solomon intentionally associates the siege of the city with those adversities that might suddenly come upon either an individual or a community.[54] Provan points to the account of the Assyrian king Sennacherib that describes his siege of Jerusalem in the time of King Hezekiah as shutting Hezekiah up in 'his royal residence, like a bird in a cage.'[55]

---

52. Longman, *Ecclesiastes*, 232.

53. Huwiler, 'Ecclesiastes,' 212.

54. Bartholomew, *Ecclesiastes*, 313.

55. Provan, *Ecclesiastes, Song of Songs*, 192. For the Assyrian record, see Mordechai Cogan, 'Sennacherib's Siege of Jerusalem (2.119B),' in *The Context of Scripture*, 3 vols., ed. by William W. Hallo and K. Lawson Younger, Jr. (Leiden, The Netherlands: Brill, 2003), 2:303.

The margin of NASU notes that 'he delivered' could be translated alternatively as 'he might have delivered' (v. 15). Thus, some commentators prefer to see the verb as speaking of a hypothetical situation.[56] However, the context appears to favor an actual past event, since Solomon claims to have observed the situation he describes (v. 13).

The story about the wise man draws out four conclusions: (1) Wisdom proves superior to might (v. 16a), (2) people do not always respect or honor wisdom (v. 16b), (3) powerful people can make it difficult to listen to the voice of wisdom (v. 17), and (4) no matter how superior wisdom might be, one foolish act by a sinner can destroy the good results of wisdom.[57]

What are 'the words of the wise heard in quietness' (v. 17)? Does the statement refer to the words being spoken in quietness or calm ('heard in quietness'), or does it mean that those who hear the words should listen in quietness, without interruption ('in quietness is heard')?[58] The parallel ('the shouting of a ruler among fools') favors the first understanding. Other commentators prefer to take the word 'heard' in the sense of 'hearable' or 'worth hearing.'[59] Thus, the words of the wise spoken quietly or calmly possess value and ought to be taken seriously.[60] The wise also face disrespect among their fellow citizens (cp. Matt. 13:57; Mark 6:4; Luke 4:24; John 4:44).

Verse 18b reminds readers that even wisdom can be foiled: 'but one sinner destroys much good.' 'Often,' writes Barton, 'the brilliant plans of a leader, faithfully followed by many, have been brought to nothing by the stupid incompetence of one man.'[61] In the biblical account of Israel's entry into Canaan and the disastrous defeat at Ai, the example of Achan's disobedience provides just such an occurrence (Josh. 7:1-26).

At this point in the book, Kidner observes that Solomon 'has made his case against our self-sufficiency.'[62] Indeed, he has 'finished his work of demolition. The site has been cleared:

---

56. E.g., Gordis, *Koheleth*, 309, 'Most probably Koheleth is inventing a *typical* case (or generalizing) in order to illustrate his point, rather than invoking a specific historical incident.'

57. Cf. Kaiser, *Ecclesiastes*, 105.

58. Eaton, *Ecclesiastes*, 132 footnote 2. See, also, Longman, *Ecclesiastes*, 236.

59. Whybray, *Ecclesiastes*, 149.

60. Cf. Longman, *Ecclesiastes*, 236.

61. Barton, *Ecclesiastes*, 165-66.

62. Kidner, *A Time to Mourn*, 86.

he can turn to building and planting.'[63] Kidner lays out the closing chapters as reminders to be

- sensible (chapt. 10)
- bold (11:1-6)
- joyful (11:7-10)
- godly (chapt. 12)[64]

STUDY QUESTIONS

1. In what ways does God reveal His control over your life?

2. Why do we fill our lives with distractions and squander what little time we have on insignificant worries?

3. What other hard questions can you think of besides, 'Why did you walk away from your family?'

4. What is the significance to the revelation that 'God has already approved your works' (9:7)?

5. In what ways can Christians enjoy God's gifts 'under the sun'?

6. How can we prepare ourselves and our families for our inevitable departure from life 'under the sun'?

---

63. Ibid., 87.
64. Ibid.

10

A Final Reflection about Folly

In conclusion, *the Preacher* determined
to fear God, obey God, and
enjoy life *(9:1–12:14)*, Part 2

Having discoursed on the nature and examples of wisdom (9:10-18), Solomon turns to its opposite, foolishness in chapter 10. The first verse of the chapter picks up where chapter 9 leaves off – with a comparative statement regarding wisdom and foolishness. In 9:18 he uses the 'better than' type of proverbial statement to bring out the contrast between the success of wisdom and the destruction of good by foolishness. In 10:1, an illustrative proverb depicts dead flies corrupting the perfumer's oil. In general, chapter 10 reveals that the wisdom literature topic of the *two ways* (e.g., Ps. 1 contrasts the way of the righteous with the way of the wicked) applies to nations as much as to individuals.[1]

Recognizing Fools (10:1-4)
Whereas 9:18 refers to a community situation in which one sinner destroys what is good, 10:1 looks only at an individual situation.[2] The phrase 'dead flies' could mean 'deadly flies' (literally, 'flies of death;' cp. Ps. 7:13 [Heb. 14], 'deadly weapons'

---

1. Bartholomew, *Ecclesiastes*, 327.
2. Eaton, *Ecclesiastes*, 133.

literally, 'weapons of death'). However, the proverb does not focus on their deadliness, but on their effect on the perfumed oil.[3] Since that is the obvious intent of the author, some commentators believe that it means 'dead flies.'[4] Gordis, implementing the analogy of 2 Samuel 19:28 (Heb. 29; NRSV, 'doomed to death'), prefers 'dying flies' or 'flies about to die.'[5] Flies were persistent pests in the ancient Near East. Landing on the surface of perfumed oil might result in their entanglement and death. The dead flies would spoil the oil.[6] The writer actually verbalizes the action of the flies in the oil ('make stink') with two separate Hebrew verbs without the conjunction 'and' to connect them. Literally, the text reads, 'makes stink makes bubble up' or 'causes stench pours forth.'[7] That is, when someone opens the bottle of perfumed oil, the foul smell pours out of it, overwhelming the senses. Since ancient peoples used such oils to disguise the smell of decaying bodies (cp. 2 Chron. 16:14), the picture here might be that the oil itself exudes a fouler stench than even a decaying corpse.[8]

Eaton explains that the fool's 'small mistake makes the smell of his folly greater than the fragrance of his wisdom.'[9] The truth thus conveyed is that a little thing can bring about unacceptable results. Other ways to express the proverb include: 'an ounce of folly can destroy a ton of wisdom;'[10] 'it takes far less to ruin something than to create it;'[11] 'it is easier to make a stink than to create sweetness;'[12] or, 'wisdom is acquired at great expense … but stupidity comes easy.'[13]

Yet another contrasting proverb opposes wisdom and foolishness (v. 2). Literally, the verse reads, 'A wise man's heart is at his right hand and a fool's heart is at his left hand' (or, 'A wise man's heart is to his right and a fool's heart is to his left'). Translators handle the text in a variety of ways in the English versions:

---

3. Ibid., 133 footnote 1.
4. Murphy, *Ecclesiastes*, 97.
5. Gordis, *Koheleth*, 314.
6. Barton, *Ecclesiastes*, 166.
7. The second verb could mean 'ferment' (Longman, *Ecclesiastes*, 238).
8. Provan, *Ecclesiastes, Song of Songs*, 194.
9. Eaton, *Ecclesiastes*, 133.
10. Adapted from Murphy, *Ecclesiastes*, 100.
11. Kidner, *A Time to Mourn*, 88.
12. Ibid.
13. Kelley, *The Burden of God*, 135.

- 'A wise man's heart *is* at his right hand,
  But a fool's heart at his left' (NKJV, KJV).

- 'A wise man's understanding is at his right hand;
  but a fool's understanding at his left' (JPS).

- 'The heart of the wise inclines to the right,
  but the heart of a fool to the left' (NRSV, RSV, NIV).

- 'A wise man's heart inclines him to the right,
  but a fool's heart to the left' (ESV).

- 'A wise man's mind tends toward the right hand,
  a fool's toward the left' (NJPS).

- 'A wise man's heart *directs him* toward the right,
  but the foolish man's heart *directs him*
      toward the left' (NASU, NASB).

- 'A wise person's good sense protects him,
  but a fool's lack of sense leaves him vulnerable' (NET).

- 'The sage's heart leads him aright,
  the fool's leads him astray' (NJB).

- 'A wise person chooses the right road;
  a fool takes the wrong one' (NLT).

All of these translations furnish the same basic concept: the wise person tends to or goes to the 'right,' but the fool to the opposite. The 'right' (or, 'right hand') speaks of the correct route – a road to favor, while the 'left' speaks of the path of error – a road to disfavor and rejection (v. 2; cp. Gen. 48:13-14; Matt. 25:32-34). This concept produces the English word 'sinister,' which originates from the Latin word for 'left hand' (*sinistra*). Note that the text does not speak of the feet and walking, but of the heart and its inclination. The heart represents the inner person. The wise person possesses a mind attuned to the eternity that God has placed within it (3:11). The foolish person, however, yields to the evil within (cp. 8:11 and 9:3). The axiom approximates that in 2:14a ('The wise man's eyes are in his head, but the fool walks in darkness').

More than direction discloses the foolish person, however. People can discern what sort of person someone is just by watching him walk along a road (v. 3). 'His sense is lacking' literally reads, 'his mind is lacking.' In other words, a fool exhibits an inner deficiency through his or her behavior (cp. Prov. 12:23; 13:16). The fool speaks loudly, behaves arrogantly, ignores the rights and needs of others, and rebels against spiritual things.[14] Solomon had learned to discern the nature of people by how they spoke and behaved.

'Ruler' (*moshel*) in verse 4 does not limit the reference to kings, but allows expansion to multiple levels of governing (cf. 2 Chron. 23:20; Eccles. 9:17; Jer. 51:46).[15] This verse brings to mind prior instructions regarding wise behavior in the royal court. Solomon advises remaining calm and collected even when a government leader expresses or displays anger (cp. 9:17), because a calm response prevents unwise words or actions (cp. Prov. 15:1; 16:14; 25:15). 'Do not abandon' represents the first of only three direct instructions in chapter 10 (cf. v. 20, which says twice 'do not curse') and all three are negative. Kidner applies the proverb to 'the huff.' He suggests avoiding self-inflicted damage, 'for while it may feel magnificent to "resign your post" (NEB), ostensibly on principle but actually in a fit of pride, it is in fact less impressive, more immature, than it feels.'[16] The circumstances in verse 4 differ from those in 8:3, so the advice varies accordingly.[17]

An Upside-Down World (10:5-7)

Solomon introduces the next section with yet another report of his observations.[18] The only remaining occurrence of 'I have seen' in the book comes in this same section (10:7). These two references bracket verses 5-7 with 'I have seen.' The 'evil' (cp. 5:13; 6:1) that Solomon has seen 'under the sun' refers to something that is not good – it is improper, disruptive, unjust, or even

---

14. Cf. Eaton, *Ecclesiastes*, 134.

15. Murphy, *Ecclesiastes*, 101.

16. Kidner, *A Time to Mourn*, 89-90.

17. Krüger, *Qoheleth*, 183, discusses the options for understanding verse 4 as a call for opportunistic behavior toward the ruler – 'If the ruler's displeasure rises against you, do not give up your place! For calmness covers up great shortcomings (that is, undoes them or prevents them).' In addition to this call, there could be a critique – 'Indeed, calmness allows room for great shortcomings.' Or, as a call for 'civil courage' – '(Even) if the ruler's displeasure rises against you, do not give up your viewpoint! Your calmness can prevent great shortcomings.'

18. See 1:14; 2:13, 24; 3:10, 16, 22; 4:1, 4, 7, 15; 5:13, 18; 6:1; 7:15; 8:9, 10, 17; 9:11, 13.

harmful. This particular impropriety occurs within the realm of government. A comparative sense ('like an error') seems not to fit the context well. Therefore, some versions render the phrase 'as it were' (RSV, ESV) or even omitting any form of 'as' or 'like' (HCSB, 'There is an evil I have seen under the sun, even an error ...'). The meaning could also be 'indeed an error.'[19] 'Error' refers to a 'thoughtless, culpable sort of mistake.'[20] An administrative oversight results in placing exceedingly inept people in positions of high responsibility and power.

The 'ruler' (*shalit*) in this case does not specifically designate a king any more than *moshel* in verse 4. *Shalit* is related to the word 'sultan.' Interestingly, Moses employs both words to describe Joseph's role in Egypt (Gen. 42:6, *shalit*; 45:8, *moshel*). The individual can be anyone in government leadership who is subordinate to the king (or pharaoh). Although Leupold seeks to identify the 'ruler' with God,[21] that attempt fails to satisfy the context both with regard to the individuals Solomon identifies and with regard to the fact that he identifies an 'evil' with regard to the behavior of the ruler. Greidanus warns against linking 'ruler' with God, because 'one must be careful not to identify as metaphors words that make good sense when taken literally.'[22]

Verse 6 specifies the particular governmental situation or circumstance. Too many fools sit in places of leadership, while 'rich men sit in humble places' (v. 6). Equally topsy-turvy are those governments in which slaves move around on horseback and princes walk like slaves (v. 7). In the cultural environment of ancient Israel, the common citizen did not own a horse. Normally, only the royalty, nobility, and the military used equestrian transport (1 Kings 5:6).[23] Proverbs 19:10

---

19. Gordis, *Koheleth*, 319; Bartholomew, *Ecclesiastes*, 318. Or, 'entirely an error,' Whybray, *Ecclesiastes*, 152; or, 'an error indeed,' Longman, *Ecclesiastes*, 241.

20. Fredericks, 'Ecclesiastes,' 221.

21. Leupold, *Ecclesiastes*, 235. See, also, Huwiler, 'Ecclesiastes,' 214 and Hengstenberg, *Ecclesiastes*, 225.

22. Greidanus, *Preaching Christ from Ecclesiastes*, 243.

23. Seow, *Ecclesiastes*, 315: 'Foreign to the Levant, horses were very expensive to acquire and maintain. Hence, they were used largely for military purposes.... Donkeys and camels were ordinarily used for transportation of ordinary citizens, whereas horses were used to carry only kings and nobles (see Esth 6:8-9; 2 Chron. 25:28). Ownership of horses was a mark of wealth and power (cf. Deut. 17:16). Horses were a status symbol.'

addresses just such a topsy-turvy situation: 'Luxury is not fitting for a fool; much less for a slave to rule over princes' (cp. Prov. 30:21-23). Such conditions in government illustrate the reality of the uncertain aspect of life: 'things do not turn out the way one expects' – even if wisdom is present.[24] Political realities are often tangled. No one knows when one official will fall from favor and another, very different individual, will rise to power.

Comparing Solomon's observations (vv. 5-7) with Hannah's song (1 Sam. 2:7-8) demonstrates that wisdom instruction in proverbs refers to general truths that might not apply in every situation. Solomon himself speaks of circumstances in which he prefers a wise young king to a foolish old king (4:13-16). The elevation of a slave or a poor man to a position of political power can also testify 'to the power of God's "revolutionary" ways.'[25] Citizens cannot know whether God has purposefully produced the reversal of political roles. The sinfulness of man might have brought about the situation, but it might also be the result of the sovereign God's guiding hand. Note that Solomon does not advocate instigating a counter-revolution. Instead, he instructs the godly citizen to:

1) continue on as before without leaving any governmental position (v. 4),

2) be an observer like Solomon himself (vv. 5, 7),

3) behave wisely, taking proper precautions even for daily labors (vv. 8-10),

4) speak with grace and avoid loquaciousness (vv. 12-14),

5) remember that the future cannot be known (v. 14),

6) be diligent, not lazy (v. 18),

7) pay attention to the normal enjoyments and necessities of life (v. 19), and

8) do not speak disrespectfully of those in authority (v. 20).

---

24. Murphy, *Ecclesiastes*, 101.
25. Brown, *Ecclesiastes*, 99.

Proverbs from Everyday Life Settings (10:8-11)

Calamity awaits anyone even in common actions in everyday living. A farmer or a hunter may dig a pit and end up falling into it and being injured (v. 8a; cp. Pss. 7:15; 9:15; 57:6; Prov. 26:27; 28:10).[26] A serpent might bite the workman demolishing the wall of a dwelling or the wall of a city (v. 8b; Amos 5:19; cp. Acts 28:4). The quarryman must watch that a loosened slab might not suddenly break away and fall on him (v. 9a). The woodman splitting logs might be harmed by a piece that flies up into his face, a log that suddenly rolls over his foot, or by the axe itself glancing off the log and striking his leg (v. 9b; cp. Deut. 19:5). This last illustration might also be compounded by a dull blade (v. 10a). The axe wielder must apply more strength in order to get the dull blade to bite deep into the wood. The extra exertion might create yet another accident.

At the end of this string of common proverbs Solomon finishes with his main point: 'Wisdom has the advantage of giving success' (v. 10b). No matter what labor one pursues (digging a pit, demolishing a wall, quarrying stone, or splitting logs), the application of wisdom brings safety and success to the endeavor. It is as though Solomon said, 'Use your head. Think about what you are doing. Proceed with proper caution and attention to potentially harmful consequences.' Danger can lurk in every area of daily life. Pragmatically speaking, these illustrations speak of proper preparation for any task.[27] Wright adapts the truth to two modern axioms: 'Sharpen your knife before carving the chicken. Or, Don't blame the class for not listening if you haven't sharpened your wits with proper preparation.'[28] Speaking of the axiom's relevance, Tidball

---

26. Many of the biblical references to falling into a pit of one's own making speak of retribution and justice (sometimes called 'boomerang justice'). However, this verse deals with accidents.

27. Delitzsch's lament over the waste of paper in the attempt to find the connection between verses 1-7 and 8-11 need not be echoed in the present commentary: 'How much time, thought, and paper have been expended in seeking to find out a close connection between this group of verses and that going before!' (Delitzsch, *Song of Songs and Ecclesiastes*, 377). Delitzsch, it must be pointed out, did reach the same conclusion as above regarding v. 10b as the general truth tying the five illustrations together with a wisdom theme consistent with vv. 1-7 (ibid., 379, 381).

28. Wright, 'Ecclesiastes,' 5:1186.

writes, 'People want to lead churches or evangelize the world without training first. They want to go and live overseas without learning the language. They want to get married and have a family without saving up.'[29]

The final proverb moves from the realm of common chores to the snake charmer (v. 11). His imminent danger seems a bit more expected – snake charmers work with poisonous serpents like cobras and adders. If the charm does not work immediately, the snake might strike the charmer (or a customer) and cause his death. Eaton notes from this proverb that 'Slackness may nullify inherent skill.'[30] The dual reference to 'serpent' and 'bite' in verses 8 and 11 bracket this section, corroborating its unity and confirming its treatment as one part of the outline of chapter 10.[31]

The Words and Work of a Fool (10:12-15)

All biblical wisdom literature eventually gets around to the topic of speech (often using the figures of mouth, tongue, and/or lips).[32] Literally, verse 12 begins, 'Words of a wise man's mouth are grace.' Gracious words accompany the wise (v. 12a; cp. 8:1; Prov. 22:11; Ps. 45:2; Luke 4:22) and such grace wins favor with the people whom a wise person encounters. Indeed, the wise individual's words are 'gracious in content, winsome in spirit, affectionate in appeal, and compliant and affable in tone.'[33] The foolish on the contrary, will suffer the consequences of unwise words (v. 12b) and only succeed in alienating others. From start to finish, the speech of a fool displays a lack of wisdom and too often results in 'wicked madness' (v. 13). In spite of the dangers he faces, however, the fool just keeps on talking ('multiplies words,' v. 14a). The implied lesson is that everyone must take heed to the words they speak, for God hears and will judge each one accordingly (Matt. 12:36-37).

---

29. Tidball, *That's Just the Way It Is*, 169.
30. Eaton, *Ecclesiastes*, 136.
31. Greidanus, *Preaching Christ from Ecclesiastes*, 241, 242; Glenn, 'Mankind's Ignorance: Ecclesiastes 8:1–10:11,' 329.
32. Cp. Job 8:2; 15:5; 16:5; 20:12; 35:16; Pss. 5:9; 10:7; 19:14; 49:3; 73:9; Prov. 4:24; 6:2; 8:13; 10:6, 32; 14:3; 15:2; 16:23; 18:6; 21:23; 26:7, 28; Eccles. 5:2, 5; James 3.
33. Kaiser, *Ecclesiastes*, 110.

Just as the proverbs of verses 8-10a conclude with a practical application, so verses 12-14a unexpectedly apply their instruction to the ignorance of mankind concerning what will happen in the future (v. 14b; cp. 3:22; 6:12; 7:14; 8:7; Job 14:21). According to Kaiser, the fool's 'unbelief and failure to consider that there is a future judgment, wherein the totality of life will be reviewed, puts him at such a huge disadvantage compared to the devout, wise man that he is to be pitied.'[34]

The closing instruction indicates the futility of a fool's labor – he becomes so exhausted that he cannot figure out how to go into a nearby city (v. 15). Incompetence arises out of the failure to apply due diligence in the realm of labor and work. Eaton describes the circumstances as 'a moral and intellectual laziness which leads to a stumbling (2:14), fumbling (10:2), crumbling (10:18) life.'[35] Does the second half of the proverb refer to seeking shelter within a city when an enemy army invades the land? Or, does it refer to going into the city in order to accomplish some task, such as buying food in the marketplace? According to Garrett, 'the advice of foolish counselors is so bad that they cannot even give simple directions. Their long-winded explanations only wear out the confused traveler. How much worse to take their counsel in affairs of state.'[36] On the other hand, Kidner explains that the fool 'would get lost, we might say today, even if you put him on an escalator.'[37] Whatever the original meaning of this proverb, one thing is clear: the fool often cannot accomplish the most intuitive of tasks or make the simplest decisions. He (or she) just 'makes things needlessly difficult for himself by his stupidity.'[38] An English saying fits the fool well here: 'He does not know enough to come in out of the rain.'[39]

Due Diligence (10:16-20)

Turning to the status of a nation, Solomon introduces a woe-oracle (v. 16) and a declaration of blessing (v. 17). Thus the text

---

34. Ibid.
35. Eaton, *Ecclesiastes*, 136.
36. Garrett, *Proverbs, Ecclesiastes, Song of Songs*, 336.
37. Kidner, *A Time to Mourn*, 92-93.
38. Ibid., 93.
39. Gordis, *Koheleth*, 324. See, also, Barton, *Ecclesiastes*, 174. Lohfink, *Qoheleth*, 130, looks at the statement with regard to the city as 'a proverbial phrase meaning to become rich and to rise socially.'

describes two different national destinies: disaster or security.[40] In a context dealing with wisdom, Solomon reveals that wise people truly care about how leaders govern their home country. It is the fool who does not care and who isolates himself or herself from how a government conducts its business and from those who lead it 'in a world which is at once demanding (18), delightful (19) and dangerous (20).'[41] A nation with a young and inexperienced king and profligate leaders is doomed. Security will be lax and the business of the nation will suffer from lack of mature and serious judgment (v. 16). Isaiah 5 pronounces woes on those who get up early in order to pursue the drinking of alcoholic beverages (v. 11) and on those who, due to their alcoholism, accept a bribe to declare the wicked innocent and to remove the rights of those who are truly innocent (vv. 22-23). King Lemuel's mother taught him that kings should never fall under the power of alcohol (Prov. 31:4-5), because they will commit injustice under its influence.

Blessing, however, awaits the land with an experienced king who comes from a noble heritage and who works together with officials not given to gluttony and drunkenness (v. 17). Good national leaders exhibit personal independence, maturity, wisdom, and self-control.[42] Selfish, arrogant, and pleasure-seeking leaders bring trouble to any nation. In Isaiah 3:1-5 the Lord announces that He will judge His people in Jerusalem and Judah by removing the mature, the experienced, the noble, and the influential and replace them in leadership with 'mere lads' and 'capricious children' who will bring in an oppressive government. Such a situation brings to mind the astounding pettiness and ignorance of Rehoboam as he rejected the counsel of his wiser elders and listened instead to the unwise council of rash young men:

> The young men who grew up with him spoke to him, saying, 'Thus you shall say to this people who spoke to you, saying, "Your father made our yoke heavy, now you make it lighter for us!" But you shall speak to them, "My little finger is thicker than my father's loins! Whereas my father loaded you with a heavy yoke,

---

40. Cp. Eaton, *Ecclesiastes*, 137.
41. Kidner, *A Time to Mourn*, 94.
42. Cp. Eaton, *Ecclesiastes*, 137.

I will add to your yoke; my father disciplined you with whips, but I will discipline you with scorpions"' (1 Kings 12:10-12).

Solomon's words here in Ecclesiastes 10 are on the verge of becoming a rude reality in his own kingdom. Perhaps with his powers of keen observation he sees the trouble brewing already and with his God-given wisdom discerns what will happen when his son inherits the throne. Interestingly, 2 Chronicles 13:7 refers to Rehoboam being 'young and timid and could not hold his own against' his worthless companions. 'Young' (Hebrew *na'ar*) here is relative, since he was forty-one years of age when he became king (1 Kings 14:21). David used the same word for his foolish son Absalom (2 Sam. 18:12) who may have been in his forties when he began to conspire against his father (cp. 2 Sam. 14:27). Solomon himself, at the time of his ascension to the throne of Israel, admitted, 'yet I am but a little child [*na'ar*]' (1 Kings 3:7). That is why he asked God for wisdom to rule with discernment (1 Kings 3:9).

What takes place within a nation might also take place within each citizen's home.[43] The lazy home owner will soon find himself living in a home on the verge of collapse – literally (v. 18). The roof sags precariously and the rain causes innumerable leaks to sprout. Ancient roofs were flat and sealed with lime, 'which eventually cracked and allowed rain to seep in (cf. Prov. 19:13; 27:15).'[44] In Eaton's words, 'If attention is not paid to the everyday details of life, the results become a crippling liability.'[45] The proverb should be interpreted literally and applied liberally – it speaks in itself of a man's need to maintain his home, but within this context that same axiomatic truth applies to the government of a nation just as accurately.[46] In government, Fredericks observes, 'self-indulgent sluggards will only procrastinate the routine decisions necessary for the daily administration…. This indolence is the opposite of the urgency of the biblical work ethic.'[47]

---

43. Huwiler, 'Ecclesiastes,' 214, suggests that the context should cause the interpreter to consider the possibility that the house here is merely a metaphor for government. Delitzsch, *Song of Songs and Ecclesiastes*, 388, takes the house as figurative of the state, as does Leupold, *Ecclesiastes*, 251.

44. Murphy, *Ecclesiastes*, 105.

45. Eaton, *Ecclesiastes*, 137.

46. Estes, *Handbook on the Wisdom Books*, 367.

47. Fredericks, 'Ecclesiastes,' 225. See Eccles. 9:10; Prov. 10:4; 18:9; 20:4; and 28:2.

The opposite of laziness is diligence. The lazy will suffer loss, but the diligent will enjoy the fruits of their labors. They enjoy food enough, drink enough, and money enough to take care of every need (v. 19). This positive interpretation of the verse depends upon associating it with the appropriate behavior of wise rulers in verse 17, rather than connecting it with the irresponsible feasting of foolish officials in verse 16.[48] Verse 19 focuses on the food and drink by means of an inverted parallelism:

> a   for enjoyment
>   b   *Men* prepare a meal
>   b   and wine
> a   makes life merry

Then, in the last line of the verse, the writer places 'money' at the head of the sentence in order to focus on it, too. According to Garrett, 'The point is that at least some money is essential for enjoying life, and steps must therefore be taken to insure that the economy (be it national or personal) is sound.'[49] Some commentators think that this verse might repeat some of the previous enjoyment passages, rather than represent a description of the dissolute.[50] Kidner suggests that it teaches that 'every man has his price but that every gift has its use – and silver, in the form of money, is the most versatile of all.'[51] The teaching approximates that of Christ in Luke 16:9 ('And I say to you, make friends for yourselves by means of the wealth of unrighteousness, so that when it fails, they will receive you into the eternal dwellings'). Solomon has already addressed the positive value of money or wealth in 2:26; 5:19; and 7:11-12.

Lastly, Solomon returns to the topics of private speech and rumors to warn against speaking unwisely about the king (v. 20; cp. 7:21-22). In fact, cursing a ruler comprises a violation of the Mosaic law: 'You shall not curse God, nor curse a ruler of your people' (Exod. 22:28). Paul instructed Timothy to pray for 'kings and all who are in authority, so that we may lead a tranquil and quiet life in all godliness and

---

48. Estes, *Handbook on the Wisdom Books*, 368. The contrary view is represented by Fredericks, 'Ecclesiastes,' 225-26.
49. Garrett, *Proverbs, Ecclesiastes, Song of Songs*, 336-37.
50. Murphy, *Ecclesiastes*, 105.
51. Kidner, *A Time to Mourn*, 95.

dignity' (1 Tim. 2:1-2). 'Cursing political leaders is wrong in itself,' Ryken reminds us, 'But in addition to being wrong in themselves, our foolish criticisms may come back to haunt us.'[52] Within the royal household few words can be spoken without someone overhearing them (see 2 Kings 6:12) – even the walls of one's bedroom have ears. Words spoken can return to haunt the one who curses a king or a rich man. It is the nature of fallen mankind to use tidbits of gossip to one's own advantage. Using a bird as the illustration implies the speed with which idle words can make their way to the ears of the slandered person. If he is powerful, woe be to the speaker. In essence, therefore, a woe commences this section (v. 16) and also concludes the section (v. 20), marking its boundaries.

Verse 20 closes the chapter by twice giving an instruction to not speak a curse even within the quiet seclusion of one's bedroom. When compared with the proverb of 9:17, there is a measure of irony that, having given positive significance to a failure to listen to quiet words *publicly* spoken at the end of chapter 9, Solomon ends chapter 10 with a warning about the certainty of hearing quiet words *privately* spoken.[53] Eaton concludes that 'The verse challenges us to remain calm in days of national sloth, immaturity and indulgence, and calls for a submissive approach to authority, giving an expedient reason for obedience.'[54] It really is a matter of patriotic respect for governmental leaders. In his book, *Politics According to the Bible*, Wayne Grudem reminds his readers that 'The Bible teaches Christians to obey and honor the leaders of the nation in which they live.'[55] He identifies this instruction in both the New Testament (Rom. 13:1-7; 1 Pet. 2:13-17) and the Old (Prov. 24:21; Eccles. 10:20; Jer. 29:4-7).[56]

In concluding his sample exposition of Ecclesiastes 9:13–10:20, Greidanus suggests that thinking of the three kinds of animals

---

52. Ryken, *Ecclesiastes*, 244.
53. Ogden, 'Variations on the Theme of Wisdom's Strength and Vulnerability: Ecclesiastes 9:17–10:20,' 340.
54. Eaton, *Ecclesiastes*, 138.
55. Wayne Grudem, *Politics According to the Bible: A Comprehensive Resource for Understanding Modern Political Issues in the Light of Scripture* (Grand Rapids, Mich.: Zondervan, 2010), 110.
56. Ibid., 110-11.

mentioned in 10:1-20 will help us remember the message of the passage.[57] The diminutive size and seeming insignificance of flies, snakes, and birds conceal the great potential for harm that they possess.[58] The flies, after all, were 'flies of death' (or, 'deadly flies;' v. 1). The serpent's bite can also be deadly (vv. 8, 11) and the little bird carrying one's words to the king can bring dire consequences (v. 20). Bird flu epidemics have cost the lives of thousands of people even in the modern era of scientific medicine – evidence that small animals bring enormous consequences. If nothing else, this chapter teaches us to pay proper attention to the so-called 'little things' in life both personally and nationally. Everything a person does matters. The character of a government leader matters. Even a little word can have far-reaching effects.

Study Questions

1. What little things in life possess the potential to bring substantial harm upon an individual?

2. What seemingly insignificant factors have the potential to bring about serious consequences for a nation?

3. How can we identify a biblical fool?

4. Identify some of the preparations necessary for a wise and secure life on a daily basis.

5. What are the qualities of a good national leader?

6. Of what significance are flies, serpents, and birds in Ecclesiastes 10? What animals do other biblical writers use as illustrations to teach truths for daily living?

---

57. Ogden, 'Variations on the Theme of Wisdom's Strength and Vulnerability,' 338, 'The major rhetorical feature available as a criterion is the motif already encountered in 10:1a, 11 – that of the small animal or insect representing a potential source of danger. On this basis we are able to see how a *motif* has been used as the *inclusio* for the whole chapter; the fly in v. 1, the serpent in vv. 8, 11, and the bird in v. 20.'

58. Greidanus, *Preaching Christ from Ecclesiastes*, 258.

11

Sowing in the Morning, Sowing in the Evening

In conclusion, *the Preacher* determined
to fear God, obey God, and enjoy
life *(9:1–12:14)*, Part 3

Ecclesiastes begins with a declaration that all is futile, enigmatic, or ephemeral ('Vanity of vanities! All is vanity,' 1:2).
Then Solomon focuses on the apparent lack of human advantage
in life's labors 'under the sun' (1:3). Indeed, he characterizes life
on earth as an endless cycle of sunrises and sunsets (1:5). Now,
at the end of the book, he looks 'beyond his gloomy vistas to
see God.'[1] Solomon realizes that life's certainties (like death)
and life's uncertainties (like accidents and disasters) cannot
be predicted (cf. Prov. 27:1). However, a person can prepare
for both sets of circumstances and enjoy God's marvelous gift
of life 'under the sun.' How should someone live in the light
of Solomon's extended discourse? Kidner offers a concise, but
appropriate summary of this section of the book: 'Be bold! Be
joyful! Be godly!'[2] Thus, Solomon carries on from the advice of
chapter 10, 'Be wise!'[3] Chapter 11 continues to expand 'wise
advice in the light of an uncertain future.'[4] Such instructions

---

1. McComiskey, 'Ecclesiastes,' in *Baker Encyclopedia of the Bible*, 1:654.
2. The three referring respectively to 11:1-6; 11:7-10; and 12:1-8 (Kidner, *A Time to Mourn*, 96).
3. Cp. ibid., 97, 'Be sensible!'
4. Wright, 'Ecclesiastes,' 5:1189.

or exhortations characterize the last major section of the book (11:1–12:8), proclaiming a call to decision and obedience.[5] That tone aids the interpreter to avoid understanding any part of the text as a decline into hopelessness and hedonism.

What a Person Does Not Know (11:1-6)

Repeatedly Solomon has urged his readers to pursue the opportunities God gives 'under the sun.' Now, in verse 1, he addresses the matter of exercising some faith in making an investment that entails risk. The opportunity involves either almsgiving (the traditional view)[6] or commercial pursuits involving ocean-going ships.[7] Both of these involve the use of profits gained from one's labors. If verse 1 deals with almsgiving, then verse 2 speaks of a distribution of gifts[8] to seven or even eight needy people,[9] multiplying the odds that some are going to do exceedingly well with that which they have been given. Adherents to this view appeal to an Arab proverb ('Do good, throw your bread on the waters, and one day you will be rewarded')[10] and to Egyptian parallels ('Do a good deed and throw it in the water; when it dries you will find it').[11] Texts like Proverbs 19:17 ('One who is gracious to a poor man lends to the LORD, and He will repay him for his good deed') lend further support to this approach involving a principle of ultimate compensation for generosity.

---

5. Eaton, *Ecclesiastes*, 139.

6. Another view that has few adherents interprets the 'bread' as a figure for seed that a farmer sows by casting it on soggy or wet ground (Jamieson, Fausset, and Brown, *Commentary on the Old and New Testaments*, Eccles. 11:1); Bridges, *Ecclesiastes*, 293. Murphy, *Ecclesiastes*, 106, holds yet another view: 'Bread in the water is a metaphor for doing something that is really senseless.' His point is that it still might succeed, because the future is just too unpredictable.

7. Glenn, 'Ecclesiastes,' 1002; Whybray, *Ecclesiastes*, 158-59; Garrett, *Proverbs, Ecclesiastes, Song of Songs*, 338; Longman, *Ecclesiastes*, 256; Estes, *Handbook on the Wisdom Books*, 369-70; Bartholomew, *Ecclesiastes*, 337; Ryken, *Ecclesiastes*, 255.

8. Ryken, *Ecclesiastes*, 254-55, associates the word 'portion' here with its use in Neh. 8:10. NASU's translation ('Divide your portion to seven, or even to eight') is itself misleading, because the Hebrew reads literally, 'Give a portion to seven and even to eight.' In addition, Deut. 18:8 uses 'portion' with regard to food.

9. Fredericks, 'Ecclesiastes,' 234, suggests a potential relationship to the fact that 'Israelite law required that one distribute a portion of one's assets to the poor for at least *seven* years, if necessary (Deut. 15:7-11; cf. Prov. 28:27; Matt. 5:7; Eccles. 2:26).'

10. Longman, *Ecclesiastes*, 255-56.

11. Brown, *Ecclesiastes*, 101, referring to the 'Instruction of Anksheshonq'). See also, Krüger, *Qoheleth*, 192.

Kaiser, taking the almsgiving viewpoint, rephrases verse 2, '"Be liberal and generous to as *many* as you can and *then some*,"… So, make as many friends as you can, for you never know when you yourself may need assistance.'[12] In the New Testament a similar truth appears in Luke 16:9 ('make friends for yourselves by means of the wealth of unrighteousness, so that when it fails, they will receive you into the eternal dwellings').

If, however, verse 1 refers to investment by means of commercial shipping, then verse 2 refers to the diversification of shipments and/or investments into seven or eight consignments, so that at least some ships survive the journeys and return with their holds filled. 'Cast' (v. 1) actually provides a misleading translation that promotes the traditional viewpoint. However, the imperative more closely approximates 'Send' or 'Let loose' – more befitting a commercial enterprise for which ships are sent out to sea for years at a time before returning to their home port. Additional argumentation for the maritime understanding of these two verses includes the Solomonic history which bears witness to the ships of Solomon's commercial fleet (1 Kings 9:26-28; 10:22). Also, Proverbs 31:14 makes mention of both 'ships' and 'bread.' 'Bread' does not occur anywhere in Scripture with the meaning of 'seed,' unless it be here. As for the later Arabic proverb, it 'may have been influenced by the early "charitable" interpretation of verse 1.'[13] None of the Egyptian references parallels closely the use of 'bread,' making them weak attestation to almsgiving in Ecclesiastes.

The 'seven, or even to eight' is the same 'x + (x +1)' formula found elsewhere in the Old Testament (including Eccles. 4:6, 12).[14] This form of reference indicates that there are more potential entities that match the description than just the seven or even the eight – in other words, an indefinite number. However, in some situations the formula expresses the fullness of a condition or, here, an enterprise.[15] NEB's interpretive translation represents the commercial viewpoint, even though it takes

---

12. Kaiser, *Ecclesiastes*, 114 (emphasis his).
13. Parsons, 'Guidelines for Understanding and Proclaiming the Book of Ecclesiastes, Part 2,' 301.
14. See the discussion of 4:7-12.
15. Eaton, *Ecclesiastes*, 141.

some liberties with the text: 'Send your grain across the seas, and in time you will get a return. Divide your merchandise among seven ventures, eight maybe, since you do not know what disasters may occur on earth.'

Solomon does not mean by his words that commercial enterprise or almsgiving are 'just a roll of the dice, gamble and nothing more. He is certain that the covenant people can count on eventual success, because God will guarantee it.'[16] That which God grants, however, requires both faith[17] and patience. As Leupold declares, 'The emphasis lies upon the certainty of reward as well as upon the fact that this certain reward will not be received at once.'[18] Jesus' parable of the talents in Matthew 25:14-30 appears to illustrate the same truth. The parable condemns the man who fails to invest the one talent that his master had given him. He did not want to take any risks, so he lost all potential gain. In the end, his master took away even the gift he had received. Paralyzed with uncertainty, fear, and doubt, he lost the gift due to its disuse. Fascinating parallels with Ecclesiastes leap from the Gospel text:

- A long time passes between the giving of the money and the return of the master (Matt. 25:19; Eccles. 11:1, 'after many days').

- The good slaves who had risked their investments, enter into a state of joy (Matt. 25:21, 23; Eccles. 11:8, 9, 'rejoice').

- Fear as a factor against taking the risk for investing (Matt. 25:25; Eccles. 11:1, 4, uncertainty leading to inaction).

- Laziness as a factor (Matt. 25:26; Eccles. 11:6, 'do not be idle').

- Darkness (Matt. 25:30; Eccles. 11:8).

Even if the parable does not draw directly from Ecclesiastes 11, it certainly reflects agreement with the truths found therein.

---

16. Kelley, *The Burden of God*, 138.
17. Eaton, *Ecclesiastes*, 140.
18. Leupold, *Ecclesiastes*, 256.

As with several of the difficult interpretive issues in Ecclesiastes, none of the views regarding verses 1 and 2 warrant dogmatism. Thankfully, the variety of interpretations and translations do not destroy the foundational truths of the text. For example, whether an interpreter settles on either a charitable, an agricultural, or a commercial interpretation of verses 1-2, the concepts of investment, risk, and faith remain and the exhortation to action rather than paralysis still rises inexorably from the text. Likewise, Solomon's prior observation in 5:13-14 about hoarding one's wealth might apply to either interpretation.

Verse 2 concludes with 'for you do not know what misfortune may occur on the earth.' Three more times, Solomon highlights human ignorance (twice in v. 5 and once in v. 6). The statement serves as the key to the entire passage. In Whybray's opinion, 'since the future is hidden even the most senseless actions may turn out well, and equally the most prudent ones may lead to disaster.' [19] Knowledge of our ignorance forms the basis for a realistic outlook that depends upon a sovereign, omniscient God.

Continuing the discussion of risk, verse 3 reveals that no one has control over when the rain falls (even though it will inevitably come) or where a tree might fall (which is entirely random). Kaiser poses a few questions for consideration: 'So what if we cannot prognosticate the outcome of all of our joyful involvement in life's tasks? Is not this detail covered also in the plan of God?'[20] Whenever an individual waits for perfect conditions before either sowing or reaping (v. 4), failure and loss may very well follow. Over-hesitancy in making decisions involving risk can result in the best time passing by during inactivity. The paralysis of inaction results in lost opportunities. In the New Testament a similar agricultural metaphor makes its appearance in Paul's description of the respective tasks of mankind and God in the spread of the gospel: 'I planted, Apollos watered, but God was causing the growth' (1 Cor. 3:6; cp. Prov. 10:22).

Natural phenomena within God's control remain mysterious to a certain degree to mankind (v. 5). The wind's path[21] can-

---

19. Whybray, *Ecclesiastes*, 158.

20. Kaiser, *Ecclesiastes*, 115.

21. Lohfink, *Qoheleth*, 134, 'From v. 3 the clouds symbolize the foreseeable; in v. 5 the wind will return as the symbol of the unforeseeable.'

not always be charted (cf. John 3:8[22]) and the bones of a fetus can form in unexpected ways inside the womb (cf. Ps. 139:13-16).[23] Both are basically invisible and outside the control of mankind (cp. Eccles. 8:8).[24] God, as the Maker of all things, produces the wind's patterns as well as bones for the unborn infant. The very fact that He is in control demonstrates that He governs all things and that people are not in control. He is mightier than they. Mankind's ignorance of the work of God (cp. 8:17) forms an ongoing theme in the final chapters of Ecclesiastes.

Opportunity knocks only at certain times. If the conditions are good enough for sowing seed in the field, the farmer must remain active and pursue his occupation (v. 6). He cannot know whether the sowing should be in the morning or the evening, but the day gives the opportunity, if he works all day long. Whybray takes the phraseology to 'refer simply to a full day's work from morning to evening.'[25] The text expresses the continuous labor that a wise person must expend in order to see the harvest. God alone gives the field's increase, the enterprise's profits, or the labor's success, but wise people must labor in order to see such results (cf. 9:10). A fitting illustration involves steering an automobile. It only turns the corners if it is also moving. Each individual must be busy, must be moving, for God to steer them and bring them to success. Tidball summarizes verses 3-5 under three headings: 'Don't be paralyzed by inevitability' (v. 3), 'Don't be paralyzed by speculation' (v. 4), and 'Don't be paralyzed by ignorance' (v. 5).[26] Again, New Testament texts reflect the same instruction

---

22. Wright, 'Ecclesiastes,' 5:1190, believes that it 'is likely that Jesus Christ had this verse [Ecclesiastes 11:5] in mind.'

23. With a few changes in the Hebrew text, 'wind' can be translated as 'spirit' or 'life-breath,' resulting in the elimination of the figure involving wind and making the illustration just the entrance of the life-breath into the fetus (Seow, *Ecclesiastes*, 336-37; Garrett, *Proverbs, Ecclesiastes, Song of Songs*, 338. Cp. NRSV: 'Just as you do not know how the breath comes to the bones in the mother's womb.') However, the translation requires a slight alteration of a Hebrew preposition attached to the word 'bones.' Gordis, *Koheleth*, 332, responds that the dual reference view (wind *and* womb) would require the conjunction 'and,' which is not in the text. However, as Lauha, *Kohelet*, 199, points out, the lack of the conjunction is difficult, but not impossible ('ist allerdings schwierig, aber nicht unmöglich').

24. Compare, also, the phrase 'striving after wind' in 1:14, 17; 2:11, 17, 26; 4:4, 6, 16; 6:9.

25. Whybray, *Ecclesiastes*, 160.

26. Tidball, *That's Just the Way It Is*, 183-84.

via a similar metaphor: 'he who sows sparingly will also reap sparingly, and he who sows bountifully will reap bountifully' (2 Cor. 9:6) and 'Let us not lose heart in doing good, for in due time we will reap if we do not grow weary' (Gal. 6:9).

Rejoice in the Light (11:7-8)

Life presents wonderful opportunities that mankind must enjoy. Being 'under the sun' has its limitations, but existence in the light (being able to 'see the sun;' cf. 6:5; 7:11) is far more pleasant than the alternative (v. 7). Regardless of the number of years God might grant to any individual, 'let him rejoice in them all' (v. 8a). Another enjoyment text graces the pages of Ecclesiastes in these verses. God's gift of life should be enjoyed, not just endured. Until this point in the book, other enjoyment passages have 'followed enigmatic sections. This shift to having the *carpe diem* section preface and structure the enigmatic section about death is significant, as is the introduction of "remember," which has not yet occurred in a *carpe diem* passage.' [27]

At the same time as one must rejoice, one must also 'remember the days of darkness' (v. 8b). Since these dark days occupy a large amount of time ('for they will be many'), death does not seem an adequate reference[28] – suffering, old age, and dying do fit the description, however. These days consist of times of trouble in which a person finds no delight (cp. 12:1).[29] Krüger recommends that this instruction depicts the 'times that an old man thinks back on his life (cf. 5:16; 7:14; 12:1). The verse then determines that an old man rejoices over his long life *and* in accordance with the length of his life also remembers numerous "dark days" that he has experienced.'[30] The trials and travails of a lifetime just serve to make the joys all the more pleasant and sweeter. Psalm 118:24 reminds the godly of the right daily attitude:

> This is the day which the LORD has made;
> Let us rejoice and be glad in it.

---

27. Bartholomew, *Ecclesiastes*, 343.
28. *Contra* Barton, *Ecclesiastes*, 184.
29. Greidanus, *Preaching Christ from Ecclesiastes*, 286 footnote 24.
30. Krüger, *Qoheleth*, 196.

Disregard for rejoicing and remembering leads to great disappointment, because everything yet to come will pass very swiftly (v. 8c). 'Futility' (*hebel*) in this setting refers to that which is brief and ephemeral. 'Everything' must refer to the latter days of life, including the time of dying, rather than to the afterlife.

Again, Rejoice (11:9-10)

Just as the apostle Paul repeats the command to rejoice ('Rejoice, and again I say, rejoice,' Phil. 4:4), so King Solomon repeats the identical command (vv. 8, 9).[31] However, the second time he addresses the command specifically to the young man. Youth passes quickly, so its opportunities for enjoying life will be few. Kelley explains the Solomonic advice: 'Do not trouble yourselves over "the cycle!" The world belongs to God, and He has granted you the opportunity to build up life. Give yourself to life in all its richness and fullness. If things seem to be perverse and distorted, do not let that bother you…. Life may not turn out as you expect, but you must not permit its uncertainties and disturbances to impair your energies.'[32] The reader of Ecclesiastes should note that Solomon does not instruct young people to rejoice *that* they are young, but *while* they are young.[33] He tells the young to put in place the theological foundation for living as early as possible.[34] When the youth becomes a man, he enters yet another brief season of life. During his manhood, he needs to allow his heart to enjoy life's pleasantness. 'Like a bubble the days of our "*youth*" soon burst, so we have to clutch them while we can.'[35]

To many readers, Solomon's instruction ('follow the impulses of your heart and the desires of your eyes') sounds hedonistic and reckless. Those who interpret the text in this fashion contrast it with Numbers 15:39: 'It shall be a tassel for you to look at and remember all the commandments of the LORD, so as to do them and not follow after your own heart and your

---

31. This is the final enjoyment (or, *carpe diem*) passage in Ecclesiastes. As Fredericks notes, 'This is a more qualified refrain, however, buffered by the realities of God's judicial sovereignty and the utter brevity of each stage of life' (Fredericks, 'Ecclesiastes,' 236-37).
32. Kelley, *The Burden of God*, 141.
33. Leupold, *Ecclesiastes*, 270.
34. Bartholomew, *Ecclesiastes*, 344.
35. Hubbard, *Ecclesiastes, Song of Solomon*, 237.

own eyes, after which you played the harlot.' The verse from Numbers speaks of the way that the tassels with a blue cord on the fringes of the Israelites' garments will remind them to obey the Lord's commandments rather than their own lusts. Ignoring the context of one or both passages provides the only means by which the two can be confused or made to be contradictory. Due to the very consistent and careful conclusions Solomon reaches throughout the book (and especially in its final chapter), Longman's characterization of the writer as 'a confused, skeptical wise man who vacillates between the traditional doctrine in which he was trained and the harsh realities of life'[36] seems unnecessary and overly skeptical itself.

Solomon does not leave this instruction without qualification. In a context where 'you do not know' occurs four times (vv. 2, 5 twice, 6), he now says in a positive way, 'Yet know' (v. 9c). He reminds the young man that he must keep in mind that God will judge him for all that does not meet with divine approval (cp. 9:7). The Hebrew employs a definite article with both 'God' and 'judgment' ('the God will bring you into the judgment').[37] Such grammar might indicate that Solomon has a single, specific judgment in mind.[38] In other words, a reality exists beyond this life and that reality includes divine retribution.[39] Hebrews 9:27 proclaims the same basic theological truth: 'it is appointed for men to die once and after this *comes* judgment.' Therefore, priority must be given to God and to His will as revealed in His Word. No one should ever make his or her own desires the priority. Solomon encourages innocent, God-approved enjoyment of life's gifts. Brown compares Ecclesiastes 11:9 with texts like Proverbs 2:11-14 and concludes that 'the old sage, much like a typical grandparent, provides the necessary balance to the harsh admonitions of the parental voice in Proverbs. The combined effect is the formative education of youth.'[40]

Therefore, people must 'remove grief and anger' from their hearts and 'put away pain' from their bodies, because the times of their lives 'are fleeting' (v. 10). Mankind must never focus on

---

36. Longman, *Ecclesiastes*, 261.
37. See the concept of judgment in 3:17; 8:12-13; and 12:14.
38. Eaton, *Ecclesiastes*, 145; Leupold, *Ecclesiastes*, 271; Ryken, *Ecclesiastes*, 266.
39. Krüger, *Qoheleth*, 197, denies any such meaning, opting to identify the judgment with the transitoriness of mankind's existence.
40. Brown, *Ecclesiastes*, 106.

the negatives to the extent that they miss the pleasant opportunities that God gives for their enjoyment. Enjoying the good
things requires the proper perspective on the bad things in life.
After all, the bad is equally ephemeral. The translation 'grief and
anger' in the NASU represents a single Hebrew word occurring
seven times in Ecclesiastes. In 1:18 and 2:23 it is parallel to
'pain.' In 5:16 the NASU translates the word as 'vexation,' in the
description of eating in darkness 'with great vexation, sickness
and anger.' But, in 7:3 Solomon contrasts it with laughter and
happiness, making it an equivalent of sadness. Occurring
twice in 7:9, 'anger' seems most appropriate in that context.
As Ryken points out, 'This is not a call to deny the very real
suffering that everyone experiences. Nor is it a call to escape
pain by living for pleasure. Rather, it is a call to take care of
our mental and physical health.'[41] In Garrett's opinion, the two
phrases should be taken as a hendiadys, resulting in a single
reference to casting away grief over the condition in which
human beings live.[42]

The last clause of the chapter gives the reason why one
should remove grief and put away pain, 'because childhood
and the prime of life are fleeting.' 'Childhood' appears also in
verse 9 and in Psalm 110:3. In all three the meaning is more
that of 'youth' than of early youth ('childhood'). The next word
('the prime of life') receives several different treatments in the
English versions ('the dawn of life,' NRSV, ESV; 'black hair,'
NJPS; 'vigor,' NIV; 'a whole life,' NLT). 'Dawn of life' reverses
the order of time periods, since that would be a time prior to
childhood or youth. Thus, 'dawn' cannot survive as the most
straightforward interpretation. With the topic of age coming
in 12:1-7, the progression from youth to the prime of life to old
age seems most consistent. Lohfink's translation ('for youth
and dark hair are a breath'[43]) expresses the concept well. Black
hair turns to gray or silver all too quickly – or even to baldness.

Solomon in his old age proffers advice for the young out of
his own life of blown opportunities. He cannot undo his own

---

41. Ryken, *Ecclesiastes*, 267.
42. Garrett, *Proverbs, Ecclesiastes, Song of Songs*, 340.
43. Lohfink, *Qoheleth*, 135. Lauha, *Kohelet*, 209, takes the two words ('youth' and 'dark hair') as a hendiadys (two words but one meaning), translating them as 'youth with its bloom is vain' ('ist die Jugend mit ihrer Blüte eitel;' ibid., 204).

mistakes or cover over his sins for which he will stand before a holy God in the final judgment. However, he can exhort those who still 'see the sun' to make the most of the gifts which God has given. Life passes ever so swiftly (cf. Job 7:6; 9:25; Pss. 78:39; 109:23; 144:4). Chapter 11 sets the stage for Solomon's closing description of old age and death – the end-of-life experience for which the young are destined, if they 'see the sun' long enough. Meanwhile, the godly and ungodly alike must keep in mind that God does exist, that life 'under the sun' will be followed by a day of divine judgment of mankind, and that the judgment itself implies entry into an afterlife beyond the sun. How should we then live (cp. 2 Pet. 3:11)?

STUDY QUESTIONS

1. What plans do you have to take some risks in order to serve God faithfully and trust Him fully?

2. Over what kinds of things in your life do you feel that you have no control?

3. What are the perfect conditions for which you wait before making decisions or before doing something for Christ?

4. What are the pleasant things you enjoy in life 'under the sun'?

5. What are some of your memories regarding your 'days of darkness'?

6. How can young and old alike enjoy life with a balanced perspective and a sense of accountability?

7. How can you 'remove grief and anger from your heart and put away pain from your body'?

12

Life Under a Setting Sun

In conclusion, *the Preacher* determined to fear God,
obey God, and enjoy life *(9:1–12:14)*, Part 4

Continuing the book's grand finale (11:9–12:7), Solomon transitions from the enjoyment of 'seeing the sun' to the approach of death. Assuming temporal existence for mankind 'under the sun', 'he broadens the range of his observation to include God, who is above the sun, and death, which is beyond the sun.'[1] When the wise contemplate death, they find all aspirations to grandeur and gain exposed as illusory visions of their own arrogance. Brown says of such contemplation, that it 'purges the soul of all futile striving and, paradoxically, anxiety…. The eternal sleep of death serves as a wake-up call to live and welcome the serendipities of the present.'[2] Just as the setting sun signals the end of a day, so aging signals the approach of the close of one's life. However, preparation for the end of life must begin even in youth.

'Before' in verses 1, 2, and 6 sets up a time-oriented series of statements that favor understanding the text as a description of the time of death, rather than merely a depiction of the process of aging.[3] The first seven verses of this chapter comprise one long sentence.[4] Huwiler suggests that if someone were to read it aloud as one sentence, he or she would be '"out of breath" by

---

1. Estes, *Handbook on the Wisdom Books*, 373.
2. Brown, *Ecclesiastes*, 108.
3. Fox, *Qohelet and His Contradictions*, 286.
4. Whybray, *Ecclesiastes*, 167.

the end'[5] – a play on the key word *hebel*, which can also mean 'breath,' as well as 'vanity,' 'futility,' or 'fleeting.' However, the interpreter would be remiss to focus too much upon death in this section. Both preceding (11:9) and subsequent (12:14) contexts identify God's judgment as the real focus.[6] Therefore, a truly theological theme permeates the final chapter rather than accentuating a man or woman's physical decline and decease at the end of his or her earthly existence.

Solomonic Advice (12:1-7)

Just when one might expect either 'Remember death' or 'Remember darkness', Solomon surprises readers with 'Remember your Creator'.[7] However, given the statement in verse 7 ('then the dust will return to the earth as it was, and the spirit will return to God who gave it'), any consideration of death naturally leads one to think of the Creator (cp. Gen. 2:7; 3:19).[8] 'Creator' is actually a plural form in the Hebrew – a typical means of expressing majesty and superiority. The reader of Ecclesiastes should refer to the writer's previous mention of the Creator and His work in 3:11 ('He has made everything appropriate in its time'); 7:13-14 ('Consider the work of God'), 29 ('God made men upright'); and 11:5 ('the activity of God who makes all things').[9] Solomon's choice of this title, Garrett observes, 'is not by accident. It both looks back to the creation narrative, which plays so prominent a role in Ecclesiastes, and maintains the perspective of wisdom that a joyful life is found through adherence to the principles built into the creation.'[10] Estes argues that this title demonstrates that the writer addresses all humanity, not just Israel.[11] What Solomon has to say in these verses is for every man, woman, and child on the planet.

Some interpreters seek to eliminate 'Creator' from the text, because they think that 'allusion to God the Creator ill fits this context'.[12] Slight alterations to the Hebrew text can produce meanings

---

5. Huwiler, 'Ecclesiastes,' 215.

6. Kelley, *The Burden of God*, 142.

7. Lohfink, *Qoheleth*, 137.

8. Fox, *Qohelet and His Contradictions*, 300.

9. The Old Testament uses the divine title 'Creator' only here and in seven other verses (see Isa. 40:28; 42:5; 43:1, 15; 45:7, 18; Amos 4:13) – some of these seven could be the participle 'creating' rather than the noun 'Creator'.

10. Garrett, *Proverbs, Ecclesiastes, Song of Songs*, 340, footnote 232.

11. Estes, *Handbook on the Wisdom Books*, 373.

12. Crenshaw, *Ecclesiastes*, 184.

like 'your well' (symbolizing one's wife as in Proverbs 5:15, 18) or 'your pit' (another way of speaking of the grave) or even 'your well-being'.[13] The ancient rabbis had their own explanations. Rabbi Akabya ben Mahallalel (first century A.D.), according to the Talmud (*Abot* 3.1), combined three different potential meanings into one instruction to know from where you came (the source or well), where you are going (the grave), and before whom you will stand (the Creator).[14] Crenshaw, settling on the first meaning ('your well'), indicates that the text 'urges young people to reflect on the joys of female companionship before old age and death render one incapable of sensual pleasure'.[15]

Before one can 'remember' the Creator, he or she must believe that 'there *is* a Creator who made us, not some naturalistic process of evolution.'[16] The Hebrew word for 'Creator' involves a root that never takes a human being as the subject. Only God creates, as far as the Old Testament writers are concerned. Genesis 1:1–2:3 provides an authoritative account of the creative activity of God. The God who created all things is the 'Creator.' There is no other way that all things came into existence (cp. Isa. 45:18 and John 1:1-3). Remembering one's Creator involves more than mere memory or acknowledgment. For the Hebrew writers, 'remember' involves action,[17] or allowing the objects of remembrance to 'shape one's perspective in the present'.[18] First, we must 'drop our pretense of self-sufficiency and commit ourselves to Him'.[19] If an individual neglects serving the Creator in intentional obedience to His Word, 'the capacity for joy will be lost.'[20]

'Before the evil days come' (v. 1) relates to the previous mention of 'the days of darkness' in 11:8 and stands in contrast to 'the days of your youth' (12:1a). Both the evil days and the dark days refer to times of misery and trouble. The previous reference deals with the bad times throughout one's lifetime. However, the second

---

13. Ibid., 184-85.

14. Gordis, *Koheleth,* 341. Cf. Seow, *Ecclesiastes*, 351, 'Given his penchant for wordplays, it seems likely that [the writer] might have intended his audience to hear more than one meaning in the word.'

15. Crenshaw, *Ecclesiastes*, 185.

16. Morris, *The Remarkable Wisdom of Solomon*, 227.

17. Kaiser, *Ecclesiastes*, 118.

18. Bartholomew, *Ecclesiastes,* 346.

19. Kidner, *A Time to Mourn*, 100.

20. Eaton, *Ecclesiastes*, 148.

refers to the end of life and the process of aging and, ultimately, dying. This understanding obtains confirmation in the addition of 'and the years draw near'. Such phraseology rules out individual events of personal trouble or calamity. The threefold occurrence of 'before' (vv. 1, 2, 6) in these concluding verses of Ecclesiastes emphasizes the brevity of life and the finality of death.[21]

As Fox reminds his readers, 'No interpretation of this poem is entirely satisfactory; none (including the one I will offer) solves all the difficulties.'[22] No commentator convincingly explains these verses by means of a single consistent figure, metaphor, or allegory.[23] Garrett argues that 'a single, unified picture should not be sought'.[24] Regardless of all the difficulties involved in this passage, Kidner correctly warns interpreters not to treat it 'as a laboured cryptogram'.[25] Exercising a little common sense and a tendency toward a literal interpretation will avoid, according to Barton, 'the vagaries to which excessive zeal for anatomical identification has led.'[26]

The Gathering Storm (12:2)

The second 'before' (v. 2) speaks of 'the sun and the light, the moon and the stars' being darkened. Mention of 'light' causes confusion for some interpreters, but in the creation account 'the light' (Gen. 1:3-5) existed separate from sun, moon, and stars (Gen. 1:14-16). Thus Solomon demonstrates his awareness of the Genesis account and puts some of its concepts to work for him in speaking of the Creator and the approaching death of a human person, one of the Creator's created beings. Whether a reader understands the verse as a description of a storm or the coming of death, the context inevitably links the text to death. A gathering storm might depict the suddenness of death, 'setting forth the fear, melancholy and desolation which grip a household upon which death has cast its shadow.'[27] The returning clouds might symbolize the repeti-

---

21. Fredericks, 'Ecclesiastes,' 238.

22. Fox, *Qohelet and His Contradictions*, 284. See the chart of interpretive approaches that follows the exposition of verses 1-7.

23. Cf. Eaton, *Ecclesiastes*, 147.

24. Garrett, *Proverbs, Ecclesiastes, Song of Songs*, 340 footnote 228.

25. Kidner, *A Time to Mourn*, 101.

26. Barton, *Ecclesiastes*, 186.

27. Leahy, 'The Meaning of Ecclesiastes 12:1-5,' 378.

tive occurrences of calamities and sorrows.[28] Kidner compares the resilience of youth for absorbing tremendous difficulties and rebounding from them, in that stormy skies eventually turn sunny once again.[29] Provan admits that even an apocalyptic interpretation of these verses can be applied to aging and dying: 'The end times for the individual human being are here pictured, then, in terms of the end of the world.'[30]

The Household of the Deceased (12:3-4)

In verses 3 and 4, Solomon seems to depict a great house either in decline or anticipating the death of its master. The picture not only describes happenings within the house, but extends to the village and ultimately becomes a metaphor of death itself. According to verse 3, four classes of people experience the fear and anxiety created by the proximity of death within the household. The 'watchmen' represent the male servants who are responsible for protecting the household. 'Mighty men' depict the freemen, the landowners, the family members of the estate or the heads of nearby estates. Following the two groups of men come two groups of women: the maidservants who grind the grain and the freewomen, the mistresses of the estate, who avoid the public eye in the time of grieving.

Does the maidservants' grinding decrease due to the economic situation, or to the imminent death of the master of the house, or to the decrease in the number of the estate's inhabitants? Are the women or the windows darkened? Does the darkening refer to the wearing of black clothing in mourning? Differing interpretations arise from the seemingly enigmatic descriptions that allow for a variety of meanings. 'Those who look through the windows' most naturally refers 'to the women of the household who, according to Middle Eastern custom, were not allowed to mingle with the men in the business of the household, so they peered through the lattice-work of the house.'[31] Other biblical examples of women looking out from a house include Sisera's mother (Judg. 5:28), David's wife Michal (2 Sam. 6:16-23), and even Queen Jezebel (2 Kings 9:30). Whether due to death in the

---

28. Eaton, *Ecclesiastes*, 148.
29. Kidner, *A Time to Mourn*, 101-02.
30. Provan, *Ecclesiastes, Song of Songs*, 217.
31. Davis, 'Death, an Impetus for Life, Ecclesiastes 12:1-8,' 358.

house, calamity in the village, or the arrival of a severe winter storm, these women have become more isolated from the life they once knew.

Verse 4 continues the description of the stricken household and, perhaps, its village. 'Doors' literally means 'two doors'. However, most houses in ancient Israel possessed but one door. The dual number favors a reference to a city gate through which people would enter the bazaar and the nearby judgment seat where the elders of the city held court. 'The sound of the grinding mill is low' thus indicates a decrease in the normal economic and commercial activities common to everyday life. The village activities slow nearly to a halt for the death of a key citizen and his funeral. Rising at the sound of a bird may refer either to being startled to action by the sound of a bird through the silent streets or to the hooting or cooing of birds viewed as harbingers of death. 'Daughters of song' could refer to the women whose function involves singing laments for the dying master.

Aging: The Ultimate Harbinger of Death (12:5)

Fear of either climbing heights (which might result in a heart attack or stroke – at least being left with belabored breathing) or moving about in crowded streets characterize the elderly. The blossoms of the almond tree come toward the end of winter before the leaves even sprout. The white color of the blossoms crowning the whole tree reminds one of the white hair of the aged. A locust or grasshopper, when no longer able to hop about with youthful vigor, drags itself along as though burdened – much like the awkward gait of old men and women. The ancient peoples in the Near East prized the caperberry for stimulating appetite or sexual desire. In the advanced years, however, the caperberry no longer acts as an effective stimulant.

Indeed, all of these characteristics of the aging indicate that they are on their final journey to their 'eternal home' Several commentators cite the use of this terminology in the Egyptian 'Instructions of Onchsheshonqy' (ca. fifth–fourth centuries B.C.).[32] A conservative dating of Ecclesiastes, however, places its writing prior to that of 'Onchsheshonqy. A Palmyrene inscription (second century A.D.): "the house of eternity, that grave which

---

32. Cf. Eaton, *Ecclesiastes*, 149.

Zabdeateh built.'"[33] Though Crenshaw offers this example as evidence of its use for the grave, it comes later than nearly every conceivable date attributable to the writing of Ecclesiastes. Indeed, the Palmyrene inscription might have depended upon Ecclesiastes for the phraseology. Jewish communities still refer to their cemeteries as *Beth Olam*, the same phrase as used here. To support the translation 'dark house', Youngblood utilizes parallel biblical texts describing the grave or Sheol as a place of darkness, the potential meaning of 'darkness' for the root word from which 'eternity' comes, and extrabiblical references to darkness in relation to death, the grave, the netherworld.[34] However, the more straightforward reading of 12:5 as well as 3:11 and 3:14 ('forever') would indicate that the writer of Ecclesiastes uses the Hebrew word *olam* for 'a long time', 'forever', or 'eternity'. Readers of the New Testament readily associate the description with a similar concept in 2 Corinthians 5:1 ('if the earthly tent which is our house is torn down, we have a building from God, a house not made with hands, eternal in the heavens'). Granted, Solomon does not refer to a heavenly habitation and Paul does not refer to the grave or the netherworld of departed spirits of Old Testament times. However, both texts speak of the state of existence following life 'under the sun' as a 'house' – a place of habitation.

The reference to 'mourners' going about the street (Eccles. 12:5) fits the ancient Hebrew custom of mourning the death of an Israelite (Amos 5:16-20; Jer. 9:17-22; 22:18; 34:5).

Death: Returning to God (12:6-7)

The third 'before' (v. 6) introduces the end of life when the opportunities to enjoy God's gifts cease and the individual meets his or her Creator. The 'golden bowl' might depict a lamp like that in Zechariah 4:2-3. The lamp befits the description of death, since texts like Proverbs 13:9 speak of 'the lamp' of an individual being put out at death (cp. Job 18:5-6; 21:17; Prov. 20:20; 24:20). The silver cord could be the means of hanging the golden lamp, filled with oil. Putting fire to the wicks in the oil would give light as the oil in the wicks burned. If someone cuts the cord or it breaks, the lamp of oil crashes to the stone floor and the oil is

---

33. Crenshaw, *Ecclesiastes*, 188.
34. Youngblood, 'Qoheleth's 'Dark House' (Eccles. 12:5),' 211-27.

spilled. Likewise, the pitcher that holds life-giving water drawn from a well or cistern cannot serve its task if the pitcher breaks. Crenshaw explains that, 'The picture of a fountain in disrepair suggests that the water of life can no longer be drawn, and the end has come.'[35]

The 'wheel' could be a pulley used to lower a pitcher into the depths of a well and to draw it back up when it is filled. On two occasions 'crushed' occurs with the golden bowl as an object and then with 'the wheel'. Interestingly, Hebrew derives its words for 'bowl' and for 'wheel' from the same root word meaning 'roll' or 'round'.[36] Solomon might be depicting a violent death from a crushed skull and the failure of the destroyed cranium to retain the contents of the brain.

In Eaton's estimation, verse 7 'hints … at continued existence'.[37] Fredericks states that the verse 'is not a denial of an afterlife; it is simply not an explicit affirmation of it.'[38] Although the writer does not specifically identify an afterlife, other texts in the Old Testament make the concept more explicit (cf. Ps. 49; Dan. 12:2). Elsewhere, the reference to human beings returning to the dust out of which they came (Job 34:14-15; Ps. 104:29) makes it clear that the biblical prophets and sages clearly understood the historical record of mankind's creation (cp. Gen. 2:7; 3:19).

Only by accepting the reality and naturalness of death, can a person face life with the kind of joy that Solomon encourages in the enjoyment passages (cp. 9:2-10 and 11:7-10). For the wise believer, contentment with the brevity of life produces a freedom for living the life God gives in His service and for His glory. Ryken reminds his readers that aging and death consist of 'some of the hardest experiences in life. The Bible is honest about this, but not bitter.'[39] The psalmist speaks of the death of God's saints as precious in His estimation (Ps. 116:15). After all, 'God is the owner and donor of life.'[40]

---

35. Crenshaw, *Ecclesiastes*, 188.
36. Provan, *Ecclesiastes, Song of Songs*, 218. The Hebrew name Golgotha (meaning 'place of the skull;' Matt 27:33) comes from the same root.
37. Eaton, *Ecclesiastes*, 151.
38. Fredericks, 'Ecclesiastes,' 240.
39. Ryken, *Ecclesiastes*, 271.
40. Murphy, *Ecclesiastes*, 120.

Table of Interpretations

Phrase	Aging	Death & Funeral	Storm	House	Abstract
2a *before the sun and the light, the moon and the stars are darkened*	Does not see well (Garrett, 341). Sad countenance of an old man (Targums in Garrett, 341). Failure of memory, understanding, will, affections, and imaginations (Kaiser, 119). Youth yields to old age, making life an unpromising dark, cold winter (Estes, 375).	Extinguishing the light of life (Fox, 300). Eschatological language to describe the end of human life (Seow, 353).	Rain bringing the winter (Crenshaw, 185). A storm breaks over an Eastern city – light is darkened, clouds obscure the sun (Leahy, 378). Storm symbolic of dread and sorrow with encroaching old age and impending death (Longman, 269).		An eschatological motif with something in mind larger than aging or death (Bartholomew, 348; Seow, 353-54). Surreal and apocalyptic (Garrett, 341). Clouds represent troubles (Kidner, 101-2; Hengstenberg, 245). Decrease in the joy (brightness) of life (Barton, 186-87).
2b *clouds return after the rain*	Sounds like glaucoma (Crenshaw, 185; Garrett, 341).	Contributes to the scene of gloom at death (Fox, 301).	Yet another intense storm following the first (Fredericks, 239).		

Phrase	Aging	Death & Funeral	Storm	House	Abstract
3a *the watchmen of the house tremble*	Hands (Garrett, 341). Arms (Eaton, 148). Arms and hands (Kaiser, 120).	Servants tremble at the presence of death in the house (Fox, 301).	Lightning and thunder terrorize everyone (Leahy, 378).	Guardian slaves discomfited (Crenshaw, 185-86).	Imminent destruction brought about by God affects both the mighty and the worker (Bartholomew, 349).
3b *mighty men stoop*	Major muscles of legs and back (Garrett, 341; Eaton, 148). Legs and knees (Kaiser, 120).	Men experience violent grief (Fox, 301-02).	Cringing at the intensity of the coming storm (Fredericks, 239).	Old back of freemen (Crenshaw, 185-86).	
3c *the grinding ones stand idle because they are few*	Teeth (Garrett, 341; Eaton, 148; Kaiser, 120).	Number of maid-servants grinding grain reduced by those joining in the mourning (Fox, 303).	Women grinding grain chased into their homes by the approaching storm (Fredericks, 239).	Inactivity of slave women grinding grain (Crenshaw, 185-86).	

Phrase	Aging	Death & Funeral	Storm	House	Abstract
3d *those who look through windows grow dim*	Eyes losing their sparkle rather than decreased sight (Garrett, 341). Eyes begin to lose sight (Kaiser, 120).	Women grieving because of the death (Fox, 303).	Women peep timidly through their latticed windows (Leahy, 378).	Darkening of women of substance (Crenshaw, 185-86). People growing dim (Whybray, 164).	A literary idiom evoking dashed hopes (Bartholomew, 349; Seow, 356).
4a *the doors on the street are shut as the sound of the grinding mill is low*	Ears – deafness (Garrett, 341; Eaton, 149). Lips and becoming toothless (Kaiser, 120).	Doors are shut and mills grow silent for the funeral (Fox, 303). Double doors of the bazaar closed (Brown, 111).	Doors are shut against wind and rain (Leahy, 378).	Doors closed to normal business of life (Estes, 376). Double gates leading to the large estate (Gordis, 343).	City gates opening onto the central business area of the city (Bartholomew, 349; Seow, 356-57).
4b *one will arise at the sound of the bird*	Light sleep even with deafness (Garrett, 341). Waking erratically in the early hours, when the birds start to twitter (Barton, 189; Eaton, 149). Waking at slightest sound (Kaiser, 120).	Perhaps depicting the birds themselves joining in the songs of lament (Fox, 304). Sound of wild birds rises over the silenced commercial activities of the village (Brown, 112).	Sound of the bird can hardly be heard (Leahy, 378). Birds intimidated into silence by the coming tempest (Fredericks, 239).	Sounds of scavenging birds (Estes, 376).	Eerie silence due to the imminent catastrophe or the ominous hooting of birds as a sign of death (Bartholomew, 349; Seow, 358).

Phrase	Aging	Death & Funeral	Storm	House	Abstract
4c *all the daughters of song will sing softly*	Loss of ability to make and enjoy music (Kaiser, 120). Deafness (Barton, 189; Longman, 271).	Female singers singing laments in the traditional posture of lamentation (Fox, 304).	Merry-makers terrorized into silence by the storm (Leahy, 378).		Mourners chanting laments (Bartholomew, 350). Hooting birds moving into a desolated area (Seow, 359).
5a *men are afraid of a high place and of terrors on the road*	Fears of the aged (Garrett, 341; Crenshaw, 187; Eaton, 149; Kaiser, 121).	Fear of the High One, viz., God; and, the fear displayed as the funeral cortege passes by (Fox, 304).	Men fear the stormy heavens; outdoors there is terrors (Leahy, 378).		Fear of the heights from which attacks might come and the terrors of travel in such times (Bartholomew, 350). Birds note the desolation from on high and come swooping down (Seow, 360).
5b *the almond tree blossoms*	White hair (Garrett, 341; Eaton, 149; Kaiser, 121).	The trees are reborn in the spring, but not man – cp. Job 14:7-10 (Fox, 305).	In the wake of the storm, there is destruction of almond trees, caper-shrubs, and grasshoppers (Leahy, 378; Fredericks, 239).	Contrasting the fresh birth of spring with the deterioration of the house (Crenshaw, 187).	A sign of coming judgment as in Jeremiah 1:9-12 (Bartholomew, 350). The almond blossoms become revolting (Seow, 361).

Phrase	Aging	Death & Funeral	Storm	House	Abstract
5c *the grasshopper drags himself along*	Loss of strength – even grass-hopper too heavy (Barton, 190; Garrett, 341). Problems with joints, swollen ankles, halting walk, or impotence (Eaton, 149; Kaiser, 121). Forces hostile to life in old age (Hengstenberg, 250).	Perhaps the text should be altered so that the word for 'grasshopper' can change to 'sea onion' – see 5b for meaning (Fox, 306).			Loss of the capacity for fast movement, evoking the end of nature itself (Bartholomew, 350). The locust droops – it languishes (Seow, 363).
5d *the caperberry is ineffective*	Loss of sexual desire (Garrett, 341; Kaiser, 121). Loss of bodily appetites (Eaton, 149).	See 5b for meaning (Fox, 306).	Renewal of nature (Loader and Fox in Garrett, 341).		Refers to breaking in the sense of coming to nothing, falling apart (Bartholomew, 350). The caper is defoliated – nature comes to an end (Seow, 363).
5e *man goes to his eternal home while mourners go about in the street*	A continuous decline physically toward death – a new home (Eaton, 149)	Death within a very short time and then mourners carry the man to his grave (Fox, 306).	At the end of the storm, burial of the dead bring mourners into the streets (Fredericks, 239).		Death has come comprehensively to the creation (Bartholomew, 351).

Phrase	Aging	Death & Funeral	Storm	House	Abstract
6a *the silver cord is broken*	Spinal marrow connecting brain and nerves (Kaiser, 121). The soul (Delitzsch, 421).	Death of a nobleman (Fox, 307).			This and the following all refer to the demise of ordinary, daily life 'under the sun' (Bartholomew, 351).
6b *the golden bowl is crushed*	The brain (Kaiser, 121). Body (Delitzsch, 421).	See 3a, above.			
6c *the pitcher by the well is shattered*	The failing heart (Kaiser, 121).	Death of a common man (Fox, 307).			
6d *the wheel at the cistern is crushed*	Veins and arteries (Kaiser, 121).	'Wheel' should be taken as a 'jar' depicting a poor man (Fox, 307).			
7a *the dust will return to the earth as it was*					
7b *the spirit will return to God who gave it*					

Swindoll offers three pieces of practical advice in the light of verses 1-7:

1. I must face the fact that I'm not getting any younger.
2. God has designed me to be empty without Him.
3. Now is the time to prepare for eternity.[41]

The Epilogue to Ecclesiastes (12:8-14)

Most commentators hold that an editor added these final verses. A Jewish tradition attributes them to Hezekiah's men who penned them as a conclusion to all canonical Solomonic writings.[42] Some, like Longman, believe that the final editor added verses 8-14 in order to express a positive and orthodox theology, because the editor was unhappy with the ultimate conclusion of the book as a whole.[43] Such a viewpoint finds little support from a careful reading of Ecclesiastes. Concepts of divine judgment, human accountability, and divine demands or imperatives surface throughout the book (cp. 2:26; 3:1, 17; 5:1, 2, 4-7; 7:29; 8:12, 13; 9:7-10; 11:9; 12:14).

Crenshaw states that the presence of the refrain ('Vanity of vanities,... all is vanity') in verse 8 'refutes the claim that Qohelet hoped for immortality of the soul'.[44] Such a negative treatment of the teachings of Solomon languishes for adequate support. (1) Elsewhere in the book, Solomon speaks clearly of a future judgment (11:9; 12:14; cp. 1 Cor. 4:5; Heb. 9:27). (2) Crenshaw's declaration that the writer 'hoped' for immortality rests upon an unknowable – the writer himself must specifically identify his hopes in order for later readers to claim their existence. (3) The fact that the spirit returns to God speaks of hope – it implies that the spirit does not cease its existence with the dissolution of the body in the grave.[45] Ryken cites a set of syllogisms: 'If there is no God, then there is no Judge. If there is no Judge, then there will be no Final Judgment. If there is no Final Judgment, there is no ultimate meaning to life. Nothing matters.'[46] But, 'The final message of Ecclesiastes is not that

---

41. Swindoll, *Living on the Ragged Edge,* 385.
42. Reichart and Cohen, 'Ecclesiastes,' 2:109.
43. Longman, *Ecclesiastes,* 284.
44. Crenshaw, *Ecclesiastes,* 189.
45. Cf. Bartholomew, *Ecclesiastes,* 352-53.
46. Ryken, *Ecclesiastes,* 273.

nothing matters but that *everything* does.'[47] In other words, Solomon's argument goes this way:

- God exists – He is the Creator.
- Since God is the Creator, He is also the Judge.
- If God is the Judge, there will be a final judgment.
- Since there will be a final judgment, everything we do (how we live) matters.
- Therefore, even though life is but a fleeting breath, it is not futile and insignificant.

The inclusio of 12:8 with 1:2 helps to highlight another Solomonic theme, the cycles of existence (cf. 1:4).[48] All things continue as they were from the beginning. From the Fall of man (cp. 7:29), vanity or futility entered the creation through mankind's sins. Death came because of sin (Rom. 5:12). Because of death, life is fleeting. The use of *hebel* ('vanity' or 'breath') in verse 8 follows the mention of 'spirit' in verse 7 so closely that the text seems to indicate that 'Human breath is the metre not only of one's life but of the duration of all that is done under the sun.'[49]

Verses 9 and 12 both begin with the same word in the original text (*weyoter*, 'in addition' or 'beyond this'). The use marks off two sections of the epilogue. Provan paraphrases the first part of verse 9 with 'I want to add my own perspective on all this: I consider Qohelet a wise man and someone who taught knowledge to the people.'[50]

Verses 9-10 give implicit, if not explicit, testimony to the reality of the writer's historical existence.[51] According to Eaton, 'In his concern for teaching the Preacher was akin to Moses (Deut. 6:1f.), David (2 Sam. 1:18; *cf.* Pss. 34:11; 51:13), Jehoshaphat (2 Chron. 17:7-9), Ezra (Ezra 7:10), and many other Israelite leaders.'[52] Verse 9, even if written by an editor, seems to point to the Book of Proverbs, which the writer attributes to 'the

---

47. Ibid., 281 (emphasis his).
48. Cf. Fredericks, 'Ecclesiastes,' 240.
49. Ibid.
50. Provan, *Ecclesiastes, Song of Songs*, 226.
51. Cp. Fox, *Qohelet and His Contradictions*, 316-17, who argues that this might be a common literary device to cause readers to 'suspend disbelief' in order to accept the book itself as credible.
52. Eaton, *Ecclesiastes*, 152.

Preacher'. That implies that the author of Proverbs is the same as 'the Preacher'.[53] Solomon's pursuit of wisdom displays a pastoral tone more than an academic or professional tone.[54] 'Pondered,' 'searched out,' and 'arranged' all reflect Solomon's knowledgeable pursuit of wisdom and the issues involved in life 'under the sun'. 'Pondered' (literally, 'weighed') 'points to careful evaluation, indicating his honesty, caution and balance';[55] 'searched out' implies his 'thoroughness and diligence';[56] and, 'arranged' points to orderliness and an artistic skill in his presentation (cp. 1 Kings 4:32).[57] The description of the author reminds readers of the introduction to the Gospel of Luke (Luke 1:1-4) and of the various inscriptions found in the Book of Proverbs (24:23; 30:1; 31:1). All are a straightforward account of how the respective book or collection (in Proverbs) came to be written.

Solomon attributes both delightfulness (cf. Prov. 25:11) and dependability to the words that he sought (Eccles. 12:10). These two characteristics of instruction in Ecclesiastes reveal a balance. 'To be upright but unpleasant is to be a fool; to be pleasant but not upright is to be a charlatan.'[58] Crenshaw notes that 'Many readers have not concurred in the statement that Qohelet's observations are both pleasing and trustworthy.'[59] Those who find Ecclesiastes skeptical and filled with doubt rather than faith will perhaps agree with this judgment. However, the positive message of Ecclesiastes as presented in the enjoyment passages and in the book's closing exhortations argue against a pessimistic approach to the teachings of the book. Kaiser takes a positive approach to the book: 'In no way can that be a description of the work of a pessimist, nihilist, or Epicurean with an "eat-drink-and-be-merry-for-tomorrow-we-die" mentality.'[60]

Interpreters variously take the 'one Shepherd' as either Solomon, wisdom writers in general, or God (v. 11).[61] Since the book addresses the author as 'the Preacher', it seems better to

53. Barton, *Ecclesiastes*, 197.
54. Eaton, *Ecclesiastes*, 153.
55. Ibid.
56. Ibid.
57. Ibid.
58. Ibid., 154.
59. Crenshaw, *Ecclesiastes*, 191.
60. Kaiser, *Ecclesiastes*, 123.
61. Longman, *Ecclesiastes*, 279, argues for a generic reference to wisdom teachers as just another aspect of the agricultural metaphor involving the goads.

understand 'Shepherd' as a title of deity rather than another title for the human author.[62] This title for God in this context implies a doctrine of divine superintendence in the writing of Scripture (cp. 2 Pet. 1:21).[63] Kaiser supports the conclusion that 'Shepherd' refers to God who 'is the real source of the words of this book; not cynicism, not skepticism, not worldliness.'[64] The agricultural reference to goads (cf. 1 Sam. 13:21) provides a vehicle for saying that 'Words and goads are tools to guide people on the right path, though making them uncomfortable in doing so.'[65] The 'well-driven nails' appear to be something like tent pegs for the herdsmen's tents or pegs driven into beams for use in hanging utensils from them. The two figures represent the stimulation and the steadying effects of wise words, or, as Kidner notes, 'they spur the will and stick in the memory.'[66]

In verses 12-13, the imperatives fill the air with a sense of urgency.[67] Verse 12 provides the only occurrence of the phrase 'my son' in Ecclesiastes. Crenshaw, along with other commentators, apply the nomenclature to students, as opposed to actual sons.[68] The context does not resolve the meaning for the reader. Either interpretation might be correct.

Fox takes the position that 'the writing of many books is endless' means '"Making many books is a thing of no purpose". Writing is praiseworthy, but there is no point in overdoing it.'[69] Eaton, on the other hand, sees the statement as a warning about the many pagan writings from other nations that claim to offer wisdom.[70] Understanding it as a warning, Whybray identifies it with 'poring over unsuitable literature', which will only weary and do harm.[71] As Fredericks points

62. Hengstenberg, *Ecclesiastes*, 264; Gordis, *Koheleth*, 354; Kidner, *A Time to Mourn*, 106; Garrett, *Proverbs, Ecclesiastes, Song of Songs*, 344; Bartholomew, *Ecclesiastes*, 366-69; Fredericks, 'Ecclesiastes,' 248.

63. Eaton, *Ecclesiastes*, 154.

64. Kaiser, *Ecclesiastes*, 124-25.

65. Fox, *Qohelet and His Contradictions*, 326.

66. Kidner, *A Time to Mourn*, 106.

67. Crenshaw, *Ecclesiastes*, 190.

68. Ibid., 191.

69. Fox, *Qohelet and His Contradictions*, 327.

70. Eaton, *Ecclesiastes*, 155.

71. Whybray, *Ecclesiastes*, 173. Jewish commentators sometimes make the clause a reference to the 'Oral Law' – that is, 'it would be impossible to commit the entire Oral Law to writing' (Reichart and Cohen, 'Ecclesiastes,' 2:110).

out, the writer intends more the 'use' of books than the writing of them.[72]

Verses 13-14 form the ultimate conclusion of Ecclesiastes. The Masoretes, preservationists of the ancient Hebrew text from around A.D. 700–1200, instruct the public reader to repeat verse 13 after verse 14 so that the reading does not end upon a negative note. Ending with verse 14 makes 'evil' the final (and ominous) word of Ecclesiastes.[73] The Masoretes also perform the same service for Isaiah, the book of the twelve Minor Prophets, and Lamentations, for the same reason.

Note the order of the Hebrew text in verse 13. By placing the two direct objects ahead of the imperative in each clause, the text emphasizes 'God' and 'commandments'.[74] The logical order of the two imperatives ('fear' and 'obey') supplies additional significance. As Eaton explains, 'Conduct derives from worship. A knowledge of God leads to obedience; not vice versa.'[75] The teaching in these final verses reflects the Book of Deuteronomy (4:6, 10; 6:2, 24; 8:6; 10:12-13).

'Every person' (literally, 'the whole of man'; Eccles. 12:13) occurs also in 3:13 and 5:19. However, here the construction is quite different and distinct. According to Greidanus, 'The Hebrew does not have the word "duty," so it reads literally that fearing God and keeping his commandments "is the *whole* of everyone." It's not just our duty, it's our *essence*.'[76] In Psalm 109:4 the psalmist uses a similar construction to indicate that he is characterized by prayer: 'I am prayer.' The same type of construction appears also in Psalm 120:7 ('I am peace') and Job 8:9 ('we are yesterday'). The point is that the attribute is the defining essence of the person or persons to which it is ascribed. Thus, it is mankind's very essence to fear God and obey Him. The truths of Ecclesiastes apply to everyone (cp. Rom 2:14-16). Here is the answer to the opening question (1:3): 'What advantage [or, profit] does man have in all his work which he does under the sun?'). Kaiser put it this way, 'He gets the living God! And his whole profit consists of fearing Him

---

72. Fredericks, 'Ecclesiastes,' 244.
73. Reichart and Cohen, 'Ecclesiastes,' 2:111.
74. Eaton, *Ecclesiastes*, 156.
75. Ibid.
76. Greidanus, *Preaching Christ from Ecclesiastes*, 309-10 (emphasis his).

and obeying His Word.'[77] Or, as Estes puts it, the advantage 'resides not in human achievement apart from God, but rather in human connection with God.'[78]

Solomon's pursuit of wisdom and investigation of mankind's condition 'under the sun' results in 'an incitement to true piety. The insignificance of all that is done under the sun leaves him awestruck and silent before God.'[79] Leupold sums up verse 14 as 'an excellent example of when the words of the wise man are truly "goads" and "nails."'[80] The reader's course is clear:

- Remember God, the Creator (Eccles. 12:1).

- Fear God, the Creator (Eccles. 3:14; 5:7; 8:12; 12:14).

- Keep the commandments of God (Eccles. 12:14).

- Enjoy the life God gives (Eccles. 9:7-10).

- Prepare for leaving life 'under the sun' (Eccles. 12:1).

- Prepare to stand before God in a future judgment where we will be held accountable for enjoying what He has given and for living in accord with His commands (Eccles. 11:9; cf. Rom. 2:16; Heb. 9:27).

STUDY QUESTIONS

1. What does it mean to 'Remember your Creator'? How can we do that?

2. Why is death sometimes very unpleasant and even frightening?

3. What are the characteristics of aging for most people?

4. How should we prepare ourselves for old age and death?

5. Explain the reasons for believing that the text of Ecclesiastes actually hints strongly at a life beyond the sun?

6. How does the writer of 12:9-11 describe the Book of Ecclesiastes? How does that compare to a pessimistic or skeptical approach to the book?

---

77. Kaiser, *Ecclesiastes*, 125.
78. Estes, *Handbook on the Wisdom Books*, 378.
79. Garrett, *Proverbs, Ecclesiastes, Song of Songs*, 345.
80. Leupold, *Ecclesiastes*, 301.

An Epilogue

Further Thoughts on Ecclesiastes

The epilogue to Ecclesiastes in 12:8-14 inspires epilogues to commentaries. Interestingly, not a single commentator disclaims authorship for either their commentary or its epilogue. However, they tend to deny that privilege to the author of Ecclesiastes. If Solomon penned the epilogue (12:8-14), he wrote it in order to instruct readers in how to understand and apply what he had written in 1:1–12:7. The biblical epilogue focuses on theological and practical matters. This commentator's 'Further Thoughts on Ecclesiastes' finds its motivation in those same matters from a New Testament frame of reference. As William Brown writes, 'Taking my cue from Ecclesiastes 12:9-14, I find the genre of the epilogue to be the best place in which to express certain conclusions about Ecclesiastes from an expressly Christian perspective.'[1]

Ecclesiastes puts mankind in their proper place theologically – subordinate to God and accountable for how they live 'under the sun.' Solomon writes with God-given wisdom about human wisdom apart from God. He shows, as Michael Kelley explains, that 'Man in his rebellion has proudly looked to self-generated wisdom ideals to erect paradise on earth. He confidently believes himself to be in possession of the correct agenda for life and culture.'[2] Solomon receives wisdom from God for governing Israel. He soon discovers, however, that his wisdom has limits and that other areas of wisdom that God allows him to possess are not adequate to answer the greatest

---

1. Brown, *Ecclesiastes*, 121.
2. Kelley, *The Burden of God*, 150.

enigmas of mankind's existence. His limited wisdom could not prevent his plunge into idolatry and his rapid decline spiritually.

Through it all, Solomon produces his spiritual journal to stimulate his readers' thinking. Just as he searches for what is truly meaningful in life, so he expects his readers to take spiritual issues very seriously. Kelley interprets the occasional pessimistic tone of the book as revealing to God's own people 'what is at stake.'[3] Some people only awaken to the brevity of life and the need for fearing God when they encounter the darkest of life's realities. Death plays top billing among the realities that might shake a person out of spiritual lethargy or indifference. Trials edify, produce godly patience, and instill joy for the gifts God gives day by day. 'Pastorally this is significant,' writes Craig Bartholomew, 'for Ecclesiastes, like Job, holds out hope for those struggling amid the mysteries of what God is up to in their lives and thus in his world.'[4]

Although the New Testament does not directly quote from Ecclesiastes, the apostle Paul makes two potential allusions to the book in Romans. The first potential allusion comes in Romans 3:10 ('as it is written, "THERE IS NONE RIGHTEOUS, NOT EVEN ONE"'). Paul may be referring to Ecclesiastes 7:20, 'Indeed, there is not a righteous man on earth who *continually* does good and who never sins.' Mark Seifrid points out that Paul's wording differs from both Psalms 14:1, 3 and 53:1, 3 even in the way the ancient Greek Septuagint translates those texts. In place of 'There is no one who does good,' the apostle 'substitutes 'no one is righteous,' perhaps drawing on Ecclesiastes 7:20.'[5] Whether or not Paul actually depends upon Ecclesiastes, the ultimate significance is that both Ecclesiastes and Romans teach the same propositional truth: everyone is a sinner.

The second potential allusion to Ecclesiastes comes in Romans 8:18-22: 'For I consider that the sufferings of this present time are not worthy to be compared with the glory

3. Kelley, *The Burden of God*, 138.
4. Bartholomew, *Ecclesiastes*, 371.
5. Mark A. Seifrid, 'Romans,' in *Commentary on the New Testament Use of the Old Testament*, ed. by G. K. Beale and D. A. Carson (Grand Rapids, Mich.: Baker Academic, 2007), 616.

that is to be revealed to us. For the anxious longing of the creation waits eagerly for the revealing of the sons of God. For the creation was subjected to futility, not willingly, but because of Him who subjected it, in hope that the creation itself also will be set free from its slavery to corruption into the freedom of the glory of the children of God. For we know that the whole creation groans and suffers the pains of childbirth together until now.'

The ancient Greek Septuagint translation of Ecclesiastes uses the same Greek word for 'vanity' in Ecclesiastes as Paul uses for 'futility' in Romans 8:20 (*mataiotes*).[6] Although evidence is exceedingly thin for any dependence on Ecclesiastes, the fact is that the apostle, like Solomon, recognizes the futility or vanity of life 'under the sun' as a result of Adam's sin. Mankind's sufferings cannot be resolved through human effort or wisdom. The only hope resides with God's ability to deliver creation from 'its slavery to corruption' (Rom. 8:21). Both Paul and Solomon realize that the Creator alone can make things right in a world subjected to *hebel* ('vanity' or 'futility').

James 4:14 presents a third potential allusion to Ecclesiastes: 'Yet you do not know what your life will be like tomorrow. You are *just* a vapor that appears for a little while and then vanishes away.' Daniel Fredericks notes that the New Testament echoes Ecclesiastes' message concerning the transience of life. 'If there is a NT passage that is closest to the spirit of Ecclesiastes' message of brevity, it is that found in James 4:14.'[7] Second Corinthians 4:18, Fredericks argues, presents an even better parallel:[8] 'while we look not at the things which are seen, but at the things which are not seen; for the things which are seen are temporal, but the things which are not seen are eternal.' Solomon makes the same point: what mankind experiences 'under the sun' is fleeting, but God is beyond the sun, eternal and unchanging.

Comparing Ecclesiastes to Paul's New Testament epistle to the Philippians rests on more than just a focus on joy. Both works recognize significant truths for the godly:

---

6. Longman, *Ecclesiastes*, 39.
7. Fredericks, 'Ecclesiastes,' 43.
8. Ibid.

- Some people, who appear to be doing the righteous thing, actually act out of impure motives like envy, greed, and antagonism (Phil. 1:15-17; Eccles. 4:4, 8; 8:10).

- Life 'under the sun' should engage in fruitful labor (Phil. 1:22; 2:12-13; Eccles. 9:7, 10).

- The godly need to manifest an unselfish concern for others (Phil. 2:1-4; Eccles. 4:1, 8-12; 5:14; 7:21-22; 11:1-2, if these two verses refer to charity).

- Believers need warning about evil workers (Phil. 3:2, 18-19; Eccles. 3:16, 18; 4:1; 5:1, 13; 7:6, 7, 26, 29).

- The spirit returns to God (cp. Phil. 3:21 and Eccles. 12:7).

- Believers must apply their minds to understanding truth (Phil. 1:10; 4:8; Eccles. 3:11; 7:2, 4, 13, 25; 8:1; 10:2; 12:1, 9-11).

- Contentment comes only in accepting that God provides both suffering and prosperity, hunger and abundance (Phil. 1:29; 4:11-12, 19; Eccles. 3:14; 5:18-19; 6:2; 7:14; 9:1, 7-9; 11:7–12:1).

A careful reading of the Book of Ecclesiastes results in a number of comparisons between the teachings of Jesus and Solomon's observations. Luke 12:16-21, for example, presents a number of parallels with the teaching in Ecclesiastes (see the commentary on 1:3-8 for a full description of both similarities and dissimilarities). In the Sermon on the Mount Jesus addresses the matter of fulfilling vows (Matt. 5:33). Perhaps the 'ancients' about whom He speaks include Solomon (Eccles. 5:2-6). The instruction Jesus offers implies that one ought to fear God (Matt. 5:34-37) – the same conclusion Solomon reaches (Eccles. 5:7).

Jesus warns against empty deeds of righteousness that were nothing but show (Matt. 6:1-4) and Solomon speaks of the 'sacrifice of fools' (Eccles. 5:1) and the wicked who made a practice of attending the holy place (Eccles. 8:10). In his closing instructions Solomon also warns the young man against enjoying the gifts of God in this life with a wrong attitude or purpose (Eccles. 11:9). When Jesus teaches His disciples to pray, He first reminds them that God is in heaven, but they are on earth (Matt. 6:9-10; cp. Eccles. 5:1-2). He also reminds His disciples to remember that it is God who provides their food (Matt. 6:11, 25, 31), their drink (Matt. 6:25, 31), and their clothing (Matt. 6:25-29). Comparison with Ecclesiastes 3:12-13; 5:18-19; 8:15; and 9:7-9 are unavoidable. Jesus even refers to Solomon at this very stage of His discourse (Matt. 6:29). 'But seek first His kingdom and His righteousness, and all these things will be added to you' (Matt. 6:33) refers to the food, drink, and clothing that God gives. Although Ecclesiastes never speaks directly of God's kingdom and righteousness, the implications of passages like Ecclesiastes 3:14, 17; 5:7; 7:13, 18; 8:12-13, 17; 9:1, 7; 11:9; 12:1, and 13 certainly imply the righteousness and sovereignty of God. In addition, the statement that 'Each day has enough trouble of its own' (Matt. 6:34) echoes the 'days of darkness' in Ecclesiastes 11:8.

Then Jesus cautions His disciples about judging others too quickly and strictly, when they themselves might be equally guilty (Matt. 7:1-5). Solomon gives very similar instruction in Ecclesiastes 7:21-22 concerning what a person's servants might be saying behind their master's or mistress's back. Jesus concludes the Sermon on the Mount with yet another reminder of the gifts of God (Matt. 7:11), with an exhortation to keep the Law (Matt. 7:12; cp. Eccles. 12:13), with yet another caution against hypocrisy (Matt. 7:21-23; cp. Eccles. 5:1-7; 8:10), and a closing contrast between the wise and the foolish (Matt. 7:24-27; cp. Eccles. 9:13-10:3; 10:12-15; 12:11).

The content of the final verse of Ecclesiastes (12:14, 'For God will bring every act to judgment, everything which is hidden, whether it is good or evil') also recurs in Jesus' teaching in Matthew 12:36-37 and Luke 12:1-3. Death will come to every human being, but so will God's judgment (Heb. 9:27).

What do all of these comparisons prove? First, the comparisons made above are only a fraction of all that might be drawn between Ecclesiastes and the New Testament. The warp and woof of Ecclesiastes exhibit theological and practical truths that remain the same centuries later when Jesus, the Master Teacher, addresses first-century disciples about living a godly life. Second, focusing on Jesus might give the impression that His instruction bears a closer relationship to Ecclesiastes than the writings of the apostles. Such is not the case. A brief foray into the epistolary literature of the New Testament demonstrates that those same truths continues through the apostolic era. Third, characterizing the writer of Ecclesiastes as pessimistic, skeptical, and unworthy of proclaiming theological truth cannot obliterate the clear testimony of the book. The internal consistency of the canon of Scripture speaks emphatically to its unity and integrity.

No wonder Walter Kaiser concludes his brief commentary with 'What a book! What a good God! What a life! And what a plan!'[9] The Book of Ecclesiastes does not present the full panorama of divine revelation, but it certainly sets a person on a firm foundation upon which a solid spiritual life might be erected. Face today and tomorrow with Solomon's journal in hand. Enjoy life 'under the sun,' but prepare for life beyond the sun.

STUDY QUESTIONS

1. What evidence is present in Ecclesiastes to demonstrate that Solomon expects his readers to take spiritual issues seriously?

2. What do New Testament texts like Romans 3:10 and 8:20 teach us about the teachings present in the Book of Ecclesiastes?

3. Identify various examples of truths taught by Jesus in the Sermon on the Mount that Ecclesiastes also emphasizes.

4. Why should New Testament believers give serious attention to the message of Ecclesiastes 12:14 about divine judgment?

5. Which New Testament book(s) might someone identify with the message of Ecclesiastes besides Paul's epistle to the Philippians?

6. What is one life-changing truth that you have learned from studying Ecclesiastes?

---

9. Kaiser, *Ecclesiastes*, 125.

Bibliography

Books:

Barr, James. *Comparative Philology and the Text of the Old Testament, with Additions and Corrections*. Winona Lake, Ind.: Eisenbrauns, 1987.

Bartholomew, Craig G. *Ecclesiastes*. Baker Commentary on the Old Testament Wisdom and Psalms. Grand Rapids, Mich.: Baker Academic, 2009.

Barton, George Aaron. *A Critical and Exegetical Commentary on the Book of Ecclesiastes*. International Critical Commentary. 1908. Reprint, Edinburgh: T. & T. Clark, 1971.

Bridges, Charles. *A Commentary on Ecclesiastes*. 1860. Reprint, Edinburgh: Banner of Truth, 1961.

Brown, William P. *Ecclesiastes*. Interpretation. Louisville, Ky.: John Knox Press, 2000.

Bullock, C. Hassell. *An Introduction to the Old Testament Poetic Books: The Wisdom and Songs of Israel*. Chicago, Ill.: Moody Press, 1979.

Crenshaw, James L. *Ecclesiastes: A Commentary*. Old Testament Library. Philadelphia, Penn.: Westminster Press, 1987.

Delitzsch, Franz. *Commentary on the Song of Songs and Ecclesiastes*. Translated by M. G. Easton. Commentaries on the Old Testament. By C. F. Keil and Franz Delitzsch. Reprint, Grand Rapids, Mich.: Wm. B. Eerdmans Publishing, 1970.

Drane, John. *Introducing the Old Testament*. Revised edition. Oxford, U.K.: Lion Publishing, 2000.

Eaton, Michael A. *Ecclesiastes: An Introduction and Commentary*. Tyndale Old Testament Commentaries. Downers Grove, Ill.: Inter-Varsity Press, 1983.

Eissfeldt, Otto. *The Old Testament: An Introduction*. Translated by Peter R. Ackroyd. New York: Harper & Row, Publishers, 1965.

Ellis, Havelock. *The New Spirit*. New York: Houghton and Mifflin, 1926.

Estes, Daniel J. *Handbook on the Wisdom Books and Psalms*. Grand Rapids, Mich.: Baker Academic, 2005.

Fadiman, Clifton, ed. *The Little, Brown Book of Anecdotes*. Boston, Mass.: Little, Brown and Company, 1985.

Fox, Michael V. *Ecclesiastes*. JPS Bible Commentary. Philadelphia, Penn.: Jewish Publication Society, 2004.

——. *Proverbs 1-9: A New Translation with Introduction and Commentary*. Anchor Yale Bible 18A. New Haven, Conn.: Yale University Press, 2008.

——. *Qohelet and His Contradictions*. Journal for the Study of the Old Testament Supplement Series 71. Sheffield, U.K.: Almond Press, 1989.

Fredericks, Daniel C. 'Ecclesiastes.' In *Ecclesiastes & The Song of Songs*. By Daniel C. Fredericks and Daniel J. Estes. Apollos Old Testament Commentary 16. Nottingham, U.K.: Apollos, 2010.

——. *Qoheleth's Language: Re-evaluating Its Nature and Date*. Lewiston, Penn.: Edwin Mellen Press, 1988.

Garrett, Duane A. 'Ecclesiastes.' In *Zondervan Illustrated Bible Backgrounds Commentary*. 5 volumes. Edited by John H. Walton, 5:504-17. Grand Rapids, Mich.: Zondervan, 2009.

——. *Proverbs, Ecclesiastes, Song of Songs*. New American Commentary 14. Nashville, Tenn.: Broadman Press, 1993.

Ginsburg, Christian D. *The Song of Songs and Coheleth*. 2 volumes in 1. New York: KTAV Publishing House, 1970.

Glenn, Donald R. 'Ecclesiastes.' In *The Bible Knowledge Commentary: Old Testament*. Edited by John F. Walvoord et al., 975-1007. Wheaton, Ill.: Victor Books, 1985.

Goldberg, Louis. *The Practical Wisdom of Proverbs*. Grand Rapids, Mich.: Kregel Publications, 1990.

Goldman, Y. A. P. 'Ecclesiastes.' In *General Introduction and Megilloth*. Volume 18 of *Biblia Hebraica Quinta*. Edited by A. Schenker et al., 25-53, 13*-17*, 28*-30*. Stuttgart, Germany: Deutsche Bibelgesellschaft, 2004.

Gonzalez, Guillermo, and Jay W. Richards. *The Privileged Planet: How Our Place in the Cosmos Is Designed for Discovery*. Washington, D.C.: Regnery Publishing, 2004.

Gordis, Robert. *Koheleth – The Man and His World: A Study of Ecclesiastes*. 3rd edition. New York: Schocken Books, 1968.

Gray, John. *The Legacy of Canaan: The Ras Shamra Texts and Their Relevance to the Old Testament*. Leiden, The Netherlands: E. J. Brill, 1957.

Greidanus, Sidney. *Preaching Christ from Ecclesiastes: Foundations for Expository Sermons*. Grand Rapids, Mich.: William B. Eerdmans Publishing Co., 2010.

Grudem, Wayne. *Business for the Glory of God: The Bible's Teaching on the Moral Goodness of Business*. Wheaton, Ill.: Crossway Books, 2003.

——. *Politics According to the Bible: A Comprehensive Resource for Understanding Modern Political Issues in the Light of Scripture*. Grand Rapids, Mich.: Zondervan, 2010.

Hallo, William W., and K. Lawson Younger, eds. *The Context of Scripture*. 3 volumes. Leiden, The Netherlands: Brill, 2003.

Hawking, Stephen W. *A Brief History of Time: From the Big Bang to Black Holes*. New York: Bantam Books, 1988.

Hengstenberg, Ernest W. *A Commentary on Ecclesiastes*. 1869. Reprint, Minneapolis, Minn.: James and Klock Christian Publishing Co., 1977.

Hubbard, David A. *Ecclesiastes, Song of Solomon*. Preacher's Commentary Series 16. Nashville, Tenn.: Thomas Nelson, 1991.

Huwiler, Elizabeth. 'Ecclesiastes.' In *Proverbs, Ecclesiastes, Song of Songs*, by Roland E. Murphy and Elizabeth Huwiler. New International Bible Commentary. Peabody, Mass.: Hendrickson Publishers, 1999.

Jamieson, Robert, A. R. Fausset, and David Brown. *A Commentary, Critical and Explanatory, on the Old and New Testaments.* Electronic edition. Oak Harbor, Wash.: Logos Research Systems, 1997.

Jarick, John, ed. *A Comprehensive Bilingual Concordance of the Hebrew and Greek Texts of Ecclesiastes.* Society of Biblical Literature Septuagint and Cognate Studies Series 36. Atlanta, Ga.: Scholars Press, 1993.

Johnston, D. *A Treatise on the Authorship of Ecclesiastes.* London: Macmillan and Co., 1880.

Kaiser, Jr., Walter C. *Ecclesiastes: Total Life.* Everyman's Bible Commentary. Chicago, Ill.: Moody Press, 1979.

Kautzsch, E., ed. *Gesenius' Hebrew Grammar.* 2nd English edition. Translated and revised by A. E. Cowley. Oxford, U.K.: Clarendon Press, 1910.

Kelley, Michael. *The Burden of God: Studies in Wisdom and Civilization from the Book of Ecclesiastes.* Minneapolis, Minn.: Contra Mundum Books, 1993.

Kidner, Derek. *A Time to Mourn, and a Time to Dance: Ecclesiastes & the Way of the World.* The Bible Speaks Today. Downers Grove, Ill.: InterVarsity Press, 1976.

——. *The Wisdom of Proverbs, Job & Ecclesiastes.* Leicester, U.K.: InterVarsity Press, 1985.

Krüger, Thomas. *Qoheleth: A Commentary.* Translated by O. C. Dean, Jr. Hermeneia. Minneapolis, Minn.: Fortress Press, 2004.

Lauha, Aare. *Kohelet.* Biblischer Kommentar Altes Testament 19. Neukirchen-Vluyn, Germany: Neukirchener Verlag, 1978.

Leupold, H. C. *Exposition of Ecclesiastes.* Grand Rapids, Mich.: Baker Book House, 1952.

Lohfink, Norbert. *Qoheleth*. Translated by Sean McEvenue. Continental Commentary. Minneapolis, Minn.: Fortress Press, 2003.

Longman III, Tremper. *The Book of Ecclesiastes*. New International Commentary on the Old Testament. Grand Rapids, Mich.: William B. Eerdmans Publishing, 1998.

McComiskey, Thomas E. "Ecclesiastes, Book of." In *Baker Encyclopedia of the Bible*. Edited by Walter A. Elwell and Barry J. Beitzel, 651-54. Grand Rapids, Mich.: Baker Book House, 1988.

Metzger, Bruce M., ed. *The Apocrypha of the Old Testament, Revised Standard Version*. Oxford Annotated Apocrypha. New York: Oxford University Press, 1977.

Morris, Henry M. *The Remarkable Wisdom of Solomon: Ancient Insights from the Song of Solomon, Proverbs, and Ecclesiastes*. Green Forest, Ark.: Master Books, 2001.

Murphy, Roland E. *Ecclesiastes*. Word Biblical Commentary 23A. Dallas, Tex.: Word Books, 1992.

Olyott, Stuart. *A Life Worth Living and A Lord Worth Loving*. Welwyn Commentary Series. Hertfordshire, U.K.: Evangelical Press, 1983.

Peters, Benedikt. *Das Buch Prediger: 'Sphinx' der hebräischen Literatur*. 2nd edition. Dillenburg, Germany: Christliche Verlagsgesellschaft, 2006.

Pritchard, James B., ed. *Ancient Near Eastern Texts Relating to the Old Testament*. 2nd edition. Princeton, N.J.: Princeton University Press, 1955.

Provan, Iain. *Ecclesiastes, Song of Songs*. NIV Application Commentary. Grand Rapids, Mich.: Zondervan Publishing House, 2001.

Rankin, O. S., and Gaius Glenn Atkins. 'The Book of Ecclesiastes.' In *The Interpreter's Bible*. 12 volumes. Edited by George Arthur Buttrick, 5:3-88. New York: Abingdon Press, 1956.

Reichart, Victor E., and A. Cohen. 'Ecclesiastes.' In *The Five Megilloth*. 2 volumes. Edited by A. Cohen. Revised by A. J. Rosenberg. London: Soncino Press, 1984.

Reyburn, William David, and Euan McG. Fry. *A Handbook on Proverbs*. UBS Handbook Series: Helps for Translators. New York: United Bible Societies, 2000.

Roman, Colin. *Lost Discoveries: The Forgotten Science of the Ancient World*. New York: Weathervane Books, 1976.

Rosscup, James E. *An Exposition on Prayer in the Bible: Igniting the Fuel to Flame Our Communication With God*. Electronic edition. Bellingham, Wash.: Logos Research Systems, Inc., 2008.

Ryken, Philip Graham. *Ecclesiastes: Why Everything Matters*. Preaching the Word. Wheaton, Ill.: Crossway, 2010.

Seifrid, Mark A. 'Romans.' In *Commentary on the New Testament Use of the Old Testament*. Edited by G. K. Beale and D. A. Carson, 607-94. Grand Rapids, Mich.: Baker Academic, 2007.

Seow, C. L. *Ecclesiastes*. Anchor Bible 18C. New York: Doubleday, 1997.

Steveson, Peter A. *A Commentary on Proverbs*. Greenville, S.C.: BJU Press, 2001.

Swindoll, Charles R. *Living on the Ragged Edge: Coming to Terms with Reality*. New York: Bantam Books, 1988.

Tidball, Derek. *That's Just the Way It Is: A Realistic View of Life from the Book of Ecclesiastes*. Geanies House, Scotland: Christian Focus, 1998.

Toy, Crawford H. *A Critical and Exegetical Commentary on the Book of Proverbs*. International Critical Commentary. New York: C. Scribner's Sons, 1899.

Waltke, Bruce K. *The Book of Proverbs: Chapters 1-15*. New International Commentary on the Old Testament. Grand Rapids, Mich.: William B. Eerdmans Publishing Co., 2004.

Walton, John H., Victor H. Matthews, and Mark W. Chavalas. *The IVP Bible Background Commentary: Old Testament*. 570-76. Downers Grove, Ill.: InterVarsity Press, 2000.

Watson, Wilfred G. E. *Classical Hebrew Poetry: A Guide to its Techniques*. 2nd edition. Journal for the Study of the Old Testament Supplement Series 26. Sheffield, U.K.: Sheffield Academic Press, 1995.

Whybray, R. N. *Ecclesiastes*. New Century Bible Commentary. Grand Rapids, Mich.: Wm. B. Eerdmans, 1989.

Wilson, Robert Dick. *A Scientific Investigation of the Old Testament*. Chicago, Ill.: Moody Press, 1959.

Wright, J. Stafford. 'Ecclesiastes.' In *The Expositor's Bible Commentary*. 12 volumes. Edited by Frank E. Gaebelein, 5:1135-1244. Grand Rapids, Mich.: Zondervan Publishing House, 1991.

Zuck, Roy B., ed. *Reflecting with Solomon: Selected Studies on the Book of Ecclesiastes*. Grand Rapids, Mich.: Baker Books, 1994.

Journal Articles and Essays:

Archer, G. L. 'The Linguistic Evidence for the Date of "Ecclesiastes".' *Journal of the Evangelical Theological Society* 12, no. 3 (Summer 1969): 167-81.

Brindle, Wayne A. 'Righteousness and Wickedness in Ecclesiastes 7:15-18.' In *Reflecting with Solomon: Selected Studies on the Book of Ecclesiastes*. Edited by Roy B. Zuck, 301-13. Grand Rapids, Mich.: Baker Books, 1994.

Crenshaw, James L. 'Nothing New Under the Sun: Ecclesiastes 1:4-11.' In *Reflecting with Solomon: Selected Studies on the Book of Ecclesiastes*. Edited by Roy B. Zuck, 241-48. Grand Rapids, Mich.: Baker Books, 1994.

Davis, Barry C. 'Death, an Impetus for Life, Ecclesiastes 12:1-8.' In *Reflecting with Solomon: Selected Studies on the Book of Ecclesiastes*. Edited by Roy B. Zuck, 347-66. Grand Rapids, Mich.: Baker Books, 1994.

Day, John. 'Foreign Semitic Influence on the Wisdom of Israel and Its Appropriation in the Book of Proverbs.' In *Wisdom in Ancient Israel*. Edited by John Day et al., 55-70. Cambridge, U.K.: Cambridge University Press, 1998.

Glenn, Donald R. 'Mankind's Ignorance: Ecclesiastes 8:1–10:11.' In *Reflecting with Solomon: Selected Studies on the Book of Ecclesiastes*. Edited by Roy B. Zuck, 321-29. Grand Rapids, Mich.: Baker Books, 1994.

Hildebrandt, Ted A. "Proverb." In *Cracking Old Testament Codes: Interpreting the Literary Genres of the Old Testament*. Edited by D. Brent Sandy and Ronald L. Giese, Jr., 233-54. Nashville, Tenn.: Broadman & Holman Publishers, 1995.

Jarick, John. 'The Hebrew Book of Changes: Reflections on *hakkœl hebel* and *lakkœl z^eman* in Ecclesiastes.' *Journal for the Study of the Old Testament* 90 (2000): 79-99.

Kidner, Derek. 'The Search for Satisfaction: Ecclesiastes 1:12–2:26.' In *Reflecting with Solomon: Selected Studies on the Book of Ecclesiastes*. Edited by Roy B. Zuck, 249-56. Grand Rapids, Mich.: Baker Books, 1994.

——. 'Wisdom Literature of the Old Testament.' In *New Perspectives on the Old Testament*. Edited by J. Barton Payne, 117-30. Waco, Tex.: Word Books, Publishers, 1970.

Leahy, Michael. 'The Meaning of Ecclesiastes 12:1-5.' In *Reflecting with Solomon: Selected Studies on the Book of Ecclesiastes*. Edited by Roy B. Zuck, 375-79. Grand Rapids, Mich.: Baker Books, 1994.

Ogden, Graham S. 'The Meaning of the Term *Hebel*.' In *Reflecting with Solomon: Selected Studies on the Book of Ecclesiastes*. Edited by Roy B. Zuck, 227-31. Grand Rapids, Mich.: Baker Books, 1994.

——. 'Variations on the Theme of Wisdom's Strength and Vulnerability: Ecclesiastes 9:17–10:20.' In *Reflecting with Solomon: Selected Studies on the Book of Ecclesiastes*. Edited by Roy B. Zuck, 331-40. Grand Rapids, Mich.: Baker Books, 1994.

Parsons, Greg W. 'Guidelines for Understanding and Proclaiming the Book of Ecclesiastes, Part 1.' *Bibliotheca Sacra* 160, no. 638 (April 2003): 159-73.

——. 'Guidelines for Understanding and Proclaiming the Book of Ecclesiastes, Part 2.' *Bibliotheca Sacra* 160, no. 639 (July 2003): 283-304.

Simian-Yofre, H. 'נחם,' In *Theological Dictionary of the Old Testament*. 16 volumes. Edited by G. Johannes Botterweck, Helmer Ringgren, and Heinz-Josef Fabry, translated by David E. Green, 9:353. Grand Rapids, Mich.: William B. Eerdmans Publishing

Company, 1998.

Whybray, R. N. 'Ecclesiastes 1:5-7 and the Wonders of Nature.' In *Reflecting with Solomon: Selected Studies on the Book of Ecclesiastes*. Edited by Roy B. Zuck, 233-39. Grand Rapids, Mich.: Baker Books, 1994.'

Youngblood, Ronald F. 'Qoheleth's 'Dark House (Eccles. 12:5).' In *A Tribute to Gleason Archer*. Edited by Walter C. Kaiser, Jr., and Ronald F. Youngblood, 211-27. Chicago, Ill.: Moody Press, 1986.

Subject Index

Scripture Index